VINCENT THE RIPPER

Vincent Van Gogh Was Jack The Ripper Case Closed

Volume 1

by

Dale Larner

Black Crow Publishing

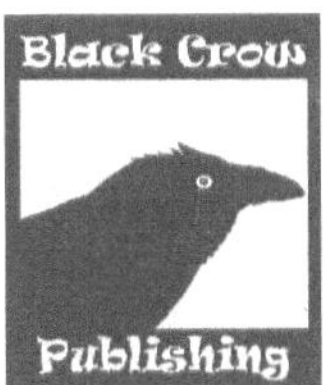

"Blood of the Lamb."

CONTENTS

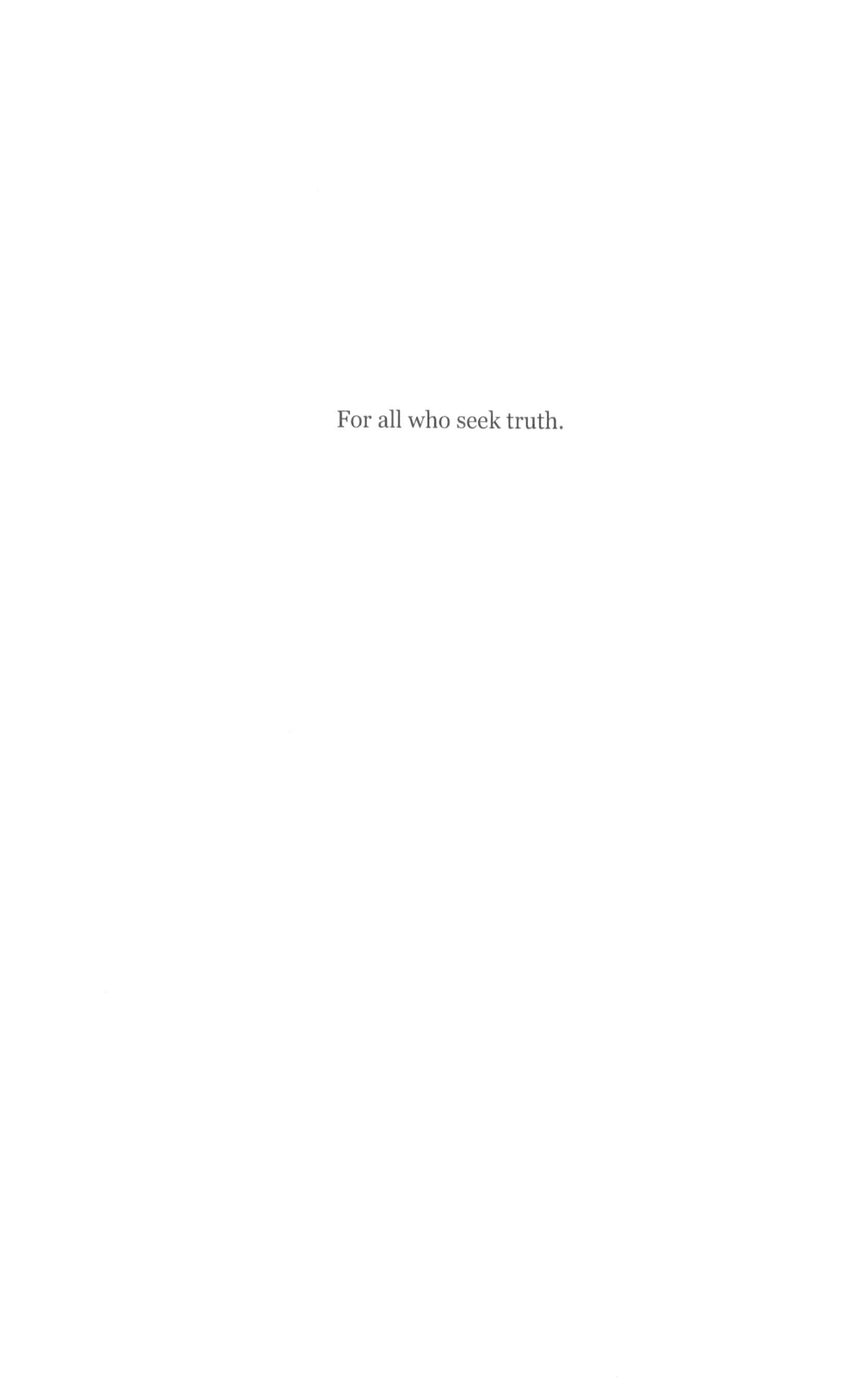

For all who seek truth.

INTRODUCTION

We live in a time when it seems the things of the past are being shifted out of their place and transported closer to where we are currently riding along on this ever-unfolding timeline of the ages. Old forgotten things are being seen with eyes enlightened by the cracking open of digital treasure chests filled with newly discovered information. And we are realizing many things were not as they seemed.

The story of the hidden life of Vincent van Gogh is one such thing. What is known about his life has been laid out before us for over a century, and with each passing decade, researchers have dug at the edges to help refine the details. It has been the same for the details of the forever unsolved murders of Jack the Ripper.

Both subjects are full of mystery and create within many a desire to hunt for unrealized information to uncover something new. With Vincent, it has been a quest to understand the painter and his torturous struggles as an artist. With Jack the Ripper, it has been about unearthing missing evidence which will lead to the killer's true identity.

For myself, I was seeking to better understand my favorite artist. I wanted to be more productive with my own art, and I thought looking deeper into Van Gogh's life might help explain why he was so productive. I could then apply that to myself. This led me to the book *Dear Theo*, which is a collection of Vincent's letters to his younger brother, Theo. While reading Vincent's own words, my view of him changed dramatically. I found him to be a much different person, especially with how he continually demanded his thoughtful brother send him more money.

Vincent did not have a job once he took up painting. He relied solely on Theo's financial support for the last ten years of his life. In exchange for this, he would send his paintings to Theo, who was an art dealer. But he wouldn't allow Theo to sell them, dispelling the notion no one wanted to buy his paintings. Vincent was using part of Theo's money for alcohol and regular visits to the brothels. He had an attitude of being entitled to Theo's money and didn't believe it was any of Theo's business how he spent it. At one point, he even secretly had a pregnant prostitute and her child living with him while he demanded Theo send more money for his rent and food. Vincent relentlessly created great difficulty for Theo, and many others, but he never blamed himself. It was always someone else's fault.

By the time I finished reading *Dear Theo*, I had a much different perspective of my favorite artist. I didn't like the sort of person he was, and I found this depressing. The artist I most wanted to paint like was not a person I wanted to *be* like. Also, I didn't discover anything related to why he was so productive, so that was also a little depressing.

Within just a few weeks of completing *Dear Theo*, I was on a trip to Arizona for my grandfather's 90th birthday and had to change planes in the Houston airport. While waiting to board the plane, I noticed a bookstore located across from my gate. I dropped in to seek out something to read. Not only was I looking to become a more productive artist, but even more so, I was on a path to becoming a writer. I wanted books that would not only be enjoyable to read but which I could also learn from as a writer.

I wasn't finding anything, and they announced the boarding for my plane. I could see the gate from the bookstore, and I watched as my fellow passengers lined up for boarding. I was now in a rush to find something, but this particular bookstore had a strange bookshelf which made it difficult to hurry. It was slanted with slots where paperbacks were dropped down into, so you had to lift them up to see the full cover. I was lifting and dropping books one after another, "Nope, nope, maybe, nope," all the while looking back at the gate, watching the line get shorter and shorter. And then I lifted up one book with the title, *Portrait of a Killer, Jack the Ripper, Case Closed*. I dropped it back down. But after a few more "nopes," I came back and pulled it out again. It was by Patricia Cornwell. I knew of her from her popular novels about a forensic detective named Scarpetta. She wrote fiction. Was this Jack the Ripper book fiction? Was the legend of Jack the Ripper mostly fiction anyway? I knew very little about Jack the Ripper at the time.

I examined the book further, wondering if Cornwell was using the Ripper case to create a fictionalized story around the murders. They announced final boarding. I turned and noticed the line at the gate was gone. I needed to go. I flipped to a section of photos and saw an old grotesque sepia-colored photo of a mutilated woman lying on a bed, and I thought, "Well, this is a real story." With no time left to think about it, I bought it and boarded the plane just in time.

Once we got in the air, I stared at that photo again. It's an awful photo. The Jack the Ripper victim was a London prostitute named Mary Kelly. Her body was slashed to pieces, and some of those pieces were piled on a bedside nightstand. Her face was unrecognizable. I kept looking at her face, though, trying to distinguish what this poor woman looked like. But I couldn't make out anything identifiable. I found I couldn't look at the photo for very long. It felt spooky to me, even surrounded by others on the plane. But I kept coming back to it and would during the entire reading of the book. We are known by our face, and I wanted to know what she looked like, but I just couldn't make out her features.

I read Cornwell's book on the plane and between the interactions with my family over a few days, then jumped back into it on the plane ride back and finished it a week or so later at home. A good book will bring you into another world. It becomes part of your life, and I wanted to take my time with this one. The details of the Ripper murders were enthralling, and I kept going back to the Mary Kelly photo trying to somehow decipher the details of her face. There are photos of the other victims after their murders, but none had disfigured faces, and I could at least see what they looked like, so I wasn't looking at those photos as much.

While reading the Cornwell book, I was living in an eerie and murderous Victorian world I knew very little about, so it was especially intriguing to learn the details of each murder as they were happening. The experience had a palpable feeling of bringing a spookiness into my existence—which was a curiosity to me. I already had an interest in reading about serial killers and watching documentaries about them and also watching true crime shows about husbands and wives killing each other thinking they could get away with it. So, I already knew that sense of having something spooky slip into my own world when learning about the evil those who kill inflict on others.

But there was something more with Cornwell's book. She was putting forward a suspect who she believed was Jack the Ripper, and that suspect was an English painter named Walter Sickert. A painter? How interesting. And me just reading about Van Gogh and having an epiphany about who he really was and not liking it. That was still with me as I read about this English painter Cornwell was attempting to connect to the Ripper murders. In the back of my mind I kept saying, "That sounds more like something Van Gogh would do." This was nothing serious to me. It related to my view that, even though Cornwell's book was thrilling to read, I did not accept the evidence she was putting forward as matching to her suspect. Walter Sickert was a spooky character, for sure, and he painted spooky kinds of paintings, but the connections to Jack the Ripper were not convincing to me. So, every time something was put forward as behavior Sickert was accused of doing, I would repeat in the reaches of my disheartened mind, "That sounds more like something Van Gogh would do." It was just a playful thing because Cornwell's suspect was a painter and because I was so disappointed to learn Vincent was different than I thought.

However, once I finished reading Cornwell's book, because that phrase had echoed in my mind repeatedly, I had a playful thought: "Well, if Van Gogh was Jack the Ripper, then it would show in his paintings." I partly thought this because Sickert's paintings look like the sort of paintings a serial killer would paint, so there must be something in Vincent's paintings that would reveal this other, hidden self, if he were truly a serial killer.

I had been looking at Vincent's paintings for years, so they were very familiar, but I grabbed one of my Van Gogh books off the shelf and started flipping through searching for any sign of a hidden serial killer's hand at work. However, looking at painting after colorful painting, all I could see was what I had seen before—brightly colored paintings filled with painterly strokes by someone who loved to express what he was feeling.

As I drifted along each page, I began to lose the playful thought of Vincent being Jack the Ripper, and about three-quarters of the way through, I turned to his *Irises* painting and paused and thought how much I loved this painting. I had an idea. In order to spark myself into becoming more productive, I should paint a copy of his *Irises* to get the juices flowing and learn more from his style. I had previously painted a copy of his *Starry Night* for the same reason.

Deciding on this conclusion, I leaned the Van Gogh book against my dresser and went to sleep. The ridiculous thoughts of Vincent being Jack the Ripper were gone, replaced by a new excitement about deciding to paint the *Irises* painting.

The next night, while lying in bed before going to sleep and wanting to see the *Irises* painting again, I lazily reached down and opened the Van Gogh book on the floor and began to push a group of pages aside to get further back to where I knew the *Irises* painting was located. As I was pushing the group of pages, I realized I was turning directly to the *Irises* painting, and when the pages were about to separate and fall back, I stopped them. I bring up this minute detail because what happened was I had stopped on the *Irises* painting so that only about a third of the right side was visible. With the rest of the painting blocked from view, a face immediately jumped out. The face of Mary Kelly. The spookiness returned.

What in the world? I looked at the entire painting and then would block three quarters of it, same thing, her face. Why? Crazy. How to understand this? I reasoned it was simply because I had looked at the photo of Mary Kelly so much, and specifically at her face, trying to find some identity, that now my mind was simply using what I had seen to recreate Mary's face by combining the flower pedals, stems and leaves in a way that it would look like her face. I retrieved Cornwell's book and looked at Mary Kelly's photo again, then back to the *Irises*. If my mind was creating it, why does the image in the *Irises* painting resemble so much what Mary's face looks like in the photo—which is not so definable. In fact, the painting had more definition to a face than the photo. In the painting, there are two eyes represented, the mouth is lifted up on one side like a kind of grin, and the nose is represented but looks more like a skeleton with the nose cut off. And Mary's dark hair in the photo is then painted black in the painting above and to the sides of the face, as would be expected.

This was a face intentionally painted within the *Irises* painting, and it was the hard-to-define, mutilated face of Mary Kelly, but why and how? For me, there was no denying what I was seeing, and it brought back to the forefront of my mind the question of Vincent being Jack the Ripper, but now it was a serious question. Crazy and spooky, but now a real question, not play.

I'm a rational-minded person, so I was trying to think of other reasons why Vincent would paint the face of a Jack the Ripper victim hidden in his *Irises* painting. Did he somehow come across this same photo of Mary's mutilated body and thought it was intriguing, and just for some creative fun he decided to play around and paint her face hidden in a painting? Was he having the same trouble I was having trying to see her identity and wanted to flesh it out in paint to try and see if that helped, and he just painted over and around it with irises? It couldn't possibly be that he was actually the killer and knew exactly what her face looked like before and after he cut it up, and painting her mutilated face in the Irises was just a little hidden fun he was having. It was too outrageous to imagine this could be the case. I closed the books and went to sleep.

Over the next days and weeks, I kept going back to the photo and the *Irises*, comparing and analyzing, and all it did was confirm for me to be the same face. I showed this to someone at work and talked about it to family on the phone. Their reaction was expected. I was just seeing things, and I could see and hear their concern over my mental state. I've always had a touch of having a few weird ideas, but in a fun way, a creative way, not in an actual "this guy might need some serious therapy" way.

Because of this, I quieted down about it, but it stuck with me. I really didn't know what to do with it. I looked up some info about Van Gogh, believing I would quickly see how ridiculous I was being and could let this go. I knew Vincent lived during the same time as the Ripper murders, but where was he living in 1888? He was in Arles, which is way down in the south of France, so far away from London. And I thought, like anyone would, that's way too far to travel back and forth several times to commit murder during that time period. And that was good enough for me. So, I set it aside and stopped thinking about the crazy thing.

Two years went by, and one day at work, after I had gotten some long-standing issues straight which were causing me difficulty, my peace of mind returned, and a question popped into my head: "Why didn't I look more into that Van Gogh thing?" I don't know why that specifically jumped back to mind, but there it was. I realized I hadn't actually looked at very much information to be able to throw aside the notion that Van Gogh was not Jack the Ripper. Sure, it was a long way to travel for murder, but they had trains and steamers. How long did it take? Was there anything in Vincent's life that matched to him being a serial killer? He certainly was different than what I had thought before, and he did cut off his ear. Could it be he was even more different than I thought? It's as if this weird thing had sat there in my subconscious, unresolved, waiting for more information before it could be moved into permanent storage and forgotten.

I started seeking out more information about Vincent's life, Jack's murders, and about what travel was like back then, and a terrible thing began to happen.

I believed I would be approaching doors and find them locked tight and be done with this. However, the more I learned about Vincent, the Ripper murders, and travel, those doors kept opening with just a turn of the knob. I truly wanted to find locked doors and set this weird thing aside. It was too crazy to keep looking into. But I kept it quiet. As the doors kept opening, I ordered more and more Van Gogh biographies and more and more Ripper books. I also searched out more books about how things were in the Victorian era, especially traveling around France and England. I also ordered more books about psychopaths and serial killers to better understand what I was dealing with.

The more I learned over the months about Van Gogh, Jack the Ripper, psychopaths and serial killers, and about travel during 1888, what I believed to be highly impossible moved to possible and then to probable. Then, one day, after continuing to uncover numerous matches, I was struck with a rush of butterflies, and I concluded what had become unavoidable—Vincent van Gogh was indeed Jack the Ripper!

As that initial research advanced, and as I continued on my path to becoming a writer, the somewhat obvious thought came to mind that I should write a book about this. I had spent years learning about creative writing with the idea of writing novels—lots of books of fiction. I was excited about creating characters and conjuring up creative new plots to twist. I had no plans of ever writing a non-fiction book. Too hard. I liked the idea of researching subjects to know more about and use within a creative story, but I had no desire to whittle away my time lost for months and years in research and to then compile it all into a book.

But now I had spent months falling deeper into the world of the late 1800's and learning more about the Jack the Ripper murders and how big a story it was back then and how much Vincent's psychology was fitting that of a psychopath. It was becoming clear how much his words, his lifestyle, and the events in his life were matching to murders. I found I was highly enthusiastic about the research, and the thought of putting together a book from so much information began to seem like something I would enjoy. But so much work. I didn't want to spend all that time doing all that research and put together the matches and then devote so much more time to actually writing it unless I was absolutely certain Vincent was the Ripper. I didn't want to end up writing a book like Cornwell's—attempting to force bits and pieces together to make them fit, having no real matches between the suspect and the Ripper. I didn't want to just think it might be possible and go from there. And I definitely didn't want to spend so much time on research and use that to loosely use the information to create a work of fiction just to have some fun with it and sell a book.

No, I was only going to do all the research needed and write a book about this if the real matches were there and the evidence was conclusive that Vincent van Gogh was definitely the serial killer known as Jack the Ripper. When I reached that point in the research where I knew there was overwhelming evidence Vincent was the man, I was faced with whether or not to write the book. I knew it would be a long road ahead, and I tried to think if it were better just to create a website. I could put some information out there for the world to have a look at and maybe at some point everyone would understand it was true. But that wasn't appealing. That would take lots of time too, and I wanted to get on with my writing career. So, it was either drop this all together and get to work on some wonderfully unrelated novel and see what I could come up with, or completely turn my attention to this and do the heavy research and write this book, no matter how long it took.

I had no idea just how many years I would work on the book, or how much it would impact my life in difficult ways, or how difficult it would be to get it published. I never imagined how many years it would continue to be my main focus, forgoing the many novels I had planned to write over all that time. But I wouldn't go back and change my mind. I know the premise is true beyond a shadow of a doubt. I believe it's important the world see the evidence which connects the famous painter Vincent van Gogh to the infamous serial killer Jack the Ripper. I think it's a worthy endeavor to undertake.

Thank you for having an open mind to what is possible and picking up this book. I believe you will be rewarded for your curiosity. If you will, just step this way, please, over towards this red door. I'll take you with me on a journey back in time to the late 1800's. All vestiges of our technological age will fall away. The sights of the burgeoning industrial age will burn your eyes with black smoke from burning coal stoves, your ears will be surrounded by horses' hoofs and wagon wheels clattering on cobbled streets, and your nose will fill with the warm aroma of strong coffee and freshly baked bread. Watch your step and mind the gap.

Yours Truly,
Dale Larner

AUTHOR'S NOTE

Vincent van Gogh rarely dated his letters. Therefore, researchers have gone to great lengths over the years to determine the most accurate dating of the undated letters. Unless otherwise noted, I have relied on the dating provided by Ronald Pickvance, as presented in his books: *Van Gogh in Arles,* 1984, pp. 260-63; and *Van Gogh in Saint-Rémy and Auvers*, 1986, pp. 291-92.

Also, the Jack the Ripper letters contain many misspellings and wrong grammar and word usage. Unless otherwise noted, the quotes are presented as originally written.

I would like it known that I have sought to present the facts of Van Gogh's life and the Jack the Ripper murders in their proper context with the intent of always seeking to maintain the integrity of the material and present the truth. I believe the evidence exhibited against Vincent van Gogh being Jack the Ripper is conclusive, and therefore I have presented the evidence as a prosecutor would—which is to presume his guilt. You, the reader, will determine whether or not I've made my case.

VIEWING IMAGES

In order to provide high resolution and color images covered in this book, the complete catalog of images referenced have been made available for ease of viewing at the following book website link:

https://vincenttheripper.com/book-images-volume1-p1

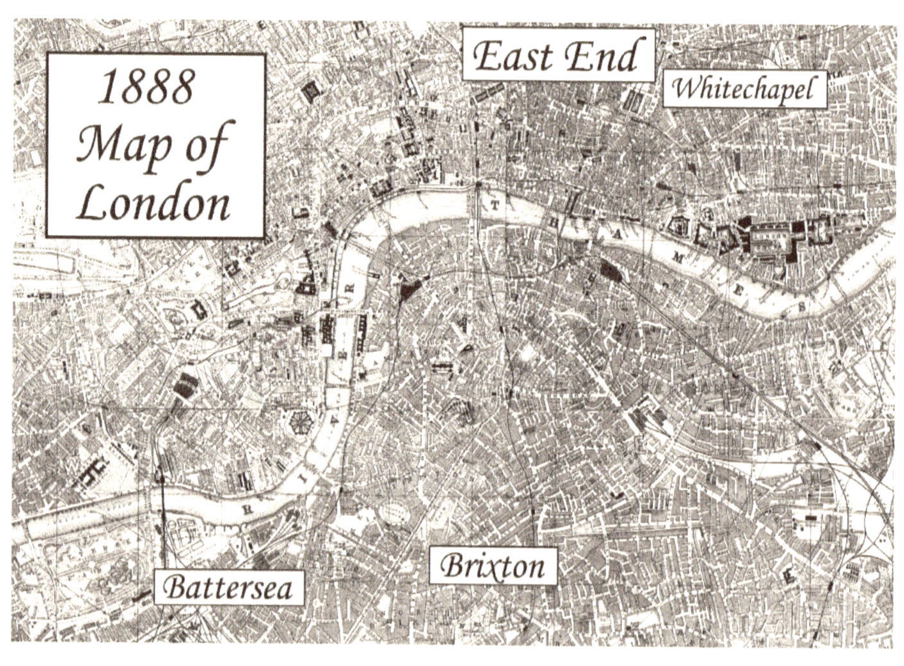

1888
Map of
London
East End
Whitechapel
Battersea
Brixton

"The whore is like meat in a butcher's shop."
—Vincent van Gogh, July 1888

1

Fair And Sunburnt
February 1888

In February of 1888, at the age of 34, Vincent van Gogh was anxious to get out of Paris and begin something new. He had a strong desire to head south to find fresh scenery and create unique paintings to exhibit at the World's Fair—which was set to open in Paris the next year. Exhibitions at large galleries for the well-known artists of the day, such as Claude Monet, were being planned, but it was also a chance for the lesser-known and unknown artists, like Vincent, to have their paintings exhibited for all the world to see.

The construction of the Eiffel Tower for the fair was under way. Seeing the massive metal base of the tower completed by February may have helped inspire Vincent to get started and make a move right away. Many other artists were of the same mind, and two of Vincent's artist friends, Paul Gauguin and Émile Bernard, were heading to Brittany on the East Coast for new scenery to paint. They invited Vincent to come along, but Vincent wanted instead the colors of the hot south near the Mediterranean.

However, a problem existed for Vincent. He didn't have the money to make the move or to support himself. He didn't have a job. In fact, he had done nothing other than pursue painting for the past eight years. This was only possible due to the financial backing provided by his younger brother, Theo (figure 1.1, photo of Theo), who had risen up the ranks to become the manager at a Paris branch of the art gallery Boussod, Valadon & Co. (which was more commonly known by its founding name of Goupil & Co.).[1] Theo had taken it upon himself to provide Vincent the means to pursue his art.

Previously, Vincent had moved back in with his parents in Holland a few times to reduce expenses at the beginning of his new journey in art. Then it was on to Antwerp, Belgium to attend the art academy. But in March 1886, against Theo's wishes, Vincent had decided he would move to Paris and live with Theo in his apartment. This was a pattern of Vincent's—to do as he wished, regardless of what Theo or others had to say, all the while expecting Theo to continue to pay his expenses.

Being a supportive brother, Theo had given in. Vincent was already there, after all, and it was true, as Vincent pointed out, the move saved Theo the expense of paying for Vincent's rent. But Vincent had a difficult nature. He tended to cause trouble, and within a year, Theo had reached his limit with Vincent and wanted him to move out and find his own means of support. Somehow, though, the two brothers worked things out, Vincent stayed, and Theo continued to pay his expenses.

But now, in February of 1888, the two were once again arguing, this time about Vincent's desire to move to the south to paint. Theo didn't want to take on the added expenses this would cost him and wanted Vincent to find a place nearby in Paris instead, but Vincent had his mind set. He demanded Theo support his decision and agree to continue to pay for everything.

On February 19, things boiled over, and Theo left his apartment proclaiming to a mutual friend he would not return until Vincent had moved out.[2] That same day, determined to do what he wanted regardless of Theo's objections, Vincent packed up his paints and brushes and headed to the Paris-Lyon train station to catch a train to the south.

By this point in his life, Vincent had exhibited a pattern of pushing others to their breaking point as a means to get his way, and this time was no different. He wanted to leave Paris and move to the south, so he argued with Theo until Theo grew frustrated and demanded he move out of his apartment. This gave the desired result of Theo being tagged the aggressor, while lowly Vincent sulked away as the hurt victim who, after all, never meant any harm.

Ever since Theo attached himself to Vincent's wellbeing by sending him money, Vincent had worked at honing his technique of using his brother's goodwill to manipulate him into continuing to pay his expenses—all the while demanding Theo accept what he spent his money on and even continue to pay more. Vincent played on his brother's sympathies with the ease of a master violinist, but he was also the conductor, orchestrating every stanza and note.

Vincent's manipulation worked again this time. All was forgiven. Theo rushed to meet Vincent at the train station to see him off. Most importantly, Theo agreed he would continue to provide Vincent with his only means of financial support. Vincent boarded the southbound train for the dusty French town of Arles, and the first step towards Vincent seeking something new was taken.

Upon his arrival in Arles, Vincent found a room above a restaurant and wrote about it to Theo,[3] who quickly responded with 50 francs.[4] Theo had also likely handed Vincent some money at the train station, and with an additional 50 francs, Vincent was well-funded. The room he took was only 1 franc a night,[5]

and he noted he could get a meal for 1 to 1½ francs,[6] so 50 francs could go a long way.

However, whenever Vincent received money from Theo, it caused an immediate change in his character. He often became boastful and reckless and tended to quickly spend what he had without the slightest thought for the future, choosing instead to put it towards alcohol and visits to the brothels. Vincent knew once the money was gone, he could write Theo, tell of his woes and hardships, and Theo would sympathize, give-in, and send more money.

Arles had its own brothels and bars where Vincent could blow his money, but he had become accustomed to the variety and excitement of the establishments available to him in Paris. Arles only offered the bare minimum needed to ply his vices and he, no doubt, yearned for something more.

London, like Paris, was another city which had the variety Vincent craved. Although he had moved in the opposite direction, I believe Vincent desired to make the trip back to Paris and then over the English Channel to London where he had once lived and indulged in his vices many years before. Like the magnetic pull of magnetic north, so too was Vincent always drawn back to London. It was a strong force he couldn't resist.

Later in the same week Vincent left Paris and arrived in Arles, a woman was attacked with a knife in the East End of London on Saturday, February 25. The London-based newspaper, the *Eastern Post*, reported that Annie Millwood had been stabbed numerous times in the legs and lower body but miraculously survived. She said her attacker was a stranger who stabbed her with a clasp knife he had taken from his pocket.[7]

A month later, Millwood had recovered and was discharged from the hospital. Unfortunately, though, ten days later on March 31, she suddenly dropped dead from natural causes.

Three days before Millwood's untimely death, in the early morning hours of March 28, another woman was attacked with a knife in the East End and also survived. According to the weekly London newspaper, *The Illustrated Police News*, the victim, Ada Wilson, said a stranger knocked at her door and demanded money.[8] She refused, and the stranger then drew a clasp knife from his pocket and stabbed her twice in the neck. Wilson lost a lot of blood, but she recovered fully after being taken to the hospital. She described her attacker as about 30, 5' 6", face sunburned, having a fair mustache, and he wore a wide-awake hat.

A witness named Rose Bierman, who lived in a room above Wilson, provided additional details which conflicted with Wilson's account. She said

Wilson came into the house that night accompanied by a male companion.[9] She added Wilson often had visitors. About midnight, she heard terrible screams and saw Wilson in the passage partially dressed and ringing her hands. She then saw "a young, fair man rush to the front door" and make his escape.

The difference in the two accounts seems to relate to a question of decorum. Wilson still had some self-respect and didn't want her true profession known, whereas Bierman didn't seem to mind if others knew Wilson was a prostitute.

In the lore of Jack the Ripper, these two attempted murders are where the story begins, and I believe this too is where Vincent's story of becoming Jack the Ripper begins.

When Vincent moved to Arles, he substantially reduced his accountability to others by removing himself from Theo's watchful eye and being out of the presence of other artists and friends he had in Paris. He had the freedom to come and go as he pleased without the need to explain himself.

Leaving Paris on Sunday, February 19, Vincent had arrived in Arles the next day. I believe he then left Arles later that same week on Friday the 24th, arrived in London on Saturday the 25th, and wasting no time, he then attacked Annie Millwood that night. He then began the journey back to Arles the next day, which brought him back on Monday the 27th, a week to the day after he had first arrived in Arles. For Vincent, nothing to it.

It seems a bit much to believe an artist seeking something new in art who had just traveled thirteen or more hours by train from Paris to Arles would just four days later take that same long train ride back to Paris and even continue on to London. Then, after all that travel, attack and stab a woman multiple times, hop right back on a train and make the return trip all the way back down to Arles. Not only this, but accepting this same artist did it all over again just a month later, attacking another woman and stabbing her twice in the neck before fleeing and traveling back to Arles, seems a stretch.

This was a great deal of travel in a short period of time, making it difficult to imagine the average artist, average person, or even average serial killer, going to such lengths. But Vincent was by no means an average artist, person, or serial killer, and traveling to him was not something he looked on as an inconvenience. He had a proven physical endurance and a matching psychological endurance which allowed him to consider such trips as nothing more than what was necessary.

It's important to understand that the distances Vincent needed to travel were not such great distances, and because he was traveling on the heavily used routes between the major cities of Marseille, Paris, and London, the travel times were in actuality reasonable. According to the March 1888 issue of

Bradshaw's Continental Railway Guide, the South Eastern Railway company boasted in their advertisements of trips from London to Paris in as little as eight hours by use of the fixed mail routes (figure 1.2, Bradshaw Ad). Choosing the express route, a passenger would be carried from London to Folkestone in about two hours, where a steamer would be waiting which would get them across the English Channel to Boulogne, France in another two hours. A well-timed French train would then carry them on the four-hour ride to Paris.

For those passengers, such as Vincent, who wanted to continue on from Paris down to Arles, they would be in for a minimum of a thirteen-hour ride to Tarascon, where they could then catch a train for a short half-hour ride to Arles. Allowing for an approximate minimum wait time of an hour for the train in Paris and another hour for the train in Tarascon, the fastest total travel time from London to Arles was about twenty-four hours. It was possible for Vincent to leave Arles and arrive in London the next day, and vice versa. London was not so very far away, after all.

Depending on Vincent's available resources, he had the option of purchasing the higher priced mail-train routes which ran during the day, but he also had other routes and schedules which offered cheaper third-class tickets, which would take longer. He could also choose the faster mail-train schedules which ran at night to save money, but these could involve longer waits between catching the steamer or the next train.

Choosing to keep costs low by using night trains and buying third-class tickets for the entire trip or parts of it could, depending on the timing and availability of steamers and trains, add as much as another five or more hours to Vincent's total journey. This didn't bother Vincent. Besides his strong stamina, he was highly motivated for what he wanted to do in London.

✳ ✳ ✳

The information available for the two attempted murders in London is limited, but what is available offers some similarities. Both Millwood and Wilson were attacked in the Whitechapel District by a stranger who had stabbed them with a clasp knife which he pulled from his pocket.

Relating to the attacker's choice of a clasp knife, it wasn't uncommon for men in the East End to carry a knife. Vincent was also known to carry a knife. He mentioned in a letter to a fellow artist in 1883, when speaking of painting, "Now and then I scrape with my pocketknife."[10] Another fellow artist also recollected about Vincent, "He often said: 'I have my whole elementary knowledge from my pocket knife.'"[11]

Vincent also shared some similarities with the descriptions of the attacker in each case. Ada Wilson had said her attacker was about 30, 5' 6", had a fair mustache, and she noted he had a sunburned face. Vincent was a few days shy of turning 35 at the time, and according to his sister-in-law, "he was of medium height."[12] As for being sunburned, Wilson may have been referring to a temporarily reddened face from a sunburn, or she may have been referring to someone who had regularly spent time out in the sun and had a tanned look. Vincent spent many hours outdoors painting landscapes, so it would be expected he had a tanned or sunburned look. Another artist who knew him, Dimmen Gestel, described him in this same way: "His sunburned, weather-beaten face was framed in a somewhat red and stubbly beard."[13]

So far, Vincent fits the attacker's profile, but Gestel's noting of Vincent's "red and stubbly beard" doesn't match with Wilson's description of a fair mustache. There's no mistaking Vincent's facial hair was red. However, his head hair was mostly blond with some red mixed in (figure 1.3, Van Gogh self-portrait), and Bierman's description that Wilson's attacker was a "young, fair man," goes along with this. A pastor named Bonte, who knew Vincent, described him in a similar way, as a "blond young man."[14] Matching generally to Wilson's description of her attacker's height, the pastor also described Vincent as being "of medium stature."

Combining Millwood's basic description of a stranger who pulled a clasp knife on her with the description provided by Bierman and Wilson, it could only be said Vincent might be stopped for questioning. There wasn't much to go on, and there would have been a wide circle of possible suspects who fit the basic details provided. However, two pieces of information in Vincent's life help to tighten the circle. First, Vincent's father had died suddenly three years prior on March 26th,[15] and Vincent's birthday was on March 30. With these dates so near to Wilson's March 28 attack, it could be Vincent took a trip to London to celebrate and have a spree for his birthday and get some emotional relief from the reminder of his father's death.

Vincent had spent the previous two years drinking heavily and living it up in Paris, and his indulgences had taken their toll. Excessive amounts of alcohol, especially for someone who continues to indulge heavily over long periods of time, could possibly lead to a difficulty in making a spree all it should be. Impotency was a difficulty Vincent struggled with at times. Sometimes he referred to it indirectly as his blood not circulating, and at other times he was surprisingly frank, admitting more directly he was dealing with an impotency issue.

I believe Vincent left Paris for Arles in the midst of this problem and, surrounded by a kind of drunken fog and seeking to find a solution to the problem, he thought each of the visits back to London would revive his senses. He had lived in London when he was younger, and the memories of what had happened there were powerful and pulled him back. But when he sought out prostitutes in the Whitechapel District on each of the trips, he continued to drink heavily, and therefore his impotency issue also continued.

Each of the attacks were triggered by his frustration and humiliation due to an inability to perform. On both occasions, in a burst of drunken rage, he pulled out his pocketknife and stabbed the women. The jabbing with the knife acted as a substitute for the sex he was incapable of. This was more clearly displayed with the Millwood attack by the various stabs to her lower body. The frustrated and drunken Vincent fled in each case without completing his rage-filled attacks, leaving his victims alive.

As for having the money necessary to make the trips to London from Arles, Theo had unwittingly provided Vincent with the amount he needed. He would have given Vincent money before his departure, and then he immediately sent him another 50 francs, which must have totaled enough for Vincent to at least purchase the cheaper tickets to London for the attack of Millwood. Based on *Bradshaw's Continental Railway Guide*, a third-class roundtrip ticket on the cheaper mail-train night service from London to Paris could be purchased for 33 shillings and 6 pence, which, using an exchange table provided in *Bradshaw's* guide, converts to 41 francs and 88 centimes. Then a third-class roundtrip ticket from Paris to Arles by way of Tarascon is listed as 52 francs and 65 centimes. This gives the lowest total amount Vincent needed for a trip to London and back at 94 francs and 53 centimes.

As for the funding of the Wilson attack on March 28, Vincent had written to Theo on March 3 to thank him for 50 francs he had received. Then again on March 24, just three days before the attack, he thanked Theo for another 50 francs in a letter. This 100 francs, together with any money he may have already received from Theo, provided him with enough for the trip.

In the March 24 letter, Vincent ended it by noting, "I'll write again in a few days."[16] This was not something he commonly wrote before this time and helps to reveal he wrote it for a purpose. By noting he would write again in a few days, he was attempting to keep Theo from responding to his letter while he was away on a trip to London.

Vincent and Theo wrote each other regularly, each responding to the other's letter as soon as they had received it. Because of the express mail-trains which ran throughout Europe, a letter sent from and to just about anywhere in Europe was expected to arrive at its destination by the next day. This was expected especially so between Vincent and Theo, since Theo was in Paris and Arles was just off the main train route from Paris to Marseille.

But on this occasion, by stating he would "write again in a few days," Vincent was attempting to prevent Theo's expected quick return response.

Vincent was planning ahead. He would be leaving that day or the next for a secret trip to London. He didn't want Theo sending him a letter while he was away. If he did, Vincent's response might be delayed because he hadn't yet returned from London. This could cause unnecessary suspicion from Theo, who was always on the lookout for signs of Vincent's already established bad behavior.

With his victims surviving their attacks and there also being a witness who described him to the papers, Vincent must have felt uneasy about remaining in London after the Wilson attack on March 28. He either left later that same day or the next, bringing him back to Arles either on the 29th or the 30th.

Looking through his mail upon his return, Vincent found Theo had either ignored or had missed his comment and had promptly written him back, even sending another 50 francs. Finding he had received a letter from Theo while he was away, Vincent had to respond quickly to avoid any suspicion of being up to something, especially since Theo had sent money. In a letter from March 30, which was Vincent's 35th birthday, Vincent thanked Theo for the 50 francs. He then wrote an uncharacteristically short letter in which he noted, "I should have liked to write you in leisure, but must do it in great haste."[17] He ended with, "In great haste, Ever yours, Vincent." He was in a hurry to get the letter off in time for the daily post so it would be on the mail-train that day for Paris. He was already late in responding, so he had to be brief and quick.

After arriving back in Arles and getting a quick response off to Theo's letter so that Theo wouldn't wonder about the delay, Vincent must have paused to take a look at his current situation. He had been careless in taking the two trips to London and in attacking the two women. His heavy drinking had clouded his judgment, and he wasn't in full control of his faculties during each attack. He had put himself at risk of being captured by being sloppy and leaving his victims alive.

His foggy head was also preventing him from producing the new art he had come to Arles to create. The opening day of the World's Fair was inching closer, and if he couldn't get it together, he would not have a large enough number of quality paintings completed in time. He needed to sober up and get his mind on the reason why he came to Arles, and he needed to find a way to gain a unique perspective that would set his paintings apart from all the others. He was progressing along nicely towards becoming Jack the Ripper.

2

A New Self
March 1888

Recognizing his excessive drinking and sloppy behavior were hampering his ability to paint and knowing he had a lot of work to do, Vincent wrote home to Holland to his youngest sister, Wilhelmina, who went by Wil, on March 30, 1888, noting, "I shall have to produce an enormous number of things against next year—when the World's Fair will be held—seeing that my friends will not fail to have many interesting things on hand by then."[1]

Vincent's competitive drive to match the output of other artists gave him a discipline to overcome his alcoholic stupor and get control of his drinking so he could become productive. He wrote to Theo in May of his progress: "I am better than I was in Paris . . . Most likely due to the bad wine, which I drank too much of. The wine is just as bad here, but I drink very little of it."[2] He was fighting to overcome his blurry state of unproductive drunkenness, and he was winning.

As May moved along, Vincent continued to make real progress, and he wrote Theo, "It is precisely that sense of stupefaction that I'm getting rid of. I do not feel so much need of distraction, I am less harassed by my passions, and I can work more calmly."[3]

With his drinking controlled, Vincent could occasionally visit the brothels without the impotency issue, and he expressed to Theo how things were going well in that area too. Referring to sex as "hygiene," he wrote, "I think there is proof good hygiene not only prolongs life, but above all can make it more serene, a clearer stream; whereas bad hygiene not only muddies the current of life, but that in addition the absolute lack of it may put an end to life before its time."[4]

Things were getting better for Vincent. He was beginning to produce studies and paintings of the quality he was after. He was on the right track now. This was the reason he came down south.

He also began to meet with some artists in the area, and this must have reminded him of a long-held idea of his to bring together an association of artists. He took it upon himself to put Theo's money towards this effort and rented a two-story house which he dubbed the Yellow House (figure 2.1, Yellow

House painting).5 There were four rooms, and the plan was for Vincent and another artist to live in the two upper rooms, leaving the bottom floor for the studio. Later, other artists could join and share the expenses.

Vincent then moved, but not yet into the Yellow House—he still needed a bed and furniture. Instead, he moved into a different hotel. He would paint at the Yellow House and sleep at the hotel until he could acquire the needed items to fully move into the Yellow House.

Surprisingly, Theo didn't put up a fight against Vincent taking on the extra expense. In fact, he welcomed the idea of combining artists. Being the manager of a Goupil's art gallery, Theo was becoming successful at bringing in new artists and selling their paintings at a time when the Impressionists were beginning to blossom. A group of Post-Impressionists were also building on their style to create new things, and Theo was right in the thick of it. He was working with artists such as Seurat, Pissarro, Lautrec, and even with Monet— who was well known by this time.

A major shift was underway in the art world, and Theo was in just the right position at just the right time to be part of this growing beehive of successful artists. The buzz of the coming World's Fair had the painters eager to be productive, and the astute Theo was looking for ways to bring in more of these artists. However, at this important moment in art, Goupil's unexpectedly proposed a transfer for Theo to their branch in New York.6

In Vincent's mind, he was Cain and Theo was Abel. Vincent was cursed and had lived a life fraught with failures, whereas for Theo there seemed to be a new blessing around every corner. Success always came his way. The offer for Theo to go to New York was one more indication of his success. The thought of Theo again advancing at a time when Vincent was headed for an opportunity to do something great was eating at Vincent's gut like an angry ulcer, reminding him he was the forever-cursed Cain. Being Cain, Vincent made it his life's work to prevent Theo, the blessed Abel, from enjoying or achieving additional successes.

This was at the heart of everything Vincent did in his life. He never outgrew the envy he had developed for Theo early on. In fact, his envy only grew stronger over time as Theo became more successful as an art dealer. Now, here again, when Vincent had a real chance to overtake Theo through his art, Theo was being offered something better that would take him out of Vincent's controlling grasp. Vincent couldn't allow Theo to go to New York.

As weeks passed without Theo deciding on the offer, I would suggest, the green poison of envy turned and twisted in Vincent's mind until all the old memories were squeezed out into the forefront again. All the old hurts Theo had caused him by being what Vincent should have been came back to life. It was Vincent who first followed in their wealthy Uncle Cent's footsteps by becoming an art dealer at Goupil's.[7] He was to be the replacement and heir to Uncle Cent's throne. But Theo had come up behind him and snatched away his crown. It should have been Vincent who was the manager of the Paris branch and being offered the position in New York. It was he who should have been in the right spot at the right time as an art dealer when the Impressionists came to fruition. Instead, Vincent was stuck with struggling to paint something impossibly unique while living off the crumbs Theo threw his way.

Always calculating, Vincent added a variable to the equation to help keep Theo from taking the New York proposal. He went ahead with his idea of an association of artists and invited his struggling artist friend, Paul Gauguin, to come and live with him in Arles where they could share expenses at the Yellow House.[8] Gauguin was in debt, ill, and his paintings weren't selling. Gauguin had previously written Theo asking for help, and now Vincent began to push Theo to represent Gauguin and go along with the idea of them living and painting together in the Yellow House. Theo decided representing Gauguin was a good idea, and Gauguin agreed to this. However, Gauguin didn't agree to the Arles move. It was left up in the air.

In June of 1888, everything remained uncertain for Vincent. He didn't know if Theo would move to New York and ruin everything or whether Gauguin would agree to move to Arles. If Gauguin agreed, this would help keep Theo in Paris and keep him paying Vincent's way, which would allow Vincent to stay in Arles and continue to seek to paint something unique.

The pressures surrounding Vincent were building. All the difficulties he believed Theo had caused him were resurfacing. Along with this, the memories of how his parents, uncles and a cousin had betrayed him and disrupted his life must have also risen to the surface. And then there were the women he had loved who had not returned his love. They had jilted him and treated him like a leper. The most difficult was his first rejection, which was served up to him at the age of 21 by a girl he had met when he lived in London and was working for Goupil's. He forever felt the sting of failure when he thought of London.

London was where everything went wrong for Vincent. It was where all of his great hopes were dashed. And now, with the return of all those painful memories and unable to cope with the situation, Vincent-the-alcoholic turned back to what soothed his thoughts. He began again to drink heavily.

Drinking and painting went hand-in-hand for Vincent. An artist who knew him a few years earlier remarked on this: "He liked to have some brandy in his flask on his rambles, and he would not have liked to do without it."[9] More and more, Vincent was taking day trips out into the countryside with his trusty flask in hand to find new things to paint under the hot June sun.

Adding to his already scorched thoughts, Theo had written to say he had sent Gauguin 50 francs.[10] This was not what Vincent had intended. He wanted Gauguin with him in Arles to share the expenses, not to share his allowance.

Vincent expressed his anger at losing what rightfully belonged to him in a letter back to Theo: "But if Gauguin isn't on the rocks, then I am in no great hurry. And I withdraw my proposal categorically."[11]

Cracks were beginning to show in Vincent's wall of sobriety. Fissures were splitting down to the base, and his drinking increased. He couldn't cope with the memories of his past. Everything was going wrong again. Theo was ever advancing in life, while he was left to shrivel up and die down south in the hot sun, like a helpless worm stranded on a sidewalk.

Vincent had screwed up his courage in April and had fought with his demon of alcoholism and had prevailed. He had cast out the demon. But by June, the woes of his life took him by the hand and led him back to the bottle, and it wasn't just the one demon that returned, but legions, and Vincent was happy to see them. The tone of his letters began to change. He was talking of madness and of death. He was becoming something different.

Vincent had long ago accepted he was Cain, but he now gave-in more completely to the idea. If he was Cain, then he would be Cain like no one else had ever been Cain before. He was now fully committed to overtaking Theo and defeating him, and with a willingness to see this to the end, he could let go of any worries or fears which had held him back before. He was now willing to risk everything and throw all to the wind to prevail. If there still remained even a small bit of brotherly love hidden in his heart for Theo, he would now blacken it out and make the whole thing dark.

With this new, unfettered determination, Vincent reaffirmed his commitment to complete enough paintings for the 1889 World's Fair, adding in the same letter to Theo, "Before next year I mean to do my share of 50 pictures."

As the old memories were allowed to bubble up again, pockets of previous fantasies, no doubt, also reemerged. Adding a steady flow of liquor helped to shift and shape the fantasies into darker and deeper visions of blood and revenge. A magical brew began to blend together in the caldron of Vincent's mind. His past rejections by women and his ever-growing envy for Theo were stirring together with the hatred he had for his family. They had all betrayed him and had turned his sweet water bitter.

Vincent continued to spend his afternoons in the fields painting and drinking, and his fantasies swirled and mixed together until a growing idea drifted up to the surface. During his Paris years, he had begun drinking absinthe, a popular drink in France at the time. It was a strong liquor with essence of wormwood as an ingredient, which is a powerful extract proven to cause hallucinations.[12] Vincent was sipping his brandy by day as he painted in the fields, and then at night, he visited the cafés and let glasses of absinthe paint fairytale visions across his mind.

The brew in Vincent's head was stirring faster, and a wicked witch of sorts was whispering in his ear, filling his fantasies of sex and revenge with new thoughts of how he could obtain power and glory. The witch knew Vincent was already a murderer. And the witch knew, and then Vincent knew, it was the spilling of blood which gave him power. He then realized, I believe, he could act again on his revenge and use murder to gain the power he needed to paint something unique. This would be the secret power he had over other artists who were aspiring to create great things for the World's Fair—the power that could only be gained by the taking of a life.

Vincent was becoming a new being, and he was beginning to paint more vigorously. Just having the fantasies of murder gave him a motivation to paint great paintings, and he completed one after another. His new attitude was not only showing up in his paintings and in his letters to Theo, but he also let it spill out into a letter to John Russell, an Australian artist he had met in Paris.[13]

Writing in English, Vincent wrote a sloppy and lighthearted letter, speaking of how he had been too "abstracted" with painting recently to finish a letter to him. As he often did, Vincent drew a sketch on one of the pages to give an idea of the painting he was working on. The sketch was of a sower in a field. He drew the sketch and wrote the letter with a reed pen, which was not commonly used by others, but was common for Vincent.

A reed pen is basically a thick reed with the end sharpened at an angle on one side and then notched in the middle. It creates a distinctive writing style, generally thicker and sloppier than a fountain pen, as can be seen in the Russell letter in figure 2.2. Vincent had previously discovered the use of a reed pen for drawing, but because he liked it so much, he occasionally used it for letter writing too—as opposed to using the standard fountain pen of the day, or a pencil.

But Vincent did more than include a drawing in this letter. Within the drawing, he whimsically expressed that new being he was becoming. As he directed the dance of his reed pen across the page, laying down his familiar stoke, he let some of what was playing in his mind have a twirl too. In the background, he dropped in a fence across the drawing, mostly using quick down strokes. As he moved from left to right, he stopped before the sower, picked up the reed pen and put it down again on the other side of the sower. Then, a little of Vincent's thoughts leaked out, and he wrote the word "Ha" hidden in the fence, as shown in figure 2.3. A few more quick strokes, and he wrote the same word again but in lower case—"ha." The two were meant to be together as one expression—"Ha, ha!"

There was more play in the drawing with the reed pen. At the bottom of the drawing, beginning above the word "violet," a series of swoops like the top stroke of a capital "R" and of a capital "P" travel to the right, as shown in figure 2.4. They look like capital "R's" and "P's" because they are. He repeatedly wrote the word "RIP" and overlapped and included other strokes nearby for cover.

Vincent was allowing his dark side to come out and play. It was a slight risk to hide a few English words in a drawing in a letter to a fellow artist whose native language was English, but what fun it was. Besides, Russell wouldn't know what to make of it even if he did notice the words. It would only be another one of Vincent's eccentricities.

In an entry in his journal many years later, Paul Gauguin wrote about a curious story which Vincent had told him. There were two recent cases of murder in Paris which were heavily followed by the public in the newspapers—one committed by Pranzini, and the other by Prado. Surprisingly, Vincent shared with Gauguin he had a connection to the murderers. Gauguin wrote about Vincent:

> As he was very much in love with La [Segatori], . . .
> he had a good many confidences from her about
> [Pranzini]. . . . According to Van Gogh, the whole
> [Pranzini] affair, as well as many others, was
> hatched in this place, with the connivance of
> [Segatori] and [her] lover. From this [Pranzini] case
> sprang another case, also, according to Vincent,
> hatched in this famous cafe, the Prado case. [14]

Segatori was the manager of the Paris café, Le Tambourin. While living in Paris, Vincent had developed a relationship with her and had worked out a deal to trade his paintings for food at the café.

Pranzini had murdered a woman, her maid and the maid's daughter—hacking their necks horribly with a large knife.[15] He fled to Marseille where he made a gift of the dead woman's jewelry to another woman, leading to his capture and conviction. His head was then cut off in public by the guillotine in 1887.[16]

Prado had committed a similar crime, cutting the throat of a woman and fleeing Paris.[17] He returned to Paris in early 1888 where he was captured and awaited trial.

As Vincent evolved into something different in June of 1888, his mind must have drifted back to those days in Paris in the café with Segatori and her stories of Pranzini and Prado. It was their notoriety which currently tickled his fancy. The newspapers had covered every detail of the trial and execution of Pranzini, and now the details of the capture of Prado and his swindling and murdering ways created a similar stir in the papers.

Something was percolating in Vincent. He wanted something big in art, but he also wanted something big in another way, like Pranzini and Prado. Their names were well known for their murders because they had been captured. Vincent certainly didn't want that, but he wanted a similar notoriety.

The new Vincent was emerging from his cocoon and saw the world with new eyes. His creative mind grabbed hold of the desires in his fantasies and came up with a way to make them reality with the intent of receiving the acclaim he desired. He would become two. He would create another entity—a persona that could receive the notoriety for his darker work while leaving his true identity hidden.

If one wished to create a separate entity, the first order of business was to come up with a good name—a name which represented the persona well, like properly naming a new painting. By mid-June, Vincent had the beginnings of the name of his new persona, and being the devious imp that he was, he couldn't keep it to himself. He had to share it in some hidden way, just as he had done when he had allowed his darker side to leak out in the Russell letter. Now, he let it leak out again, this time in a letter to his sister, Wil. Vincent described how he looked in a recent self-portrait, noting his yellow straw hat was "like a *hannekenmaaier's*."[18] The Dutch word *hannekenmaaier* was where Vincent revealed his new name without Wil knowing it. A footnote to this letter defined the word as "'Little Jack the Mower (or Reaper),' seasonal laborers who in past centuries came to Holland from Western Germany as mowers or harvesters."

Little Jack the Mower is only slightly interesting, but the second option, Little Jack the Reaper, is enormously more interesting. The similarity of Little Jack the Reaper to Jack the Ripper is remarkable. Vincent was describing himself as a Little Jack the Reaper.

Vincent had not only come up with the concept of creating a persona he fantasized of murdering by, but now he had the beginnings of the name for this other being. He would think on the name some more until he got it just right.

* * *

The newness of Arles was wearing off, and Vincent was growing restless. Referring to the depiction of the area as presented in the novels by the writer, Alphonse Daudet, Vincent wrote to Theo, "I see nothing here of the Southern gaiety that Daudet talks about so much but on the contrary, all kinds of insipid airs and graces, a sordid carelessness."[19]

His irritability was growing too. Theo hadn't accepted the proposal to go to New York but hadn't declined it either. And Gauguin still hadn't decided whether or not he would accept Vincent's invitation to move to Arles. Everything remained frustratingly suspended in midair.

Even in this state of uncertainty, Vincent was painting like a madman, but he didn't believe he was making enough progress. Expressing his frustration to Theo in a letter, he wrote, "I have not yet done half the 50 canvases fit to be shown in public, and I must do them all this year."[20]

His edginess and feverish state of mind then came out in full when he responded in late June to a letter from a young artist he had befriended in Paris, Émile Bernard. He had a much looser relationship with Bernard than he had with Theo, and his current frustrations and agitations spilled out onto the page in the form of strong opinions about prostitutes. Bernard had started the discussion, and Vincent added his own personal touch:

> The whore reminds us of meat in the market place. That's all right, the whore is like meat in a butcher's shop. I, though, having become a mere brute; I understand, I feel it, I rediscover a sensation in my own life.[21]

Referring to prostitutes as "meat in a butcher's shop" seems a tad startling coming from Vincent-the-painter, but for a psychopath who had previously played the part of a butcher and had carved up some of that meat in the past, it's a reasonable and satisfying description.

Admitting he had become "a mere brute," he was revealing what affect this topic had on him. Like a captured wolf reintroduced back into the wild who catches a sniff of rabbit on the wind and feels its killer instinct return, Vincent told of how he understood and felt the meaning of his words and how they caused him to "rediscover a sensation" in his life. He was rediscovering his hunger for the kill.

Throughout June and July of 1888, Vincent continued to paint furiously, but he had also begun to drink just as furiously. He wrote to Theo about how hard he was working and described how he dealt with the stress he was under:

"If the storm within gets too loud, I take a glass too much to stun myself."[22] He had given up on sobriety and was back to drinking full swing. He embraced his alcoholism and didn't even try to hide it. Writing to Theo again, he noted, "As for drinking too much, . . . if it is bad, I can't tell."[23] He believed he needed to drink to paint, and to paint with such fervor, he had to drink excessively and continuously.

With his increased drinking, Vincent's old problem of impotency returned, which meant he had to limit his trips to the brothel. He advised Bernard in a letter to do the same, writing, "You ought to live like a monk who goes to a brothel once every two weeks—that's what I do myself."[24] He then informed Theo in a letter of his problem by relating to a character he said was from a Guy de Maupassant story who discovered after he was married that he was impotent.[25] Vincent wrote, "I begin to resemble him physically." He then elaborated and added, "Man becomes ambitious as soon as he becomes impotent. Now though it's pretty much all the same to me whether I'm impotent or not, I'm damned if that's going to drive me to ambition."

Contrary to his declaration, Vincent was very much driven by ambition but wasn't about to let Theo know just how great it was. He would admit to something as personal as impotency, but even in this he attempted to downplay the importance of it in his life. As long as he could curb his drinking for a few days every couple of weeks, he could visit a prostitute without the problem. The two vices competed with one another, and naturally, Vincent wanted both worlds simultaneously and continuously.

In July, some of Vincent's stress was relieved when Gauguin finally responded and accepted the offer to move to Arles. But Gauguin's debts had grown too large.[26] It was difficult for him to afford to move, so it didn't appear he would be coming any time soon.

Vincent also had debts, and when he had left Paris, he left them unpaid. He didn't bother to let Theo in on this, but his debtors visited Theo looking for their money. One of these was Père Tanguy, the owner of an art supply store. Vincent felt Tanguy had benefited from their friendship and therefore didn't deserve to be paid. He also believed it wasn't actually Tanguy who was requesting the money, but instead, Tanguy's wicked wife. Vincent had a solution for this problem, and he wrote to Theo with it: "Old Tanguy would be right a hundred times over if he killed his lady, . . . but he won't do it."[27]

Certainly, no psychopathic killer would disagree with this. No middle ground here. Vincent didn't even bother to advise any lesser option, such as Tanguy standing up to his wife or perhaps leaving her. No, Vincent's solution for such evil women was to eliminate the problem entirely—to kill them. Vincent van Gogh was a psychopathic killer.

Theo was also visited at this time in Paris by John Russell, who had stopped by to see Vincent's paintings, and Russell wrote back to Vincent afterwards. He didn't mention anything about the "Ha, ha" or "RIP's" Vincent had hidden in his previous letter to him, but Russell did feel the need to express his opinion about Vincent's work. He informed Vincent, "That big one of yours unfortunately swamps in my opinion."[28] Vincent was never good at taking criticism about any area of his life, but especially not about his art. To amplify the indignity, this insult to his abilities came at a time when Vincent was pouring all he had into his paintings. This certainly infuriated him and drove him closer to his best friend the bottle.

But there was more news that would drive Vincent not just closer to the bottle but over the lip and down inside. Goupil's had given up on transferring Theo to the New York branch, but now they were considering transferring him to, of all places, their London branch.[29] This brought everything full-circle for Vincent's envy-filled mind. London was where Vincent had faltered on his path as an art dealer, and now, at this most important time in his life, Theo was possibly being sent there. Theo's replacement of Vincent would be complete. If Theo transferred to London and was a big success, as he was sure to be, then he would have done what was necessary to defeat Vincent.

Vincent always measured things in his life by what his family thought, and if Theo moved to London and succeeded, there would be the obvious comparison of Vincent's past failure to Theo's glorious triumph. The only thing worse would be if Theo also met an English girl and successfully married her—contrasting Vincent's failure in that area too.

With each new distraction, Vincent continued to worry whether his efforts to paint would be disrupted. His frustrations were pushing him harder towards his new persona and to what that new persona could bring him. The power he could tap into from murder could infuse something into his paintings that had possibly never before been produced by any other artist. And with each new frustration, his fantasies were becoming more refined and vivid. The glasses of absinthe made the fantasies seem all the more possible and gave him the courage to believe he could complete what he was contemplating.

If his fantasies were to be acted upon, they would involve travel, and his letters began to show signs he was looking at maps and thinking of trains and steamboats. He wrote to Bernard about an interesting idea that stars could possibly be accessible after death and compared this thought to "the black dots which symbolize towns and villages on geographical maps."[30] In a similar vein, he expanded on this poetic concept in a letter to Theo:

> Looking at the stars always makes me dream, as
> simply as I dream over the black dots representing
> towns and villages on a map. . . . Just as we take the
> train to get to Tarascon or Rouen, we take death to
> reach a star.[31]

He continued the travel theme when he then described one of his landscapes to Theo in another letter as being "like a map, a strategic plan as far as the execution goes."[32]

Vincent was looking at maps and dreaming of traveling back to London to act out his dark fantasies which were yearning to step out into the light of reality. He would need to prepare. He could easily invent the needed reason for being out of town for a few days to give to the few people he knew in Arles without any concern they would suspect he was lying. But Theo would require better excuses if Vincent were thinking of being away long enough to possibly break the pattern of their expected back and forth letters by not responding within a day or two.

With this in mind, Vincent began to develop excuses in his letters that would provide reasons for the possibility of missing Theo's letters. He wrote, "Work engrosses me so much I cannot manage to write letters."[33] And in case Theo happened to wonder why Vincent wasn't replying and thought of inquiring to others in Arles about him, he planted a possible reason for Theo to think about and therefore avoid his inquiry in the event he was delayed in London, writing, "Often whole days pass without my speaking to anyone."

He also wrote of the trips he was taking into the countryside to paint, noting how often he took these trips: "Yet I went fully fifty times to Mont Majour."[34] He also provided the length of time he was away, adding, "I have spent whole days outside with a little bread and milk, since it was too far to go back to the town every once in a while."

Vincent was establishing his cover stories in case they were needed. If he missed one of Theo's letters and didn't write back in a timely manner, Theo was to understand he had become very busy, and that sometimes he stayed out in the fields all day, or even for a few days, and even if he stayed in Arles, he might not talk to anyone for days, so don't bother to check on him. He was laying the groundwork for following through on his fantasies which had matured into plans, but he had yet to commit to the implementation of those plans.

✳   ✳   ✳

If Vincent had not yet fully understood he was creating a separate persona, then on July 24, he could have read about a coming play that dealt very succinctly with what was churning within his own soul and could have helped him draw the obvious conclusion. The London newspaper, the *Pall Mall Gazette*, reported that *Dr. Jekyll and Mr. Hyde* was to begin at the Lyceum Theater in London on August 4. The American actor who brought the play to London, Richard Mansfield, was interviewed and described Robert Louis Stevenson's conception of the story: "All he wanted to do . . . was to give one man's soul two bodies." This was what Vincent was doing. He was Vincent-the-painter, but he was developing an elixir that when swallowed down would suppress the painter and bring forth the cunning nature of a new kind of sexual serial killer who was otherwise only allowed to run loose in the chambers of his fantasies. All that was needed was a triggering event of some kind, so he could let it out into the real world.

3

Stabs And Jabs
July-August 1888

At many times in Vincent's life, the hand of fate seemed to reach in at just the right moment and pull the lever that turned the gears that determined the direction of his life. Most of those times, the mysterious hand on the lever was none other than Vincent's own hand disguised as fate's. But at other times, certain events beyond his control conveniently occurred at just the right time. Whether these events were directed by the hand of God or by the cloven hoof of the devil, Vincent did not care, but he did believe there was a force working to help him in his plight.

On July 31, 1888, this invisible power had again looked on Vincent with favor and had taken action to help. He had received a letter from his sister, Wil, informing him of their beloved Uncle Cent's death on July 28 (figure 3.1, photo of Uncle Cent).[1] Naturally, his family was terribly grieved by the news, but Vincent seemed instead to be delighted. It appeared to be just what he needed, at just the right moment, to bring his developing creation of another self to life. For Vincent, his uncle's death meant one could become two.

Vincent had become estranged from his uncle many years earlier after Uncle Cent had grown weary of Vincent's relentless self-inflicted troubles and had pulled the plug on continuing to support and communicate with Vincent. Vincent knew he would not be receiving any of his uncle's inheritance.

Theo, on the other hand, remained in good stead with Uncle Cent, and he was sure to receive at least a portion of their wealthy uncle's large inheritance. This was the reason for Vincent's delight. He knew Theo would soon be receiving a nice chunk of money, and to Vincent, anything Theo had, Vincent could get.

With more money coming to Theo, Vincent had some assurance he could remain in Arles and continue to paint. It wouldn't matter as much if Theo went to London or whether Gauguin decided to join him in Arles. He would have the resources to continue.

This released some of the pressure which had been building around Vincent's uncertainty of what direction his life would take. However, his feelings of rage and resentment towards his family, and especially towards

Theo, would not be diminished. His desire to exact his perceived revenge would also not waver. His plans would not change. In fact, they could be sped up. He didn't have to wait until September, which for him would have been the perfect time to begin. He could go to London and kill at the first opportunity he had. Then, if he so desired, because there would be the money for it, he could make the trip again in September.

With the prospect of future money, Vincent knew he could travel to London and kill under his new identity and be back on a train to Arles before the London police had their afternoon tea, and no one in Arles or in Paris would be the wiser. He could satisfy that growing bloodlust he was feeling, and he could gain the extra power that comes from murder to create magnificently unique paintings for all to see at the 1889 World's Fair in Paris—paintings no other painter dared dream of creating.

Vincent had no plans of traveling back to Holland to attend Uncle Cent's funeral, but he expected Theo would, and the thought of this started his caldron of envy bubbling again. Vincent, no doubt, imagined Theo back at home with their mother, their youngest brother, the three sisters, all the cousins and aunts and uncles, each long-faced and tormented with grief over the loss of the generous and well-loved Uncle Cent. And standing in their midst, the bastion of stability, Theo, looking just as forlorn and grieved as the others. But Theo would be a comfort to the afflicted and show strength in this time of tragedy, while all their weeping eyes looked upon him as the new leader of their family. They would see Theo as the replacement of the successful Uncle Cent. They would show such reverence and such respect for Theo.

"But where is Vincent?" nobody would be heard to inquire, for he was the bad seed. He had spoiled what Uncle Cent had tried to give him. He was Cain, and Theo was Abel.

Theo did attend Uncle Cent's funeral, but before he left, he sent Vincent 50 francs. Vincent wrote back and thanked him for the money and then characteristically asked for more. When he didn't hear back from Theo immediately, he wrote again on August 3, and even though he had just received 50 francs, he noted, "I could not pay my rent on the first, as I had had the model all week."[2] He then explained how he handled the landlord: "But it was just when I put my fellow off till next Monday for the month's rent that he said something about being able to find another tenant for the house." Vincent was playing on Theo's worry strings to elicit a quick response and to prod him into sending more money. He was ready to take a trip.

Vincent finally heard from Theo, and on Monday, August 6, Vincent responded back with a specific purpose in mind. He needed Theo to send even more money, and he needed to control when Theo would respond and send it.

"I shall not be able to manage this week," he wrote, "because this very day I am paying out 25 frs.; I shall have money for five days, but not for seven. This is Monday; if I get your next letter on Saturday morning, there will be no need to increase the enclosure."[3]

Van Gogh biographer, Ronald Pickvance, dated this letter as August 6, which makes good sense because Vincent stated it was Monday, which was the 6th, and because he had said he had put his landlord off until Monday, and now he was paying him that day. He likely had received at least another 25 francs from Theo, because he notes he paid the 25 francs to the landlord.

It was very common for Vincent to continually ask for more money, but it was not common for him to state he would have "money for five days, but not for seven." In general, he always worked at making his situation sound as dire as ever, continually emphasizing how he needed the money immediately. But here, he actually seemed to be showing some restraint by saying he could make it last five days.

He had also done something even more unusual, and I think telling, when he noted what day it was, by declaring, "this is Monday," and then by directing Theo to send him some money so that it would arrive "on Saturday morning." He wanted Theo to believe he wrote the letter on Monday, and he wanted Theo to wait until Friday to send him a letter back with money.

I believe Vincent wrote this letter and placed it in a public mailbox on Sunday, August 5, and then left Arles by train the same day. The post office was open on Sundays, but the mail in the public mailboxes would not be picked up until Monday and would therefore not be postmarked until Monday. Knowing this, Vincent made an issue of it being Monday to make it appear he was there in Arles sending the letter that day, as the postmark would verify. Vincent was using the postal system to help create cover for a trip.

Also, by saying he only had money for five days and directing Theo to send his response to arrive on Saturday morning, Vincent was attempting to avert Theo from responding too quickly to his letter. Vincent's letter would very likely be in Theo's hands on Tuesday, and if Theo responded the same day, it would arrive back in Arles on Wednesday. If Vincent were out of town on a clandestine trip to London, he wouldn't be able to respond quickly, and Theo might wonder what was going on with the ever-mischievous Vincent. To help avoid this, Vincent tried to control Theo's response. He didn't write "by" Saturday morning, he wrote "on" Saturday morning. He wanted Theo to wait until Friday to send him a letter with money so it would arrive on Saturday, giving Vincent plenty of time to get back to Arles while also providing him with money he would need after returning from his travels.

In this same letter, just as he had done in the Russell letter with the "Ha, ha" and the "RIP's" and as he had done with the Little Jack the Reaper letter to Wil, Vincent's constant need to live on the edge and toy with the reader of his letters by secretly hinting at what he was up to compelled him to add a comment related to his approaching trip to London. Remarkably, he wrote, "I always feel I am a traveler, going somewhere and to some destination."4

Vincent loved the idea Theo would be opening his letter in Paris on Tuesday, unquestioningly believing Vincent had sent the letter on Monday from Arles, while at that very moment Vincent would be sitting in a London pub enjoying a glass of beer after having been that traveler he spoke of.

Vincent also gave a hint of his serial killer side and what was on his mind for this journey. He added to a comment Theo had made about their deceased uncle looking so calm at the funeral, and he wrote, "I have often observed a similar effect as I looked on the dead as though to question them." Often indeed. Vincent was heading for London and heading for murder.

The first Monday of each August in London had been decreed an annual Bank Holiday, and in 1888, the first Monday fell on the 6th. For the extremely poor sorts who lived in an area like the East End, a Bank Holiday generated an increase in activity on the streets. Costermongers and the like, with their goods for sale, lined the main streets calling out for customers to come have a look.

But the hottest selling items were found in the many pubs. Beer and ale were the favorites because they were the cheapest, but for the hard-laboring men of the Whitechapel District, beer and ale weren't the only enjoyment to be had. The poorest of the poor prostitutes of Whitechapel knew this all too well, and they flocked to the pubs and the street corners and sold their merchandise right alongside the other tradespeople.

On that Monday night, two prostitutes picked up two soldiers, and the four drifted in and out of the pubs for a while and then off into the night to find a more secluded place to do their business.

Fifteen minutes before midnight, the four split into couples and headed in opposite directions to find their separate quiet spots. The soldiers were a corporal and a private. The corporal chose Mary Ann Connelly, more affectionately known as Pearly Poll, and they headed up Angel Alley. The private was then matched up with Martha Tabram, and they made their way up George Yard.

At about ten minutes after midnight, Pearly Poll and the corporal had returned to George Yard, but Martha Tabram and the private had not, so

Pearly left the corporal there and headed back down Commercial Road to look for more business.

Martha Tabram would not be rejoining Pearly Poll that night, nor any other night. She was found on the first-floor landing of an apartment building later that morning at 4:45. She was first noticed there at 3:30, but it was assumed she was only using the dark landing as a place to sleep for the night—not uncommon for the area. But Martha Tabram wasn't asleep. She had been stabbed 39 times and was very much dead.

Dr. Timothy Killeen was called to the scene and performed the postmortem and concluded she had been dead for about three hours.[5] He believed the wounds were caused during life by a knife, dagger, or possibly a bayonet (figure 3.2, mortuary photo of Tabram).

She had been stabbed 9 times in the throat, 17 times in the chest, and 13 times in the region of the belly. The assailant had punctured both lungs, the liver, stomach, the heart, and even the spleen.

There were no witnesses to Martha Tabram's murder. None of the residents of the apartment building heard a scream or a cry for help, even though Martha was murdered on the landing of the stairs, just feet from the doors of some of the residents.

The only possible suspect was the private who was last seen with Martha by Pearly Poll. The police tracked down Pearly and took her to two different barracks and paraded soldiers before her. She picked out two she thought might be the man, but one was proven to have been with his wife, and the other had been at the barracks during the time of the murder.

The police made every effort to uncover other witnesses and evidence, but all inquiries turned up empty, and the murder of Martha Tabram went unsolved. The inquest was held, and the jurors reached their verdict: "Murdered by some person or persons unknown."[6]

It was only natural for the police to follow up on the private as the most likely suspect, since this was who Tabram was last seen with. However, a habit of error began with the Tabram murder which would plague the police, the newspapers, and the public throughout all the Jack the Ripper murders. The always-present "red herring" was leading them into a swampy culvert of misdirection, helping to keep the real killer free from suspicion and capture.

On August 7, 1873, fifteen years prior to the very same day of the murder of Martha Tabram in 1888, a very young Vincent had written a letter to some friends in Holland, the Haanebeek family. He had recently moved to London from The Hague, where the Haanebeeks lived, and he had written, "Last Monday I had a nice day. The first Monday in August is a holiday here."[7]

The older, weatherworn Vincent of 1888, who was living far away from London in the southern French town of Arles, knew from firsthand knowledge, having lived in London, there would be a Bank Holiday there on the first Monday in August. He knew ahead of time that on the night of Monday, August 6, the streets of London, and especially the darker streets of the East End, would be a bit livelier than usual with Londoners enjoying their holiday.

Having begun to drink heavily again and having received the sad but welcome news of the passing of his uncle, the deliciously inviting aroma of a Bank Holiday in London was more than just a little tantalizing for Vincent. It fit in so well with his fantasies of returning to exact his revenge on the good people of London, and more specifically on their women of the streets—returning to them murder for the pain he perceived they had caused him, while reaping from murder a power he could use to paint things never imagined.

Being drawn by the recalled memories and smells of the streets of London, Vincent dropped the letter to Theo in the public mailbox on Sunday, August 5, and climbed aboard the northbound train to Paris. Sometime on Monday the 6th, Vincent was again standing on those same streets of London he so loved, smelling the smells and seeing the sights with evil intent in his blackened heart.

Whether Vincent left Arles on the morning, afternoon, or evening of the 5th, he still arrived in London sometime on Monday the 6th, just in time to participate with Londoners in their Bank Holiday.

He arrived with a purpose. He had come to London to murder. But Vincent-the-painter wasn't a murderer unless he built up his courage, and that required lots of alcohol. So, he likely spent the first part of the night in the pubs with the locals having a few drinks and observing their merriment. However, Vincent had learned from the two sloppy attacks in the spring that he must curtail his drinking beforehand, and he kept it controlled. Acting under the purview of his new persona, he knew he mustn't allow himself to overdo it. He needed just enough drink for courage, but not too much to be a careless mush.

Vincent had been fantasizing about murdering under the cloak of another persona all summer long. This other persona, who at this point was still early in development, and whose name was only preliminarily created as Little Jack the Reaper, would employ all the experience of his previous murders but would also become something new and murder in a new way. Vincent could let his remolded devilish side come out and run the show.

Thinking as Little Jack the Reaper, Vincent would make some adjustments. Besides limiting his drinking to keep a clear head, he would also make preparations for the murder by searching out an appropriate murder site beforehand to lure a prostitute. This new persona would be a thinker and a planner. He would make sure there were no witnesses and make sure he had a good escape route. But even more important than the careful planning, with this new persona, Vincent would employ a certain technique to make certain his victims were dead.

The two attacks in the spring were spontaneous drunken rages which left his victims alive. That could never be allowed to happen again. Also, both victims screamed, forcing him to flee before finishing the job. That too must never happen again. As Vincent mulled over these problems out in the fields over the summer, he contemplated how best Little Jack the Reaper could carry out his wishes while keeping his victim quiet and insuring death. After dreaming over and fantasizing about the various methods of murder, Vincent discovered and decided on the best method, and all he needed was a short piece of rope.

Vincent must have found his new method while looking over the collection of Japanese prints he owned, and in particular when he saw a print by Ichiyū-sai Kuniyoshi ga, which depicts a kabuki actor portraying the Buddhist deity known as Fudō.[8] In the image, as seen in figure 3.3, the actor is wearing a traditional robe and holding a sword in his right hand and a coil of rope in his left. Vincent could relate to the sword being like his knife, but with the use of the sword being so commonly depicted in Japanese prints, that wasn't what stood out for him and gave him his new method. It was the rope in the actor's left hand which was uncommon and which must have caused Vincent to stop and ponder the print further. And in pondering the rope together with the sword, he must have had an "Ah, ha!" moment.

Vincent understood he could use the rope, or cord, to first strangle his victim, and then use the sword, or knife, to stab and cut as he saw fit. He would have also liked the mystical aspect of it being a Buddhist deity that led him to this discovery. Examining the image further, he must have also uncovered the other aspect of the print which he could make use of.

Because the print was of an actor dressed up like and portraying the Fudō deity, Vincent must have furthered his "Ah, ha!" moment by understanding he could apply his new method of murder also as a kind of actor who was depicting a greater power than himself. He could create his own Fudō, a deity, or persona, which he could slip into for the planning and performing of his murders. From this one Japanese print, Vincent had established a new method of murder and had begun his development of an alter ego to murder by—who he would eventually name Jack the Ripper.

＊　＊　＊

The *Illustrated Police News* of Aug 18, 1888, described how Martha Tabram looked after her murder: "The face and head [were] so swollen and distorted in consequence that her real features are not discernible."[9] This was not noted at the inquest by Dr. Killeen, but the coroner didn't ask for further information, which was likely due to the obvious conclusion that the many stabs had caused her death and therefore nothing further needed to be considered. But taking into account that Tabram's head and face were swollen brings in the reasonable assumption that strangulation was first used before the knife.

A swollen face on a corpse could indicate strangulation, along with other such indicators as bulging eyes, a swollen and protruding tongue, and dark blood in the brain. But another indicator was the lack of any screams being heard by the tenants of the building whose doors were just feet away. It would be reasonable to believe a woman being stabbed 39 times would at some point cry out for help, in fact, be kicking and screaming and attempting to block the blows with her hands and arms. This is especially relevant when it is noted that Dr. Killeen felt all the stab wounds were made while the victim was still alive. There may have been defensive wounds on her hands and arms, but he didn't note any. All of this points to the victim first being incapacitated.

I believe Vincent, as the prowling Little Jack the Reaper, surveyed and found an acceptable location for his murder. Then later, in the same vicinity, he searched for a prostitute who he felt most deserved to die that night. Convincing his chosen prey he knew a good spot to do business, he then walked her up the stairs in George Yard and strangled her with a cord on the dark landing of the stairs. After her body went limp, he lowered her to the floor of the landing. Not hearing any approaching footsteps, he unleashed his beastly side, stabbing her repeatedly in a sexually charged fury, being sure to hit the heart and the throat several times to insure death.

With so many stabs, and with so much fury, slings of blood would have certainly flipped off the blade onto his hands, face, and clothes, but Vincent was an experienced killer. Because he was thinking as his more cautious new persona would think, he likely located a place beforehand such as a water trough for horses or some back alley well-pump where he could quickly run to and rinse off. The body wasn't discovered for three hours. Vincent was cleaned up and long gone by then.

The use of the knife in a stabbing action on Martha Tabram matches back to the two attempted murders in the spring. Annie Millwood had been stabbed multiple times in the lower body, and Ada Wilson received two jabs in the neck. All three victims can be stitched together by the related stabs and by surmising that the stabs to each of the women's bodies were sexually motivated by a man acting out from a sexually frustrated rage, likely caused by bouts of impotency. I believe this was the case and that all three were stabbed by the same hand — Vincent van Gogh's. Vincent had learned from his fantasies over the summer to limit his drinking and to strangle first.

Appropriate and fitting, the play *Dr. Jekyll and Mr. Hyde* had opened over the Bank Holiday weekend to the delight of Londoners looking for a ghoulish thrill. They didn't know a real Mr. Hyde lurked among them in their city looking to satisfy his decadent desires. Nor did they ever expect a real Mr. Hyde could be far bloodier and far more terrifying than what was portrayed on the stage. The play would soon become a tame comparison.

Making his escape and washing up after the murder of Martha Tabram, Vincent was then likely led by his thirst to find a quick drink. Afterwards, he may have looked for a good spot away from the East End, perhaps in a park or behind a church in a cemetery, where he could curl up under the stars for a few hours of sleep. Then, with the break of dawn and the light of a new day shinning on his crime, Vincent, acting under the command of his more careful persona and feeling the worry of a letter from Theo arriving in Arles, decided it was best not to dawdle in London, and he began his journey back home.

With cost in mind, Vincent had likely bought a roundtrip ticket when he was in Paris, and sometime later on the same day he had murdered Tabram on the 7th, he boarded a train back to the coast, hopped on a steamer across the channel, and then rode a train back into Paris. He had also likely bought a cheaper roundtrip ticket in Arles for the train to and from Paris, and he used that to take the long final leg of his journey home. He was back in Arles sometime on Wednesday, August 8, having only been gone three days—not enough time away to raise a suspicious eyebrow, even if any Arlesians had paid attention to his comings and goings.

Vincent had returned earlier than it appears he had planned, considering his request for Theo to send his reply and money so that it arrived on Saturday the 10th. This must have been the day he had planned to return, but because he didn't want to risk capture in London, he adjusted his plans and cut his trip short and returned early. But he must have also returned early because he feared Theo would again ignore his attempt to delay his response, and therefore a letter from Theo would be waiting for him when he returned, as had happened when Vincent had returned after attacking Ada Wilson on his trip to London in March. And if so, Theo would be expecting a quick response back.

When Vincent returned to his hotel room on Wednesday the 8th, he was relieved to not find a letter from Theo waiting for him. Therefore, he didn't need to write Theo that day to cover for a slow response. But he wanted to be sure Theo had no reason to imagine he wasn't where he ought to be and was definitely not hopping on trains and steamers all over Europe. He also needed more money, and this was likely another reason he came back from London early—he had spent more than expected on his trip.

To establish he was there in Arles on Wednesday and to pull at Theo's heartstrings to get him to send more money right away, Vincent wrote, "Already on Wednesday evening, I have exactly 5 francs left."[10] In the same letter, he added an indication the trip to London did him some good. He told Theo, "I am feeling very, very well these days."

Vincent had created something new and had succeeded at murdering under this new guise in a way which was controlled and well thought out. He had been able to pull in the reins on his drinking to keep his head clear, and he had followed through on his planning by searching out beforehand the murder site and escape route options. Then also, by applying the new method of strangulation first, he was then allowed to thrust his knife into his victim repeatedly without even a peep. He then stole away into the night leaving no clue to be traced. There was no trail of evidence that could guide a London detective back to Arles.

Vincent had obtained the power he sought, and he used it to set to work on his paintings with a restored vigor and eagerness. He could let his enlivened mind dream up new fantasies of murder while he painted out in the fields and pondered how he could improve on the methods of his other self. Part of him was now Little Jack the Reaper—a worker in the fields who reaped the wheat with the sharp edge of a swinging scythe.

The murder of Martha Tabram had gone well, but there were areas which still needed work, and with his creative and clever mind, Vincent could imagine murdering more perfectly. And having imagined, he would want to implement.

4

Down By The Gate
August 1888

Referring to art from an earlier letter to Theo, Vincent borrowed a doctor's saying, and wrote, "One starts by killing, one ends up curing."[1] This may have also been just how Vincent felt in August of 1888 after murdering Martha Tabram and returning to his painting in Arles—killing was curing him.

Like a starved man who's been fed, Vincent wrote to Theo, "Yes, really, I am as well as other men now . . . and it is rather pleasant."[2] Vincent had succeeded in murdering as Little Jack the Reaper and was reaping the benefits. It was the power that came from having total control over another human being through the taking of their life which satisfied his hunger and gave him what he needed. With that power came a renewed confidence in his art, and he channeled this new energy into painting vibrant portraits and brilliant landscapes.

The murder of Tabram not only acted as a devilish muse for his paintings, but the associated sexual aspect of the murder likely also acted as a stimulus to his problem with impotency. By subduing his victim and taking away her perceived power over him, he was taking away the power he felt all strong women had over him. Martha Tabram was a substitute for the women in Vincent's past who he wanted to exact violent and sexual revenge on.

Vincent expressed where his thoughts were when he commented on a book Theo had sent him which mentioned lesbianism. He wrote, "Why should it be forbidden to handle these subjects, unhealthy and overexcited sexual organs seek sensual delights. . . . Not I, who have hardly seen anything but the kind of women at 2 francs, originally intended for the Zouaves."[3]

Murder was something that made Vincent whole. Acting as a cure, Vincent could continue to drink without the ugly consequence of impotency. He could replay the murder in his mind and relive the sexual thrill of the kill. Murder allowed him to do the three things he most loved to do, and to do them better: drink, paint, and have sex with prostitutes. Vincent was equally obsessed with each, and each had feedlines which poked into one another and continually pumped nutrients back and forth—murder acting like an infusion of B12 to the whole system.

Years before, when Theo had tried to advise Vincent to refrain from visiting prostitutes and to have some patience, Vincent responded with, "My life must become more stimulating if I want to get more brio into my work; I do not advance a hair's breadth by practicing patience."[4] To Vincent, having sex meant more "brio" for his paintings, and he felt he needed it in order to advance in painting. The same was becoming true for murder—he needed it to advance his paintings.

Now that Vincent was back to his normal life in Arles, he was faced again with the uncertainty which plagued his existence, and his thoughts returned to wondering whether Gauguin would be coming to Arles. He told Theo he was "thinking about Gauguin a lot," and he felt that if they each lived alone it would mean "living like madmen or criminals, in appearance at any rate, and also a little in reality."[5] Here again, Vincent had some of his impish fun by admitting he was a criminal, but he kept it hidden behind brushstrokes of innocuous levity.

By August 9, Vincent had found out his intuition about his Uncle Cent was correct. He wrote to Theo that it was "kind of Uncle to have left a legacy."[6] Theo would be receiving some of the inheritance, but Vincent pondered how much he could get for himself.

With the money on his mind, he began to grow cold to the idea of Gauguin moving to Arles. Speaking of Gauguin, he wrote in the same letter, "If one listened to him, one would go on hoping for something vague in the future, and meantime stay on at the inn, and go on living in a hell with no way out." He was frustrated from still not knowing what Gauguin would be doing but also worried Theo would use some of the inheritance to help Gauguin. His worries were founded.

Vincent wrote Theo on August 18 and thanked him for a 100 franc note. He then said, "It's very good of you to promise the two of us, Gauguin and me, that you'll put us in the way to carrying out our combination."[7] Vincent's plan to have Gauguin move to Arles continued to backfire. Theo had previously sent Gauguin money to support his painting and was now planning on spending the inheritance on them both instead of only giving a portion of it to Vincent. Naturally, this didn't sit well with Vincent. He felt Theo should give him his share and allow him to decide what to do with it. Any money for Gauguin should come from Theo's portion.

Vincent then got to what he was after when he then added about Gauguin and money, "But haven't I, with less desire than he for the struggle in Paris, the right to go my own way? Look here. As soon as you can, would you, not give, but lend me 300 francs in one lump sum for a year?" Vincent wanted his share.

He added a few well-crafted comments towards the end of the letter to be sure and touch on Theo's sympathy, writing, "Under the present conditions, . . . I do not feel I have strength enough left to go on like this for long." Adding to this, in the spirit of all melodramatic stage actors, he figuratively placed the back of his wilted hand to his forehead and wrote, "I am going to pieces and killing myself." That should do the trick.

On August 27, Vincent wrote Theo thanking him for 50 francs. It wasn't the 300 he had tried for, but it gave him enough for what he was after. Not even a full month had passed since the murder of Tabram, but the vibrancy of reliving the memory of the murder may have already been dimming. The power he had gained from it was lessening, and like a vampire who needs more blood to thrive, Vincent craved another murder. He still enjoyed reliving the details of Tabram's murder, but as he painted thick impasto landscapes and nursed his flask of rum out in the fields under the hot Mediterranean sun, he fantasized of another murder and saw how he could improve on the last one. He added improvements to his fantasies with the goal of giving Little Jack the Reaper another successful kill but with less risk and even greater skill. And while he was making adjustments and taking his new persona more seriously, he knew he also needed to adjust the name.

To Vincent, everything he did was big, not little. He couldn't be *Little* Jack the Reaper, so he dropped the "Little" and settled on Jack the Reaper. He was the Grim Reaper of death who held in his hands the power to take life. He could wield his scythe in the direction he chose, and death would come to whomever he decided deserved it.

As he thought on the adjustments, the most important change needed was a way to not be so covered in blood. The strangling of Tabram to first subdue her kept her quiet, but the blood from stabbing her sloshed and spewed and flipped and splattered on his hands, face, and clothing. Afterwards, he had to quickly find a secluded spot to get cleaned up. It added too much risk, and Jack the Reaper was a crafty devil who looked for ways to reduce risk.

In the previously mentioned August 27 letter to Theo, it appears Vincent revealed how he handled being covered in so much blood after Tabram's murder. He told Theo, "Only last week I bought a black velvet jacket of fairly good quality for 20 francs, and a new hat."[8] With so much blood on his hat and coat, he didn't bother trying to wash them clean. Instead, he discarded them in the gutter of some back alley and bought a cheap hat and coat off a street vendor. He couldn't afford to continue this practice, though. He needed to find a better way to kill which would keep his clothes clean. His continued fantasies would lead him to the answer.

In the same letter, Vincent noted an American artist he had been meeting with named Dodge MacKnight, who had lived in the nearby town of Fontvieille, had left. Earlier in the month of August, a Second Lieutenant of the Zouaves who Vincent had befriended and painted named Paul Milliet had also left. He still had a few other acquaintances in and around Arles, but having these two leave in August helped to lessen his accountability, which added to the likelihood he would take another trip for murder.

Much later on, both MacKnight and Milliet gave some insight into the Vincent they had known. MacKnight said of Vincent, "He was an interesting fellow and when he felt like it very companionable. But he was moody and quarrelsome, especially if any one did not agree with his opinions about art."[9]

Milliet lived in Arles and spent more time with Vincent, and therefore he had a more detailed description. His words convey well the contradictory nature of Vincent's personality, but even more so, they show the effect Vincent-the-psychopathic-manipulator had on Milliet. He said Vincent was a "curious fellow" who could be charming but also had a difficult personality. He became furious if Milliet criticized his paintings, but he could also be quite agreeable. He noted his demeanor could change from day-to-day, but he thought of him as a good friend.[10]

By August 29, Vincent was ready for another trip to London. With MacKnight and Milliet gone, he had a little more freedom to disappear for a few days without question. Also, having received another 50 francs from Theo on the 27th, he had the means to travel. Since returning from the Tabram murder, Vincent had actually received a total of 200 francs from Theo.

But he would be low on money when he returned, so Vincent wrote Theo a letter and worked on him for more. He also again tried to control when Theo would respond. He wrote, "I shall have to pay my rent on September 1 . . . Send the money on Sunday by letter or by a telegraph order."[11] Vincent sent this letter on Wednesday, August 29. He had enough to pay the rent for the Yellow House and to travel, so he requested for Theo to send the money on Sunday, September 2. It went against Vincent's nature to ever request for Theo to delay sending money, but now he was doing it again, just as he had done right before leaving for the Tabram murder. He again wished to delay Theo's response to avoid receiving a letter from him while he was out of town. He was ready to leave, and he expected to be back by Sunday, September 2, so even if Theo preferred to send a telegram on that very day, it would be acceptable to him.

Vincent was impatient to kill again, and the improvements he had dreamed up in his fantasies about another murder pushed him harder towards the train station. It would have been better to wait just a little while longer and go in early September, perfect in fact, but his lust for more blood had a hold on him, and he couldn't wait.

After sending the letter to Theo on Wednesday, August 29, I believe Vincent jumped on the train to Paris with visions of a more glorious, yet cleaner, murder planned for some unlucky prostitute in the East End of London.

Arriving in London later the next day, Thursday, August 30, Vincent may have had a few hours of daylight remaining and would have enjoyed returning to the center of London to walk along the Strand and eye the London businessmen in their top hats, thinking on how he had once desired to be just like them. This was how he should have been right then. However, as always, others had spoiled his plans, and instead of a top hat and tails, he had on his new cheap hat and black velvet jacket.

He was nobody special, and to him, the English gentlemen who walked along past the shop windows, some with their ladies in arm wearing pastel-colored dresses and carrying tassel trimmed umbrellas, were all looking down their noses at this commonly dressed, insignificant man. They would know who he was soon enough, though, if not as a great artist who had been resoundingly discovered at the World's Fair, then they would know him by his darker sort of artwork which he would leave for them to view on their London streets.

Little did they know they were brushing shoulders with a murderer. His back must have straightened a bit when he thought of this. If only they knew. But they didn't. He would make sure they felt some of the pain he had gone through in their fine city. He imagined their horror-stricken faces when they read of another murder in the papers. What wonderful revenge he would have against these middle-class Victorian snobs.

As darkness fell, Vincent may have used the last rays of the dying sun to look for a good place for a kill—one that fit the requirements of his detailed fantasies of sexualized murder as Jack the Reaper. He found a back street in Whitechapel that fit the bill. It was dark and had good escape routes. An area of the street in front of a fenced stable yard lacked streetlamps and the darkness was thick enough to hide even the cruelest of deeds.

Just as with the Tabram murder, Vincent needed courage before the kill, and besides, the early part of the night was no time for a murder—too many people and police on the streets. And so, he visited the local pubs and again gazed on the colorful people of Whitechapel as he swallowed down his beer and ale, all the while thinking as Jack the Reaper, enjoying his concealed power over these wretched people but not overdoing it with drink. He would reap one of their women later that night.

As the night wore on, Vincent decided it was time, and he lifted himself up and made his way back to the spot he had previously chosen. He leaned against the wall and waited, not yet for a prostitute, but for a police constable on patrol to come through so as to get the routine of his beat. After the constable passed by, it was over to where the prostitutes loitered on Whitechapel Road to choose his prey for the evening.

* * *

Police Constable John Neil's beat took him into the generally empty street of Bucks Row about every half hour. When he passed through at 3:45 on the morning of August 31, he found a woman lying on the pavement in front of a gate with her throat cut. He called another constable over and instructed him to get the doctor. The *Daily News* reported Constable Neil's description of the discovery: "He noticed blood was oozing from the woman's throat. She was lying on her back with her hands beside the body, the eyes were wide open, the legs a little apart, and the hands open. Feeling her right arm, he found it quite warm."[12]

Dr. Henry Llewellyn arrived quickly at about 4:00 a.m. and examined the body.[13] He believed the woman had been murdered only half-an-hour earlier. The body was quickly placed on a cart and taken to the mortuary. There were bloodstains left on the walkway, but most of the woman's blood had drained down the gutter. A neighbor's son helped out and washed the remaining blood off the pavement.[14]

Constables knocked on doors and questioned residents, but just as with the Tabram murder, no cries of murder had been heard, and there were no witnesses.

The next morning, Saturday, September 1, Dr. Llewellyn performed the post-mortem. The inquest was then opened that afternoon, and the doctor gave the details of what he had found. The weekly London-based, *Reynolds's Newspaper*, quoted him as saying, "I have never seen so horrible a case. She was ripped open just as you see a dead calf at a butcher's shop."[15] Vincent would have loved the butcher shop reference.

Dr. Llewellyn further deposed the throat had been cut twice, beginning on the left side. The first incision was about four inches long, but the second extended eight inches and traveled from ear to ear and completely severed "all the tissues down to the vertebrae." He noted, "No blood at all was found on the breast, either of the body or clothes," inferring her throat was cut while lying on her back.

But the killer was not satisfied with only cutting the throat. Dr. Llewellyn described a very deep cut to the left side of the lower abdomen that ran downward in a jagged manner. He also stated there were "several incisions running across the abdomen," and on the right side "there were also three or four similar cuts running downwards." He also noted bruises on the left and right side of the jaw that may have been caused by pressure from a thumb and fingers and that there was also a slight laceration of the tongue.

A police report of August 31 by Inspector John Spratling noted additional wounds that Dr. Llewellyn had observed but had omitted from his deposition. Spratling noted there were two small stabs to the "private parts."[16] Dr. Llewellyn may have felt it was unnecessary and immodest to mention this at the inquest.

The woman's estranged husband came forward and identified her as Mary Ann Nichols (figure 4.1, mortuary photo of Nichols). Her heavy drinking had apparently split them apart years ago and drove her to prostitution.[17] Her father also viewed the body and identified his daughter and noted she was 42 and had five children.[18] Emily Holland, a friend of Nichols, also came forward and said she last saw her at about 2:30 on Friday morning "coming down Osborne-street into Whitechapel-road. She was alone and intoxicated."[19] Holland tried to persuade her to go home, but Nichols told her, "I have had my lodging money three times to-day, and have spent it." Holland said Nichols then headed down Whitechapel Road after saying she was "going to get money to pay for her lodgings."

Based on Dr. Llewellyn's estimated time of death of 3:30 a.m., Mary Ann Nichols was killed only an hour after she spoke to Holland at 2:30, and just fifteen minutes before Constable Neil discovered her body at 3:45.

Vincent had achieved the murder of Nichols between the half-hour visits Constable Neil made to Buck's Row. And if Dr. Llewellyn's time of death estimation of 3:30 a.m. was correct, Vincent killed her and fled even quicker—within fifteen minutes after Constable Neil initially walked through at 3:15.

On the surface, this may seem easy enough since Vincent likely surveyed the constable's beat beforehand and knew he had half-an-hour to do his dirty work. Also, the damage done to Nichols' body could have easily been completed within fifteen minutes. But how could he have timed it so that he picked out a prostitute on Whitechapel Road, convinced her to go with him to his chosen spot, murdered her, added some cuts to her body, and still have fifteen minutes to spare so as to escape before the constable returned?

It was possible, but acting as the ever-prepared Jack the Reaper, Vincent would not have only used the timing of the constable's beat to try and see how quickly he could choose and lure a prostitute to the exact spot he had chosen and kill her. As Jack the Reaper, he could use his cunning, and his previous fantasies provided him with a better way. The key to understanding Vincent's new technique was the gate.

Constable Neil said he found Nichols' body outside a gateway with her body "lying lengthways along the street, and her left hand touching the gate."[20] He also said the gateway was closed and was about "nine or ten feet high and led to some stables." A person standing in the dark behind this gate could easily remain hidden, and I believe that was what Vincent did.

Before the murder, Vincent likely slipped behind the gate and waited for the constable to pass. Having already timed his beat, he knew he had half-an-hour before the constable returned, so he simply followed behind Constable Neil to Whitechapel Road where he began his hunt for the right victim. But he didn't need to rush things. He didn't need to find his prey, convince her to follow him to his chosen spot, kill her and cut her up, all within half-an-hour. He only needed to pick one out and get her behind the gate and quieted down within the thirty minutes.

So, he likely chose Nichols only within minutes of Constable Neil passing the gate on Bucks Row at 2:45 a.m.—which was just fifteen minutes after Emily Holland had last seen her. Vincent then knew he had until 3:15 to make his choice for the night and get her to follow him back behind the gate before Constable Neil's beat brought him back around.

Vincent may have chosen Nichols because, as Emily Holland had stated, she was noticeably intoxicated. This would have made it a little easier to convince her to come along with him to a spot he had chosen, but with Vincent's psychopathic skills of manipulation, it wouldn't have mattered. He likely chose her because, as he eyed the ladies of the night with the eye of Jack the Reaper, he was looking for the one who most deserved to die that night. For some reason, perhaps because of her wanton drunkenness, the hate in his heart was most stirred by Mary Ann Nichols. So, he slithered up beside her offering a little extra money to come along with him. He could offer all he had. He would get it back soon enough.

Walking Nichols back up Bucks Row, he stopped at the gate and told her there was a nice dark spot behind it. He may have put a finger to his lips as he quietly opened the gate and corralled her into the stable yard. Not wasting any time, he would have stated his preference for the act he was paying for by requesting she face the other direction. When she turned away, Vincent pulled from his pocket a piece of cord. Lifting it over her head, he pulled and twisted it tight around her neck. She struggled for her life, but her struggling soon stopped, and he lowered her seemingly lifeless body to the ground.

In the quiet of the night, Vincent waited for the police constable to pass by again. After Constable Neil did so at 3:15 a.m., Vincent waited a little more for him to turn off the street, and then he pulled open the gate. Seeing the street deserted, he lifted Nichols' body and set it down just outside the gate, closing the gate behind him.

Vincent was not interested in whether or not the strangulation had killed his victim. His only interest was incapacitation, and it's possible Nichols was still alive and only unconscious when he placed her on the pavement. If she was alive, his next act made sure she was dead.

In his fantasies, while painting out in the fields, Vincent had not only thought up the method of using the gate, but he had also decided on the best way to avoid being covered in all that blood. Kneeling next to the right side of his victim's head, Vincent grabbed hold of her chin and tilted back her head. Then, reaching across her with his knife, he plunged it into the left side of her neck, puncturing through her left carotid artery. The blood spurted and gushed away from him, keeping his clothes clean.

If only unconscious, his victim may have squirmed. Tightening his grip on her face to hold her still would then account for the bruises on each side of her jaw. Vincent then removed the knife and started a new cut, pushing the knife down through to the bone and carrying it all the way around.

With the throat cut and the bloodletting having begun, if Nichols wasn't already dead, then that stopped her heart. The pump that pushed blood through her veins was no longer pumping. Therefore, any other cuts he made wouldn't be so messy.

With this fantasized act realized, Vincent moved down to her right side, lifted and pushed her dress out of the way, and imitating sex, he quickly jabbed the knife two times into her "private parts." He then jammed the knife into her left side and dragged it downward. A few quick cuts down and across her abdomen satisfied his bloodlust, and he ended his use of the knife for the night.

Dr. Llewellyn concluded all of this could have been done in five minutes. With Vincent's skill and eagerness, he likely did it in two. Wiping the blade and his hands on her dress, Vincent checked the street and chose the best escape route. If the road remained clear, he could go in either direction on Bucks Row, but if he saw someone or felt uneasy, he could disappear behind the gate and find a way out through the stables, which he would have checked beforehand.

Having plenty of time before Constable Neil returned, and the deserted street likely remaining so, he may have settled on simply walking casually down Bucks Row towards Whitechapel Road, where he blended in with the late-night crowd of drunks, hawkers, and other wanderers of the night. He kept his hands in his pockets to hide any traces of blood which remained, but he felt confident his hat, coat, and face were free of blood spatter this time. From Whitechapel Road, he slipped down a side street and was quickly out of Whitechapel all together. He was long gone before Constable Neil came back around and discovered the body at 3:45 a.m. (figure 4.2, murder sites of Tabram & Nichols)

* * *

As the weakening autumn sun lifted itself above the horizon of London on the last day of August 1888, there was no panic in the streets, and no crowds gathered at the crime scene. The papers didn't rush out the news of another murder. It was business as usual for Londoners. They would take no notice of a man sleeping on a park bench or huddled on the grass under some primrose bushes.

Vincent's after-murder routine was likely the same for the Nichols murder as it was for Tabram's. Finding a pub open a few streets away, he quelled his excited nerves with a quick drink and then found a nice place to lie down for a nap. Then, with the dawn of a new day, he must have been reminded of the tight schedule he was on and rose up and headed to the train station.

Once again, Vincent worried Theo may have missed or ignored his attempt to control the timing of his response, choosing rather to respond immediately. If Vincent wasn't back in time to write back in a timely manner, he again feared possible suspicion from Theo. So, he used his roundtrip ticket to board a train back to the English coast on Friday, August 31.

As the steam whistle blew and the train left the station, the rhythmic churning of the heavy wheels thrummed and rumbled the train further and further away from London, carrying the murderer further and further away from the searching eyes of the Metropolitan Police and away from the searching minds of the Scotland Yard detectives. Vincent could lean his head against the window and rest without worry of a sudden grasp to his collar by a policeman. There was nothing to connect him to the murder. He was just another traveler on a train.

In a half dream state, and in the safety of his own thoughts, Vincent may have drifted back to the murder scene and relived every delightful detail, enjoying the power he had again obtained from taking a life. It was not only the power he had reaped from the kill which gave him what he desired. There was also an aftereffect which acted as a soothing agent to his nervous soul. It was sadness that soothed Vincent. Sorrow was his joy.

The whole thing was just so sad, and he loved it. The deepest sense of fulfillment he got out of killing was the enjoyment of pain and sorrow. He preferred the dark cloud of melancholy to the bright sun of happiness, and he regarded prosperity and happiness in others and in himself as something evil.

Vincent had great aspirations of success, but he could never allow himself to feel he had ever done anything worthwhile or that things were going well for him. He preferred trouble and difficulty, and he did everything he could to keep both continually stirring in his life. He was Cain, after all, and being cursed like Cain, he learned to prefer curses over blessings. He needed trouble to function. It was trouble that gave him the excuses to keep drinking, and it was pain and sorrow that motivated him to paint and to murder.

That strange and sometimes elusive muse artists seek is so often found on the backside of grief. Sometimes out of a foggy depression there arises that mysterious optimum "just right" mood for creating. It was no different with Vincent, but for him everything in life was an obsession. He had to paint more, paint better, and paint in a hurry. This required continuous sorrow and deeper pain. But there's only so much going on in one person's life, so he had to gin up conflict in other's lives to get the pain and sorrow he needed. And the ultimate pain and sorrow is the taking of a life. He murdered for the mood.

As a child, Vincent's preacher father took him along on his visits to the parishioners of his small church in their Dutch village. Vincent observed his father when they called on a solemn house that harbored a sick family member or one that carried the stench of the recently deceased. He grew accustomed to seeing his father comfort the afflicted. It was the sick and grieving who received his attention. Difficulty and sorrow attracted the preacher and therefore also God.

In Vincent's young, psychopathically developing mind, he made sorrow part of his life, and he used it to create sympathy in others. This kept the cycle of sadness going which he craved. One of his favorite Biblical phrases early on was "sorrowful yet always rejoicing."[21] He likely heard his father and others use this scripture frequently during his childhood to remind one another that when sorrow came to a person's life, they could still have joy. As he grew older, he turned it into something different. It was no longer about remaining joyful through the great sorrows of life. For Vincent, he twisted it into something more like always desiring sorrow and rejoicing in it. He expressed this best in an earlier letter to Theo when he wrote, "I prefer feeling my sorrow to forgetting it . . . I find my serenity in 'worship of sorrow.'"[22] Sorrow was his joy.

The train stopped in Dover, and Vincent followed the other passengers onto a steamer which chugged them across the English Channel to Calais, where he then followed them off the steamer and back onto another train headed for

Paris. Arriving in Paris, he found the next train for Arles and used his roundtrip ticket to get aboard. He arrived back in Arles without fanfare on Saturday, September 1. Nobody even noticed the eccentric artist had been gone for another three days.

However, the newspapers back in London started to give him some attention. The murderer was called a madman and a lunatic, but there were no clues to go on. Comparisons were made to the Tabram murder, and some noted the two murders may have been committed by the same hand, but this was the Whitechapel District, the East End, Londoners had become accustomed to stories of violence and murder in this poor and decrepit area. It was certainly an exciting story to read about in the papers, but everyone had their own troubles to deal with, and London remained a city focused on the daily work of supporting an empire.

Theo had again ignored Vincent's attempt to control when he responded, and a letter from Theo awaited. Theo had likely responded to Vincent's request for money the day he received his letter on Thursday, August 30, the day after Vincent sent it and left for London. Theo's response may have arrived on Friday and sat there unopened until Saturday, September 1. Vincent had to write a quick letter and get the response to the post office so it would go off that day. His opening sentence shows his rush to respond and that Theo had responded quickly: "A hasty note to thank you tremendously for the prompt dispatch of your letter."[23] He had only missed the letter by a day, so it shouldn't be enough to make Theo suspicious of what his troubled brother was up to.

In the same letter, Vincent revealed a fear he had of "seeing the day of one's capacity for artistic creation pass." He concluded the only thing to do was to "strike while the iron is hot." This attitude was reflected in the many paintings he was creating during this period, but it also suggested he must not delay in committing more murders. He must "strike while the iron is hot" in that area too, and the fantasies continued to develop.

In just a few days, on September 10, it would be his mother's birthday, and Vincent wanted to send her something special this year, but he needed to go to London for it. Unfortunately, he had already spent all of his travel money, and time was running out. Unless Theo could come through and send more money soon, he couldn't make it to London in time to find and prepare the gift he had in mind for his mother. Whether or not he could make it there in time was ultimately up to Theo. Fortunately for Vincent, but unfortunately for those in London, Theo was always a reliable brother.

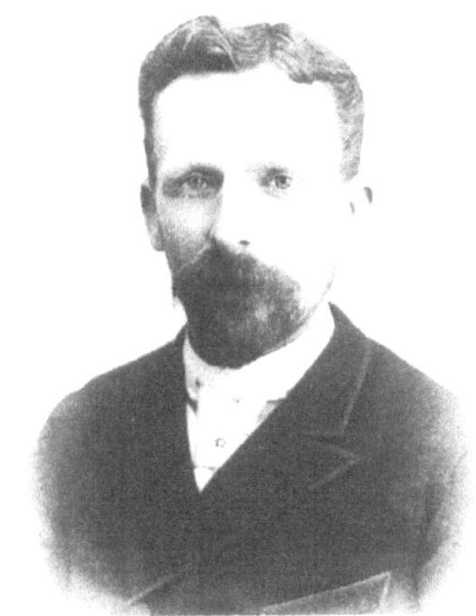

Figure 1.1
Theo van Gogh Photo
Van Gogh Museum, Amsterdam

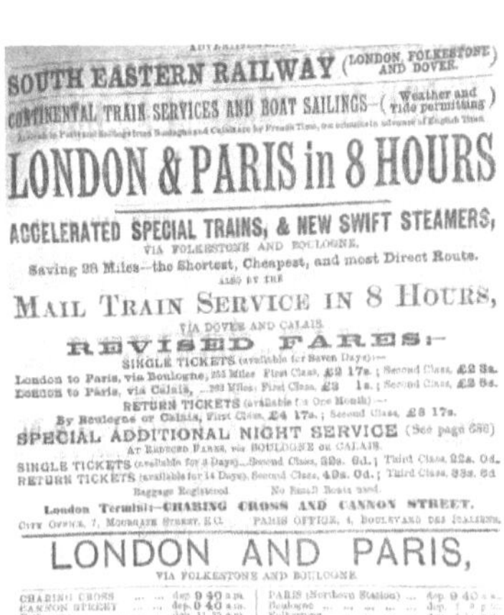

Figure 1.2
Bradshaw Ad, London to Paris
Bradshaw's Continental Railway Guide,
March 1888

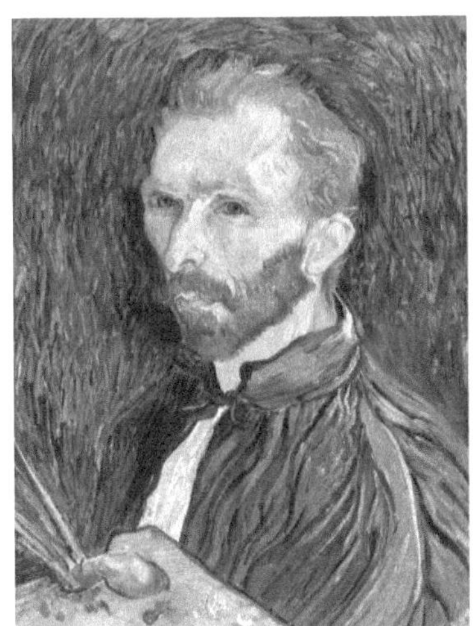

Figure 1.3
Van Gogh Self-Portrait, Aug 1889
National Gallery of Art, Washington, DC

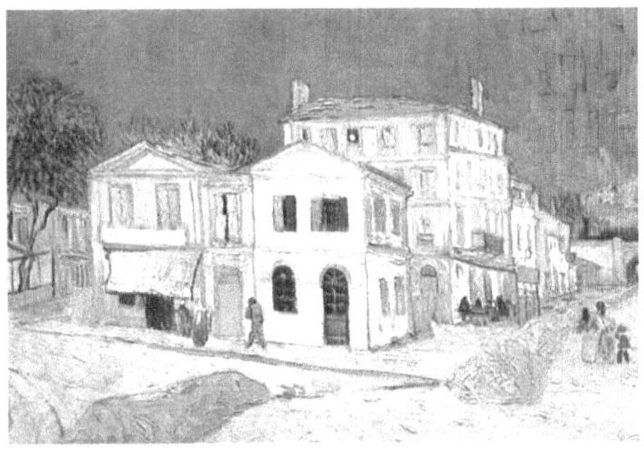

Figure 2.1
Van Gogh, The Yellow House, Sept 1888
Van Gogh Museum, Amsterdam

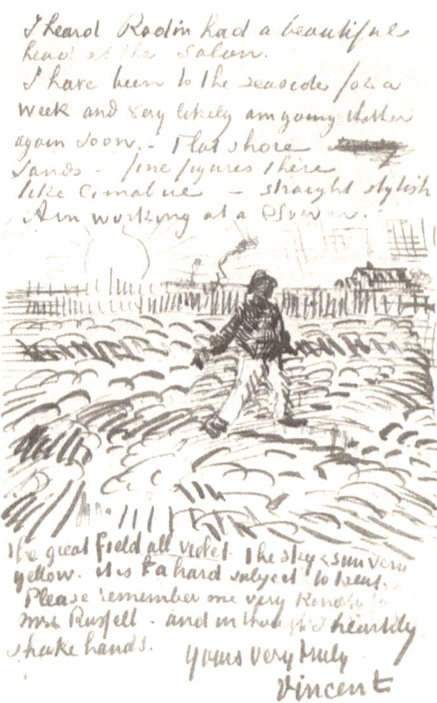

Figure 2.2
Van Gogh Letter to John Russell, p 4, June 17, 1888
Solomon R. Guggenheim Museum, New York

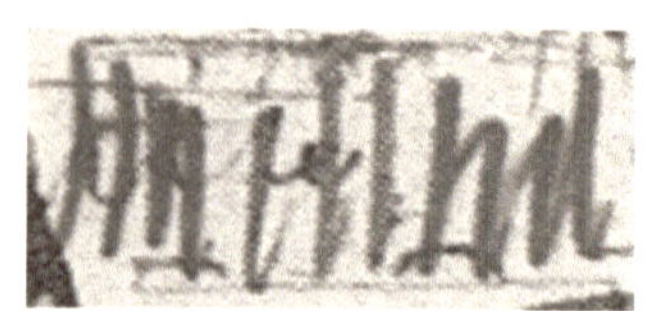

Figure 2.3
Cut showing "Haha"

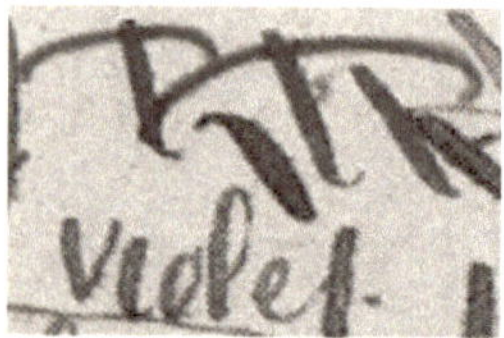

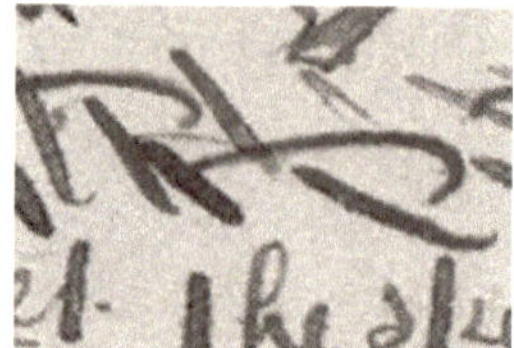

Figure 2.4
Cuts showing "Rips"

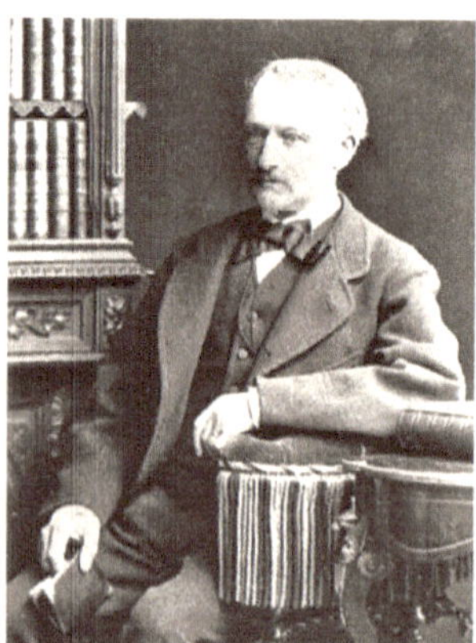

Figure 3.1
Uncle Cent Photo
Van Gogh Museum, Amsterdam

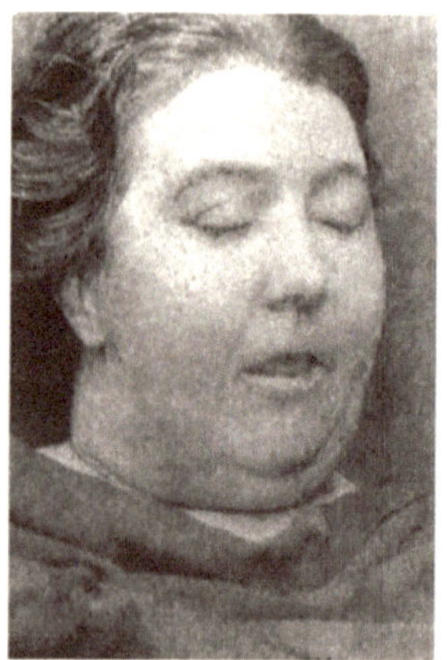

Figure 3.2
Martha Tabram Mortuary Photo
The National Archives of the UK (TNA),
MEPO 3/140

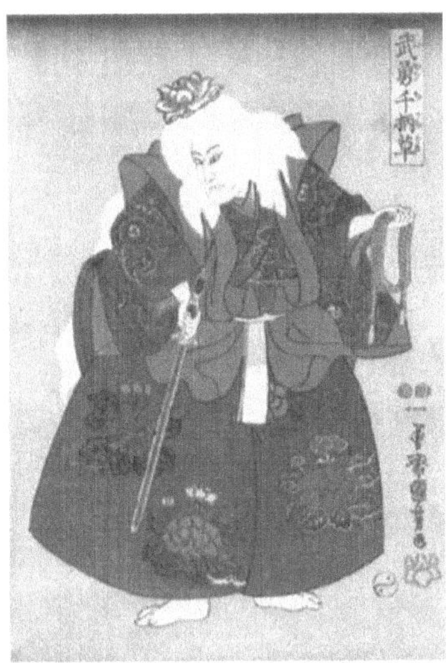

Figure 3.3

Ichiyūsai Kuniyoshi ga, Fūdo, N421 V/1962
Van Gogh Museum, Amsterdam

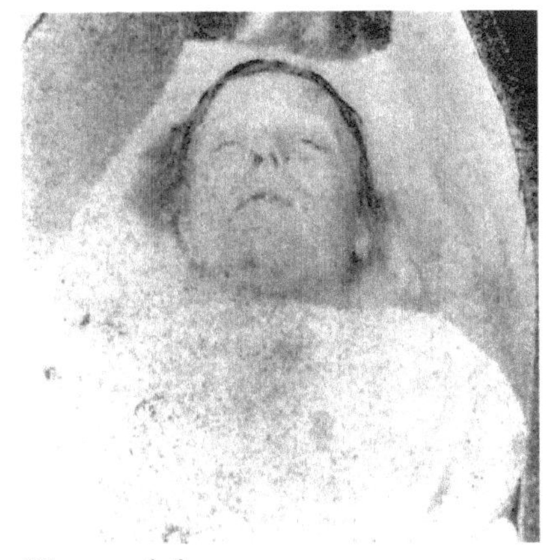

Figure 4.1

Mary Ann Nichols Mortuary Photo
The National Archives of the UK (TNA),
MEPO 3/3155

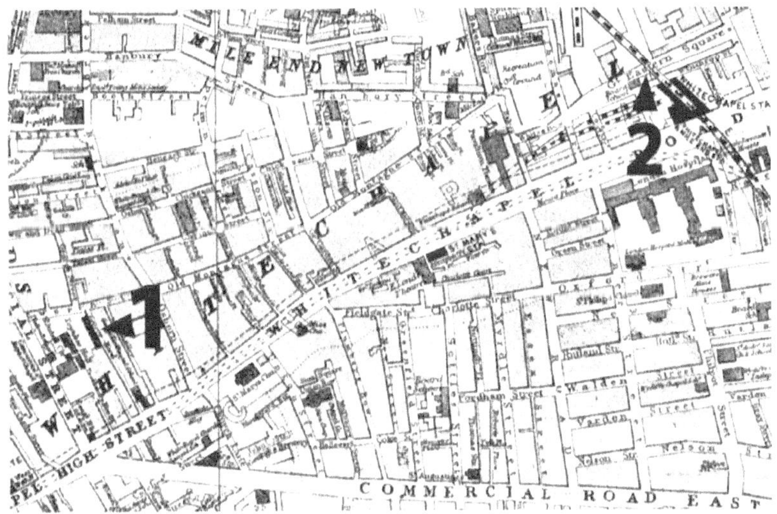

Figure 4.2

Tabram & Nichols Murder Sites
New Large-Scale Ordnance Atlas of London & Suburbs, 1888

1. Martha Tabram, 47 George Yard
2. Mary Ann Nichols, Bucks Row

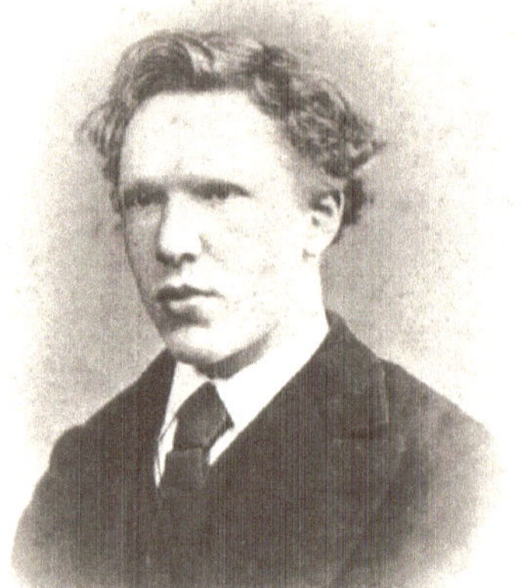

Figure 5.1
Vincent van Gogh Photo at 19
Van Gogh Museum, Amsterdam

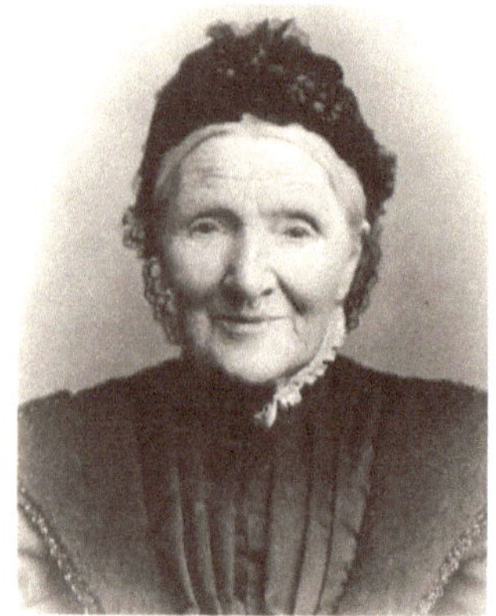

Figure 5.3
Vincent's Mother Photo
Van Gogh Museum, Amsterdam

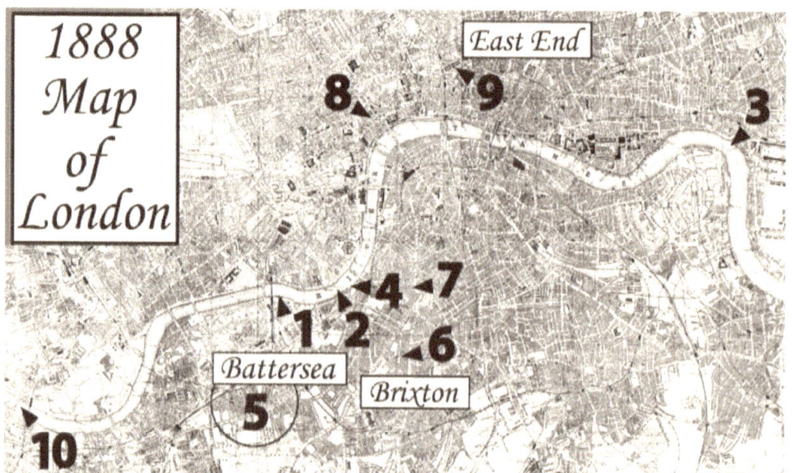

Figure 5.2
Relevant London Locations for 1873/74
New Large-Scale Ordnance Atlas of London & Suburbs, 1888

1. **1873:** Left Torso, Battersea, Waterworks, Sept 5
2. **1873:** Right Torso, Brunswich Warf, Sept 5
3. **1873:** Face, Limehouse, Sept 6
4. **1873:** Infant boy, Sept 5
5. 1st Boardinghouse, Battersea Rise area
6. 2nd Boardinghouse, 87 Hackford Rd
7. 3rd Boardinghouse, 395 Kennington Rd
8. VG worked, Goupil's, 17 Southampton St
9. **1873:** Meat Market Letter, New Meat Market, Smithfield, Sept 9
10. **1874:** Lower body, Putney Bridge, June 5

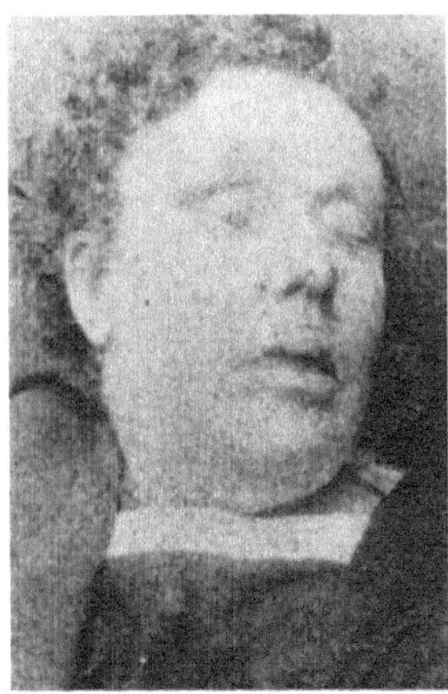

Figure 7.1

Annie Chapman Mortuary Photo
The National Archives of the UK
(TNA), MEPO 3/3155

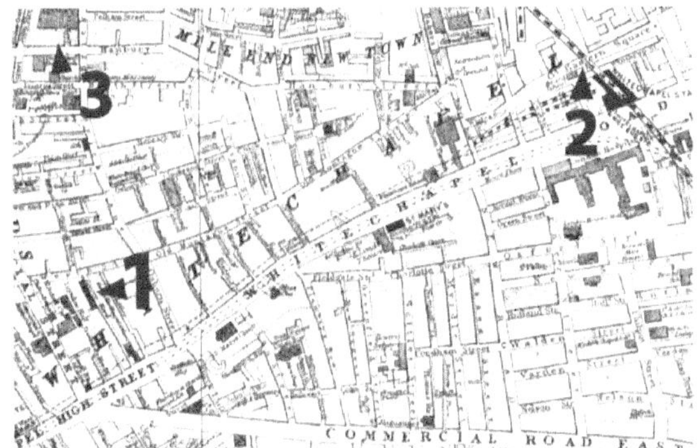

Figure 7.2

Map of Murder Sites, Tabram, Nichols & Chapman
New Large-Scale Ordnance Atlas of London & Suburbs, 1888

1. Martha Tabram, 47 George Yard
2. Mary Ann Nichols, Bucks Row
3. Annie Chapman, 29 Hanbury St

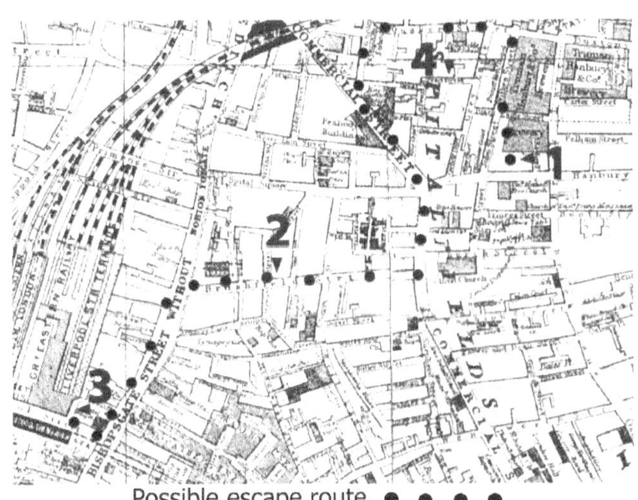

Figure 7.3

Map of Escape Route After Chapman Murder
New Large-Scale Ordnance Atlas of London & Suburbs, 1888

1. Annie Chapman, 29 Hanbury St, Sept 8
2. Prince Albert Pub, Brushfield St
3. Dirty Dick's Pub, Halfmoon St
4. Pearl St, where Rosetta Anderson deposed she saw a mysterious man the night before the Chapman murder

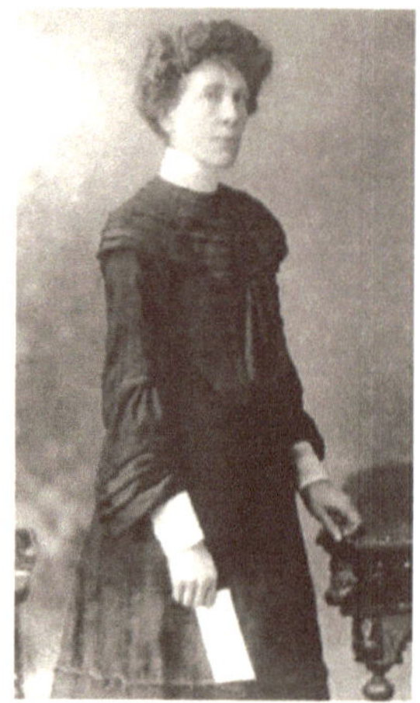

Figure 8.1
Eugenie Loyer Photo
Collection of Mrs. Kathleen Maynard
& Ken Wilkie

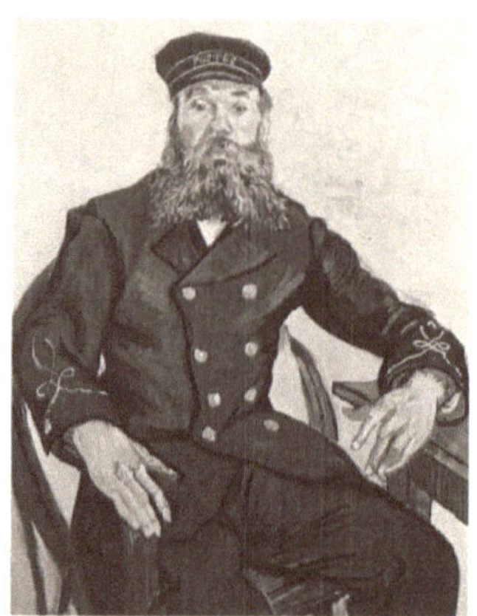

Figure 9.1
Van Gogh, Postman Joseph Roulin, 1888
Museum of Fine Arts, Boston

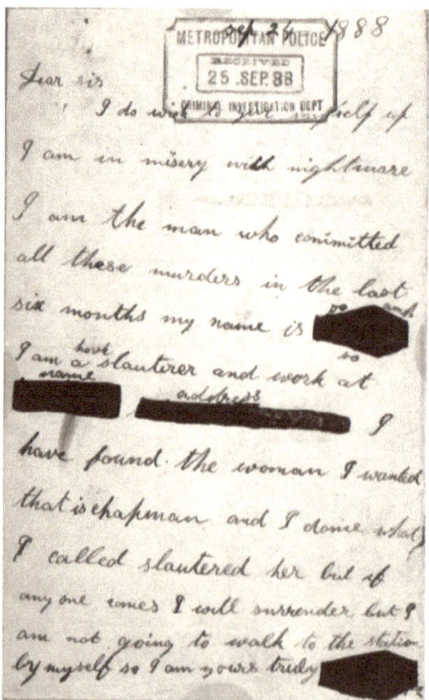

Figure 9.3
First Ripper Letter
The National Archives of the UK (TNA),
MEPO3/142, f. 4

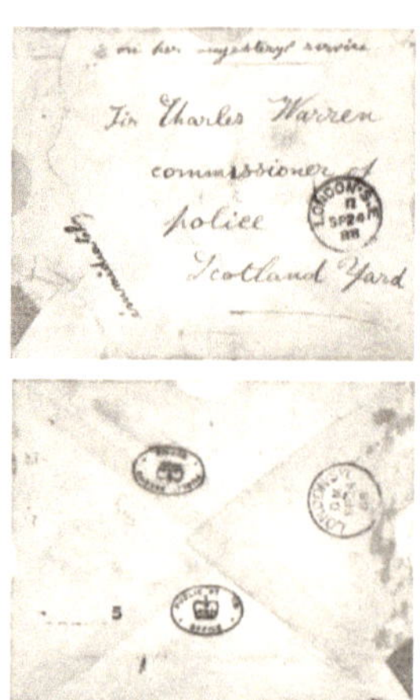

Figure 9.2
First Ripper Letter Envelope Front/Back
The National Archives of the UK (TNA),
MEPO3/142, f. 5

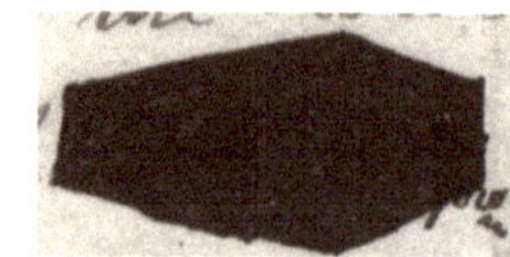

Figure 9.4
First Ripper Letter, Cut Coffin

5

She Loved Another
1872-1873

Over the summer and moving into the autumn of 1888, Vincent was, at the age of 35, transforming into something new. However, the acts of murder he had committed under his new persona were not so very new to him. Vincent van Gogh was a killer long before he began his transformation into Jack the Ripper. The murders at the beginning and end of August of 1888 were not the murders of an amateur. They were committed by an experienced serial killer who was making refinements and improvements on his previous murders.

As the important month of September began, Vincent's mind certainly must have drifted back to when it all started, back to when everything first went wrong and he was driven to his first kill. He was a young man back then, only 20, and so inexperienced at murder. It was the first time he had allowed his dark fantasies to come outside and play and when he had first dipped his knife in blood and forever became a changed being.

But it was in December of 1872, at the age of 19 (figure 5.1, photo of Vincent), that Vincent's previously dormant psychopathic mind first sparked awake and readied itself for evil intent. Vincent had received news of something that would set in motion for him a life of insatiable envy, hatred, ambition, and murder.

He was working for Goupil's at their branch in The Hague, Holland, where he had worked since his Uncle Cent had secured him a job there when he was 16. This was the same Uncle Cent who would later choose to have nothing to do with Vincent and exclude him from any right to his inheritance. But in 1872, Uncle Cent had high hopes for his intelligent nephew, and he saw Vincent as his protégé and future replacement.

Cent was short for Vincent. Vincent and his uncle shared the same name, so it seemed fitting that he should follow in his uncle's footsteps in business. Uncle Cent had amassed a large fortune in the business of art dealing, but he was forced to retire due to bad health. However, he kept financially connected and retained some influence at Goupil's. Because of this, he could have Vincent hired and direct his growth.

And Vincent was coming along well. The manager of the branch in The Hague, Herman Tersteeg, kept Vincent's parents updated on his progress. Vincent's sister-in-law noted later in her memoirs: "Tersteeg sent the parents good reports about Vincent's zeal and capacities . . . He was 'the diligent, studious youth' whom everybody liked."[1] Vincent was building a career as an art dealer, and his mentor and idol, Uncle Cent, was willing to use his influence to help him become a great success. But something was about to threaten that success.

The news that set everything in motion came in a letter from Vincent's father. It informed Vincent that his 15-year-old younger brother, Theo, was not to return to school but was to also begin working at Goupil's, but at their branch in Brussels, Belgium.

In what was just the second letter in Vincent's lifelong correspondence with Theo, he wrote, "Congratulations on the good news I just read in Father's letter. . . . I am so glad that we shall both be in the same profession and in the same firm."[2] If only Vincent had truly been glad about this news instead of being filled with envy which he had concealed with politeness, then the years of misery that followed for himself and for many others might never have occurred.

Theo started work in the Brussels branch on January 1, 1873, and a letter from Vincent showed the first touches of a young man who felt the focus of attention turning away from him. He tried to counter Theo's good fortune with a little of his own. He wrote Theo on January 18, "My new year began well: my salary was raised 10 guilders."[3]

The timing of a raise for Vincent when Theo started work was likely an intentional counter to the jealousy Vincent's family knew he would have towards the younger Theo beginning in the same company. Placing Theo at the Brussels branch also seemed like a calculated move designed to protect Theo from Vincent's influence. It would have been more logical for Theo to have been sent to The Hague branch to work alongside his older brother, but Uncle Cent and Vincent's parents knew Vincent's temperament. They were protecting the younger Theo.

Vincent believed his parents favored Theo over him, and this was noticeably the case. Vincent's sister-in-law noted later about Theo that his parents "clung fondly to him because he more than any of the other children repaid their love with never-failing tenderness and devotion, and grew up to be, as they so often said, 'the crowning glory of their old age.'"[4]

With this in mind, Vincent's envy towards Theo grew slowly in his brain like a cancerous tumor. The direction of Theo's life and how it related to their parents and to Uncle Cent, and how it compared to his own life, began to consume Vincent's thoughts. He would have wondered why Theo was not brought into The Hague branch with him, and why they had allowed Theo to begin working at 15 when he had to wait until he was 16. And then he would have also dwelled on how he was at a branch in their native country while Theo was given a bigger first step by being placed in another country. They showed more confidence in Theo's abilities. Vincent was beginning to develop a deep resentment for his family and a deep dislike for his younger brother.

Only two months after Theo started at the Brussels branch, a decision was then made concerning Vincent. Uncle Cent decided it was time to transfer Vincent to their London branch. It was likely presented as a reward, as something good for him, a counterbalance to Theo having started in the Brussels branch. This was to be a monumental decision for Vincent's life, and on March 17, he wrote to Theo with the news:

> I am looking forward very much to seeing London, . . . but still I am sorry to leave here. Now that it has been decided that I shall go away, I feel how strongly I am attached to The Hague. Well, it cannot be helped, and I intend not to take things too hard. . . . How I should have liked to stay here this summer, but we must take things as they are. . . . Theo, I strongly advise you to smoke a pipe; it is a good remedy for the blues, which I happen to have had now and then lately.[5]

It appears Vincent wanted to stay in The Hague but it had been decided for him that he should go away, and this seemed to depress him. Vincent's forlorn attitude could be thought of as simply a young man feeling sadness over leaving his homeland for a new country. However, the last line notes he had the blues "now and then lately." This suggests he was depressed about something over a period of time and not just as a reaction to being sent to London. This depressed state was, at least in part, a reaction to his envy of Theo and the resulting feeling others were no longer paying him as much attention. But it also suggests there may have been trouble in The Hague and Uncle Cent came up with the transfer as a solution to Vincent's troubles, believing it would lift up his protégé and do him some good to go out into the big world and work in London.

On May 12, 1873, Vincent left for London, but he was sent by way of Paris to first visit the headquarters of Goupil's and get better acquainted with the owners and managers. Uncle Cent was prepping Vincent for big things, but the branch in London wasn't an art gallery. It was a warehouse that sold paintings and prints to other art galleries. However, plans were underway to open a gallery in London, and Uncle Cent wanted Vincent to be part of this new expansion.

When Vincent arrived in London, Goupil's had already arranged a boardinghouse for him. The exact location is not known, but his father wrote Theo and conveyed that Vincent was "living in the outskirts of London and in the mornings, at 8:30 he goes into the city in a little steamer, which takes him an hour."[6] Vincent also wrote to Theo that he was living "in one of the suburbs of London."[7]

The Goupil's warehouse was centrally located on the west side of the River Thames in the business district at 17 Southampton Street (figure 5.2, London map). Taking the steamer to work would suggest Vincent lived in a suburb somewhere near the banks of the river. Goupil's would not have secured a boardinghouse to the northeast for a nephew of Uncle Cent's. This was the area of the East End—no place for a clerk who worked in a respectable establishment. That leaves the Thames to the south, and measuring the distance, the clue that the steamer took an hour would suggest a good distance from the center of the city. However, considering the steamer would be making stops along the way, it couldn't have been too far away.

In David Sweetman's book, *Van Gogh, His Life and His Art*, Sweetman suggested the most logical location Vincent had lived was a newly developed area near Battersea Rise (figure 5.2, London map).[8] The Battersea area fits well, and I agree with Sweetman's conclusion.

When Vincent arrived in London and settled into his new room, it wasn't murder that was on his mind, but ambition. He had turned 20 at the end of March, and now that he was truly on his own in the big city of London, he felt he was becoming his own man. Like many other 20-year-olds, he was filled with ambitious ideas of greatness. But with Vincent, the ambitious ideas had to always be bigger and greater, and the introduction of Theo into the mix ramped this up even more. He now believed he had a direct competitor in Theo and therefore believed he needed to prove himself to Uncle Cent and to his family. Vincent determined he must quickly become a successful businessman, and just as quickly, be accepted by the English people. Then things would be in their proper place. As the eldest of six, his family would then rightfully look to him as the future head of the family. Theo would be in his proper place too, as the younger brother struggling along in the Brussels branch looking up to his older brother as the supreme example of wise business dealings and high achievement.

Vincent's mother (figure 5.3, photo of Mother) wrote to Theo about Vincent's exuberance: "Our Vincent wrote that he had bought a top hat; you cannot be in London without one."9 No doubt, Vincent wore his top hat proudly as he walked each day from the steamboat pier to Goupil's, touching the brim now and then to show respect to the other gentleman he passed. He had every intention of fitting in with and being accepted by the English people and the English business class of London.

But things were not moving fast enough for Vincent. His obsessive thoughts certainly must have generated images of Theo excelling in the Brussels branch while he languished in the London warehouse. It would be some time before Goupil's opened the new London gallery. In the meantime, Vincent was left in the warehouse where he felt he was falling behind and losing time.

After only about a month in London, his disappointment was already beginning to show. He wrote in a letter to the family he knew from The Hague, the Haanebeeks, on July 2: "The business here is only a stockroom, and our work here is quite different from what it is in The Hague; but I shall probably get used to it."10

Then just a month after that, on August 7, in another letter to the Haanebeeks, it appeared Vincent's mood had darkened to despair. He wrote, "Everything is not so beautiful as it seemed to me in the beginning. Perhaps it is my own fault, so I shall bear with it a little longer."11

Vincent's dissatisfaction with being relegated to warehouse work while Theo honed his skills on customers and artists in the Brussels gallery was becoming a difficulty. The high hopes he had for achieving great success after arriving in London and purchasing his top hat had already so quickly reduced to nothing more than vanishing castles in the sky.

Vincent's worry over Theo moving speedily past him while he hopelessly stood in place pulled him back down into a state of depression. He had learned while living in The Hague, or even more so now that he was truly on his own in London, that the remedy for his depression was alcohol. In The Hague, his first taste of liquor may have only been as a casual drinker, but in London, free from the watchful eyes of friends and family, he likely drank it down in full gulps as an aspiring alcoholic.

Vincent needed a change. He needed to get out of his depressed funk. It would still be a while before Goupil's gave him what he needed by opening the new gallery, so he decided to make his own change. He decided to move.

Even though he had written to the Haanebeeks in the August 7 letter that everything was not so beautiful, he had also written, "Moving is so horrible that I shall stop here as long as possible." However, by about August 24, he had abruptly reversed himself and wrote his parents that he had moved into a new boardinghouse.[12] Vincent had decided to make this change in order to fend off his depressed state, but he also had something else in mind for changing his frame of mind, and he needed to get away from the Battersea area to do it.

✳   ✳   ✳

At 6:30 a.m. on Friday, September 5, less than two weeks after Vincent had written his parents that he had moved into a new boardinghouse, the severed left half of a woman's torso was found in the mud on the foreshore of the River Thames near the Battersea Waterworks (figure 5.2, London map). The Thames Police began searching for the rest of the woman's body and found the other half of the torso floating just a short distance downriver near Brunswick Wharf in the Nine Elms area.

The next day, the police continued the search and made an even more grisly discovery further downriver. It was unimaginable, even by 1873 standards. After finding the split torso, the police could have anticipated and prepared for finding the severed head bobbing along in the Thames, but they didn't find the head, at least not the skull. Instead, they only found the face of the woman. It was riding the current through London and was fished out near Limehouse. The skin and scalp had been cut and forcibly pulled from the skull and tossed in the river like a piece of old shoe leather.

From the 8th to the 15th, additional pieces of the woman's body were found in and on the shore of the river. Most of the pieces had been separated at the joints, and the arms and legs and feet were found in various locations. The left side of the pelvis was also found, but the matching right half and the hands were never recovered.

By chopping up the body and depositing the pieces in the Thames, the hope of the woman's killer may have been for the parts not to be found, but if a few parts were found, he still hoped the woman could not be identified. His ultimate desire may have been for the body parts to drift along and eventually float out to sea, never to be found. But because of the swirling side currents and high and low tides of the Thames, some of the parts were pushed to shore where they were stranded at low tide until they were picked up again by the high tide and carried on their way. Because of these delays in being carried away, the police were eventually able to recover many of the parts before they left the city limits.

The unusual and hideous act of removing the victim's face was, clearly, also meant to ensure the woman wouldn't be identified—a crude but highly effective method indeed. But it was sloppy of the killer to throw it in the river where it could be discovered. The entire face was intact except for the chin and a portion of the mouth and right cheek. The eyebrows, eyelashes, and even the ears remained in place. The nose had been cut off, but a flap of skin above the upper lip kept it attached.

The Divisional Surgeon of Battersea, Dr. William Kempster, examined the face and found a piece of evidence the killer never expected would be seen. Dr. Kempster deposed at the inquest: "On the right temple of the scalp was a very large bruise, three or four inches in diameter, and there was an infiltration of blood surrounding skin, and my conclusion is, that this showed there was a blow immediately before death."[13] He added, "There were two anterior incisions, much lacerated, giving the appearance of a blow or blows with a blunt weapon. I am of the opinion that these blows were received during life."

So, it was known by what method the woman was killed, but not much else was learned that could solve the case. As for uncovering her identity, Dr. Kempster had also noted, and it was reported in the papers, the woman had a wart or mole on her right breast, a large white scar on the breastbone, and a small mole on the right side of her neck. A basic description of the woman being about 40 with dark hair was also reported and inquiries were made about any missing women in the area. Some Londoners looking for missing loved ones came forward. The body parts were reassembled and viewed in a tub of spirits, but the woman was never identified.

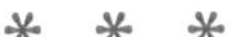

Meanwhile, with all this nastiness going on in the Thames, Vincent was safely tucked away in his new boardinghouse, sipping tea and getting to know his new landlady and her daughter. They were just far enough away from the gory discoveries in the river not to be concerned with such horrible stories.

Vincent had found a room to rent in the southeast quadrant of London in the Lambeth District within the area of Brixton. It was in a three-story row house located just off Brixton Road at 87 Hackford Road (figure 5.2, London map). The owner was a widow named Ursula Loyer, who attended to her new boarder with the assistance of her 19-year-old daughter, Eugenie.

Hackford Road is only a short distance to the east from the Battersea area where Sweetman surmised Vincent had first lived. This closeness of proximity increases the likelihood that Vincent's first boardinghouse was indeed in the Battersea area.

Because the first piece of the woman was found on the shore of the Thames at Battersea, and because all but one of the other parts were found downriver from this point, Battersea was considered the likely area where the murder was committed. The popular London-based daily newspaper, *The Times,* reported on September 15: "It is suspected, the body was cast in—at Battersea."

The likelihood Vincent had lived in the same area where the murder had occurred is no surprise, knowing his true nature. Even as an unskilled killer, Vincent knew it was best not to kill too close to home, and so he moved out of the area before following through on his dark fantasies. It looked as if by mid-August he had made up his mind and had planned to murder a prostitute in the Battersea area in early September. The impetus for the idea to move in August and to then murder in September was Vincent's desire to give his mother a gift. Her birthday was on September 10.

By August 25, Vincent had informed his parents that he had moved. Then, on September 5, only five days before his mother's birthday, as a gift for her, he murdered his first victim. He dismembered the woman's body and sent the parts to his mother—not by traditional means through the mail, but instead, he sent the parts to his mother by use of the river. He could imagine the various pieces being carried the length of the Thames and out into the English Channel where they could drift across the waters of the North Sea to Holland and into his mother's outstretched arms.

His mother certainly was entitled to receive at least a few pieces of the woman's body for her birthday. After all, as with many psychopaths, he believed his mother was one of the root causes of his desire for vengeance. Therefore, she was partly to blame for what he had done and had a hand in the prostitute's demise. She should get something for that. Others also played their part, but his mother was to blame for the envy she had ignited within him for Theo, since she did what mothers shouldn't do when she chose Theo as her favorite over him.

It was this anger at his mother for preferring Theo which awoke his envy of Theo and heightened his ambitious aspirations. This led to a dangerous need for retribution, which resulted in some poor prostitute in the Battersea area of London being slain to pay for the perceived sins his family had committed against him.

As Vincent wasted away the hours in Goupil's London warehouse, his envy-bitten brain must have replayed images of his mother and the rest of his family fawning over Theo the Golden Boy. After the murder, and after his mother's birthday, Vincent revealed in a letter to Theo of September 13 what had been swirling around in his troubled brain. He wrote, "I wonder if you were in Helvoirt for Mother's birthday and how you enjoyed it."[14] Vincent could not bear the thought of Theo returning home for their mother's birthday as the now so very mature young man who showed such promise of a dazzling future at Goupil's.

The hatred and envy which boiled within Vincent had egged him on to commit murder for his mother's birthday, but there was something more behind his choice of victim. *The Times* of September 9 reported that at the opening of the murdered woman's inquest the day before, the coroner had included, unusually, another victim's inquest. This covered "the body of a newly-born male infant found in the Thames, at the same place where the second portion of the [woman's] trunk was discovered." The *Daily News* of the same date added that the infant "was found the same morning and near to the same spot at Nine Elms (figure 5.2, London map)."

It doesn't appear anyone put the two together, but the day before on the 8th, the *Daily News* noted that the unfortunate woman appeared "to have been in an advanced state of pregnancy." Then in *The Times* of September 16, it was noted that Dr. Kempster deposed that the uterus remained attached to the left half of the pelvis, and from his examination he believed the "deceased could never have borne a child, but . . . she might have been pregnant and had a miscarriage."

The evidence seems clear that the woman was pregnant at the time of her murder and the dead infant found the same morning in the mud at Nine Elms near where the right side of her torso was found was actually her forcibly removed infant. If this had been more heavily reported in the papers, it may have led to the woman's identity.

Because no one missed her and she was not identified, it can be inferred the woman was likely a prostitute. Piecing that together with the evidence of her being pregnant, it can be further inferred the killer chose his victim based on those criteria. Choosing to murder a prostitute wasn't so very unique, but choosing to murder a prostitute who was pregnant might be.

Vincent had only been in London for about three months when he chose his victim and made his first kill. Since it was reported the victim was "in an advanced state of pregnancy," he therefore couldn't have been motivated to kill because he suspected she was carrying his baby. However, if it is accepted that the killer deliberately chose a pregnant prostitute to murder, then a possible option for his motivation was that he chose his victim as a substitute for a woman he knew who was pregnant, perhaps with his child. Relating this to Vincent, it would then follow that it was possible he had left behind a pregnant woman he knew when he left The Hague and had moved to London.

This suggests the possibility that Vincent was not only transferred to London as a counter to his envy and depression over Theo beginning at Goupil's, but the transfer may have been engineered to remove him from a sticky situation—as in he had gotten a girl, or possibly even a prostitute, pregnant.

This would give more meaning to the words Vincent's mother had written to Theo soon after Vincent had left The Hague. She had advised Theo to keep his focus on work and said, "Then you will become clever and reliable and make yourself indispensable, and this way you will have chosen the best way to be spared from temptations that you will certainly meet just like any other boy."[15] Was she thinking of Vincent when she made reference to "any other boy," warning Theo not to make the same mistakes his older brother had made?

Does this also help explain why they kept Theo away from Vincent by starting him at the Brussels branch instead of with Vincent in The Hague? This could also explain Vincent's depression and reluctance to leave The Hague. The wording in his letter to Theo had made it clear it was not his decision but that others had decided for him, having written, "It has been decided that I shall go away." It has the ring of there being a problem and suggests that others decided the best solution was for Vincent to go away. With this in mind, it is easier to see how Vincent's anger towards his family began to grow into rage.

Accepting this possibility, at the same time he had caused a problem which could bring ruin to his career and shame to his family, he had to deal with Theo coming along to replace him as the one who would keep his nose clean and not make things messy, as Vincent had done. Over those few months, from the time Vincent arrived in London to his mother's birthday, he must have mulled things over and felt the sting of his family's interference in his life, and his anger likely glowed hot because they didn't treat Theo the same. Anger and depression then opened the door for heavy drinking and visits to prostitutes in the Battersea area. Battersea was not a poor district, but prostitutes could be found all over London, and Battersea Park was a perfect place on the river for prostitutes to lure willing men to dark and secret places.

By giving-in to his family and allowing himself to be whisked away from the presumed pregnant woman in The Hague, Vincent's anger then also turned towards the woman in The Hague who had caused him so much trouble and threatened to disrupt his big plans. He couldn't return to The Hague and murder the pregnant woman. Naturally, he would be suspected. But he could release his rage on a pregnant prostitute in London by using her as a substitute for the real object of his hatred.

In the fantasies of murder that played out in his psychopathic mind, the anger and hatred he had towards the woman in The Hague became attached to the anger and hatred he had for his family, and especially for his mother, and from this combination he had concocted the perfectly fulfilling plan of murdering for his mother's birthday.

✳ ✳ ✳

When someone sends a gift, they also often send along a card, and Vincent was thoughtful enough to provide one just in time for his mother's birthday. The *Daily News* reported on September 10 (his mother's birthday), that a letter had been found the previous afternoon at the New Meat Market, Smithfield (figure 5.2, London map), which purported to be a confession by the murderer. The letter was soiled and tattered and the writing was believed to be that of an uneducated man and was written in all capital letters. The *Daily News* transcribed the lengthy letter in its entirety:

> To the Police of the City of London.—Most important.—Gents,—I have a most dreadful secret to disclose about the murder of the woman hacked to pieces and found by the officers of justice in the Thames. Gents, I am sorry to tell you that I did the deed—I who am writing on this paper, and I am truly sorry to have to tell it. As I know you will not get any murderer for the deed, I may as well make a clean breast of it. How it came to pass was this—I loved her to adoration, but she did not love me in return, and she loved another instead. When I found that out, I vowed vengeance, and minded firmly to take her life, so that no one else should have her. By the kindness of a friend of mine, a row boat was in readiness for her and me on Thursday night between Richmond and Mortlake. We floated along towards Hammersmith bridge at a late hour, and after passing the bridge about five minutes, the devil tempted me and I rose in the darkness, and clasping her as it were fondly around the neck, I gave a tremendous gash with a butcher's knife like a razor, and she fell insensible at the bottom of the boat. In the darkness I finished my bloody work, dismembered her with a sharp surgeon's saw, and scalped her in the Indian fashion. I threw the remains overboard, between Putney-bridge and Chelsea new bridge. When the boat had drifted under London-bridge among the shipping, I washed her out and tore a large hole in her side, when she began to make water rapidly. I took the first opportunity of making off. Do not take up any one on suspicion, because no one of her friends knows me, and when this reaches you I will be out of danger.[16]

It may be there has never been a more poetically morbid account of murder written in the murderer's own hand. It has a literary quality, and it drips and flows as if it were only a story of two lovers out for a romantic boat ride under the stars. What skill it shows at conveying a unique romanticism doused in morbidity, twisted together with evil sarcasm.

The letter was addressed to the police, and the tone and attitude were clearly meant as a taunt. The writer was confident his actions of cutting up his victim gave no clue to be traced back to him, and he also believed the police were too unskilled to ever capture him. He alluded to this with the line, "As I know you will not get any murderer for the deed."

Showing no fear of being discovered, amazingly, the writer then told his story of why and how he had committed the murder, actually revealing his motive and his method. This was a love story and, according to the writer, it was unrequited love which had led to the murder. He expressed this as, "I loved her to adoration, but she did not love me in return, and she loved another instead." Having found this out, he then "vowed vengeance, and minded firmly to take her life, so that no one else should have her." It can be gleaned from this that the murderer was an extremely jealous and insecure person who was incapable of dealing with rejection. If he couldn't have her, then no one would. He was a selfish person who demanded he get what he wanted, and if he didn't, then he would react with extreme violence.

Being a murderer, he was then also, by default, an unreliable writer. He exaggerated and romanticized certain aspects of his story. For instance, the killer-turned-writer described his evil act as, "Clasping her as it were fondly around the neck, I gave a tremendous gash." But the evidence of the heavy bruising to the right temple which Dr. Kempster reported contradicts this description. He cut her throat, but only after first knocking her senseless.

He also said he had used a "butcher's knife" and a "surgeon's saw" and that he had "scalped her in the Indian fashion." Each of these descriptions were used to add some flair to his story and to play into what the papers had previously reported.

The writer also exhibited a flair for manipulation when he wrote, "Do not take up any one on suspicion, because no one of her friends knows me." This was an attempt to control the idea the police had of the killer. If they did find out the identity of the woman, and they questioned her friends, they were to dismiss anything the friends might say about someone they saw with the victim because, as the writer implied, the killer was a stranger.

It is uncanny how similar the style and wording of this letter is to Vincent's own words. That same jealous nature and selfish sense of entitlement, and those same obsessive and extreme views about love and others not returning his love comes across, both in the Meat Market letter and in Vincent's own life and letters. The poetic line, "I loved her to adoration, but she did not love me in return, and she loved another instead," is vintage Vincent. This is so unmistakably Vincent for good reason—Vincent wrote the letter and dropped it in the meat market on the 9th in hopes it would be found and then published in the papers the next day for his mother's birthday, which it was. And it was also Vincent who had cut up some poor woman in a boat four days earlier, throwing her face and body parts into the Thames. Vincent van Gogh was a callous psychopathic murderer, and this was only his first.

In the letter to Theo of September 13, Vincent also shared the details of a nice day he had, writing, "One Saturday some time ago I went boating on the Thames with two Englishmen. It was glorious."[17] It may have been that this enjoyable boat ride came just as Vincent was in the throes of planning a murder. With his fertile mind ready to receive the seeds of possibilities, he may have been led to imagine how well a boat would work for his evil purposes.

On the night of the murder, he may have returned to the same dock where the two Englishmen had taken him, stealing the same boat they had used. This gives more understanding to the line Vincent wrote in the Meat Market letter: "By the kindness of a friend of mine, a row boat was in readiness for her and me."

Vincent wrote the elaborate unrequited love story and dropped it in the meat market to be found as a way to fulfill part of his fantasy of revenge by expressing himself. He was justifying anonymously to the world that he was right to return murder for unreturned love. He skillfully made it sound logical and acceptable for him to have murdered the woman since she did not return his love.

Having butchered the woman, choosing to drop his letter in a meat market was another side enjoyment for Vincent. The New Meat Market at Smithfield was only a short stroll from where he worked at Goupil's on Southampton Street (figure 5.2, London map). The letter was found on Tuesday, September 9, at 3:30 in the afternoon. After deciding on the location, Vincent only had to take a short walk up the Strand to the northeast on his lunch break from Goupil's to get there. As he meandered through the meat market admiring the hanging cuts of pork and beef, he slipped the letter from his pocket and let it fall under a vendor's table where it was sure to be noticed and looked at by a curious passerby.

By dropping it on the afternoon of the 9th, he provided just enough time for it to be found and given to the police, who could then give it to the newspapers to publish the next day on the 10th for his mother's birthday. If only she were there to pick up the *Daily News*, she could have read in Vincent's own words what she had helped to cause her wicked little son to do.

With the deed done and vengeance having been meted out, not to whom his anger was directed, but to the next best thing, a near-at-hand prostitute, some of Vincent's rage was quieted. He sought to put it all behind him and begin anew. He wasn't beaten yet. Theo had not yet overtaken him and usurped his right to the throne. He might still find a way to become great amongst the English and thereby capture his rightful crown.

He found this new hope of conquest in his new lodgings and in the widow and daughter who ran the boardinghouse. The widow had a similar stoic attitude his own mother possessed. The daughter, at 19, was only a year younger than Vincent, and he immediately developed an infatuation with her. There was hope for success in business and again a reason to hope for love.

But as a reminder to Vincent that for him sunny days were only breaches in the cloudy skies of his life, he received news in November that Theo had been transferred from the Goupil's gallery in Brussels to the gallery in The Hague where Vincent had left only six months prior. His envy and hatred may have been cooled for the moment, but it was being warmed up again. Now that he had tasted the liquor of murder, he would have a difficult time, just as with alcohol, cleaning the taste out of his mouth. In fact, he would crave more of both.

6

The Money Must Come
September 1888

The cravings for alcohol and murder which began to develop in the young Vincent with his first murder back in 1873 had only intensified over the many years since. At the beginning of September 1888, as he sat down in a field somewhere on the outskirts of Arles and touched paint to canvas, he was plied, not only with sips of rum from his flask, but likely also with beautiful nightmarish recollections of his two most recent murders of Tabram and Nichols. The creative power born from the shedding of their blood surged alive within his own veins, and on September 3, he wrote to Theo about it: "Oh, my dear brother, sometimes I know so well what I want. I can very well do without God both in my life and in my painting, but I cannot, ill as I am, do without something which is greater than I, which is my life—the power to create."[1]

Using his new persona, Vincent had now murdered two women in 1888 as a means to cultivate from murder a greater power to create. The taking of their lives had given him what he was after, but there was a terrible price to be paid for this which he had not yet fully calculated—if he needed to murder to gain the power to paint great things, then he must always murder to paint.

Not only was murder now securely fastened to his need for the power to paint, it was now also firmly attached to his sexual urges. The strangulation and then frenzied stabs to Tabram were for him a wonderful expression of his sexual frustration, but the strangulation and cutting of the throat of Nichols, and then the controlled mutilation of her belly, brought more delight than he could have anticipated in his pre-murder fantasies.

Vincent's pleasure was now found less in the jabs and more in the cuts. His issue with impotency was less of an issue because of the psychological thrill of absolute power he had obtained over his victims. Once they were incapacitated, he could do what he liked to their subdued bodies. He was in control. The stabs to Tabram reflected his impotency, but after her murder, and because of her murder, his impotency could be overcome by reliving the thrilling thoughts and memories of her bloody demise.

So, his fantasies advanced from stabs to cuts. He wanted to feel more of what he was doing with the knife. Murder was no longer birthed out of sexual frustration or as a substitute for his sexual inability but had become a means by which to enhance his sexuality. The feel of the blade cutting flesh was a sexually charged act and immensely gratifying.

Vincent's new persona was emerging out of him like a locust climbing from its shell of old skin. He was increasingly becoming more this other self, who was capable of gratifying his cravings, and like the old skin, his old self was being sloughed off.

If Vincent happened to read the London periodical *Myra's Journal* of September 1, he would have surely felt a kinship with the comments from a review of the *Dr. Jekyll and Mr. Hyde* play. It noted about Dr. Jekyll: "He can, however, at first always subdue the evil part of him. But as time passes, Hyde overcomes Jekyll, and it is rarely that he can assume the virtues and shape of his original self."[2]

Vincent was already a corrupted being with no virtues, but he would not be able to return to the Vincent he once was before the Tabram murder. He could still paint as before, even better, but he now needed to murder to paint. To go back to a time when he didn't absolutely feel he needed a fresh kill to paint was now impossible.

The reviewer of the play summed up the end result nicely, writing, "Jekyll is overpowered and Hyde is master." This was also true for Vincent. His new persona was now his master, but unlike the good Dr. Jekyll, Vincent rejoiced in it. It was who he desired to be. There was no longer a Dr. Jekyll side to Vincent.

This new Vincent was alive with energy. Electricity crackled through his creative brain, powering new visions for his paintings and new fantasies of sexualized murder. He had just murdered, but already, only a few days afterwards, he may have hungered for more. It wasn't that the murder of Nichols didn't satisfy his need for blood and sex. It was instead that he had found a certain beauty in the committing of the Nichols murder, in the execution of his improvements, and he wanted more of that.

Vincent was ready to kill again. He didn't need weeks to think through and fantasize the details of his next killing. He wanted to kill immediately, and the fantasy associated with his desire was quickly conjured up. But the fantasy was not only made up of ways to best satisfy his perverted sexual urges, or how to maximize through murder the power that could be gained for painting. There was more to this fantasy, something special, and it required him to make a kill right away in early September.

The base desire of Vincent's current fantasy had to do with what he had done before on a dark September morning of long ago—to kill again for his mother's birthday.

How perfect and complete it would be to travel to London and murder again as a gift for her birthday, fifteen years after murdering for her the first time in September of 1873. This had been a crucial part of his fantasies, no doubt, since he began the creation of his new persona and had fantasized over the summer of 1888 about returning to London. Murdering in early September was keenly on his mind all along.

The two murders in August were motivated more by impatience and opportunity than specific dates. They were only precursors to what Vincent was aiming at. Uncle Cent's death and the expected receipt of a portion of his inheritance through Theo only sped up his impatience to murder. But now, when the pristine moment had arrived for the achievement of a sense of full-circled completion, he had burned up all his funds on the previous two trips and had no money left to travel to London and give his mother the gift she so certainly deserved.

In the letter to Theo of August 18, Vincent had made the request for an additional 300 francs after being perturbed at hearing Theo had set aside some of the inheritance, not for Vincent alone, but for Vincent and Gauguin. He had added the reason for the money was to buy furniture for the Yellow House. Vincent had hoped Theo would accept his impassioned plea and send along the 300 francs in time for him to travel again in early September. But Theo had not yet come through with the money, and Mother's birthday was quickly approaching.

By September 4, Vincent could wait no longer. He had to try again, but he couldn't demand the money as he had done before. That didn't work. He would try what had always worked on Theo—sympathy. He wrote him a letter which contained sympathetic markers he had used so well on him in the past. He noted another painter he had befriended, Eugène Boch, was leaving that morning.[3] This was meant to begin the pity process in Theo's mind, generating an image of Vincent being without friends and all alone. He then worked on Theo's sense of responsibility for supplying him with his paint supplies by skillfully explaining how he was out of colors and couldn't paint.

Vincent then piled atop this an implication he might be headed for a depression due to his loss of confidence in Gauguin coming to Arles. He wrote, "I think that Gauguin doesn't care a damn about it, . . . and I for my part . . . am ceasing to believe in the urgent necessity of helping him." And then later in the letter, he added about Gauguin, "And perhaps he thinks that I shall always be here and that he has our word. But it is not too late to withdraw, and really I am tempted to do so."

With the flowerbed fertilized, Vincent then planted the bulbs: "How I'd like to settle down and have a home! . . . If we had spent 500 francs on furniture at the start . . . I should have the furniture and should already have been delivered from innkeepers." It was no accident that Vincent upped the amount from 300 to 500 francs. He always tried for more.

And so, Vincent firmly laid the blame for all his woes at the feet of Theo. If only Theo had sent more money and more paints, then Vincent's life wouldn't be falling apart. He would be able to paint and be living in the Yellow House, and his dream of a shared studio with Gauguin would still be alive.

Theo always believed in Vincent. He bought into his sincerity as an artist and as a human being, and he wanted Vincent to succeed and stand on his own two feet. Theo had made many sacrifices over many years by remaining connected to Vincent, and he seemed always willing to sacrifice more. However, Theo knew Vincent well. He knew he was an extremely flawed individual. He knew Vincent had the attitude of a spoiled child who felt entitled to Theo's money and to anything their family owned. But Theo was Abel, and Abel loved his brother, despite knowing how awful Cain could be.

Theo also knew Vincent was an alcoholic who spent part of the money he sent on drink. He knew he was enabling Vincent's vice, but he was compelled to continue to provide for Vincent out of a deep desire to help his tormented brother, who he believed had been misunderstood and rejected by all others. If only Theo could have seen through Vincent's sympathy-evoking words and understood the money he was sending him was also enabling a murderer, perhaps some murders would have been prevented. But Theo was blinded by the devices of an expert conman. He didn't know about Vincent's deeper layer of complexity and depravity. And, once again, he was fooled by the strong pathos behind Vincent's words and licked an envelope and sent him 300 francs.

Theo's letter has not survived, but I believe he sent it with the 300 francs on the same day he received Vincent's letter on September 5. Vincent received the letter and money the next day on the 6th. Not wanting to waste any time, he bought a roundtrip ticket to Paris and jumped on the next train to Tarascon that same day and was on his way back to London with gleeful murder on his mind. It looked as if Mother would get his gift in time for her birthday after all.

7

No Guts, No Glory
September 1888

Dr. George Bagster Phillips had been the Whitechapel Divisional Surgeon for the past twenty-three years when those years of experience were called upon once again on the quiet morning of September 8, 1888. At 6:20, there was a knock at the door of the doctor's East End home in Spitalfields.[1] A police constable standing on his stoop explained there had been another murder and asked him to come along. After collecting his hat and coat, Dr. Phillips and the constable climbed into a waiting carriage.

The cool morning air was split by the echo of the carriage horse as it clopped along through the streets of Spitalfields. Ten minutes later, the driver pulled on the reins in front of 29 Hanbury Street. The constable and doctor stepped down from the carriage and were directed by another constable to a door at the front of a row of houses. They followed this constable through an enclosed passage which ran between two houses to the back.

The lead constable pushed open the back door and held it for Dr. Phillips, who then cautiously took a few stone steps down to solid ground on some flagstones in the backyard. There were other constables there, and they pointed down to the side of the steps.

A woman was lying on her back with her head even with the steps and her legs further out into the yard with her knees drawn up and turned outward. Dr. Phillips took off his hat and set it on the flagstones as he knelt next to the body.

There was no need to check for a pulse or for a hint of shallow breathing. It was clear to anyone the woman was dead. Even if he hadn't at first noticed the gash in her throat, it was hard to miss her intestines pulled out and dumped over her right shoulder.

The body was later identified as that of a 47-year-old prostitute named Annie Chapman (figure 7.1, mortuary photo of Chapman). She was found at 6:00 a.m. between the stone steps of the back door and a wooden fence which divided the yards. In *Lloyd's Weekly London Newspaper* of September 16, the details of what Dr. Phillips saw at the crime scene were recorded: "The small intestines, and a flap of the wall of the belly . . . were lying on . . . the ground above the right shoulder, attached to the remaining portion of the intestines inside the body by a coil of intestine." Dr. Phillips went on to say, "Two flaps of the wall of the belly were lying in a large quantity of blood above the left shoulder." The blood was from the cut throat, and Dr. Phillips noted there was also blood on the wooden fence directly above this area, suggesting the initial surge of blood from the severed left carotid artery splashed against the fence and then drained out of the neck onto the ground. (figure 7.2, murder sites of Tabram, Nichols & Chapman)

The body was removed to a makeshift mortuary where Dr. Phillips examined the wounds more thoroughly. He noted at the inquest the incisions "had been made from the left side of the neck," and that they "carried entirely round." He also found "two distinct cuts on . . . the vertebrae on the left side of the spine." He concluded it appeared "an attempt had been made to separate the bones of the neck."

Dr. Phillips also noted signs of strangulation when he observed the face and tongue to be swollen and "the tongue protruded between the front teeth." He also opened up the head and found "the membranes of the brain were opaque, and the veins and tissues [were] coated with blood of a dark character."

The doctor also noticed an abrasion and ring marks on the ring finger of the woman's left hand. It was later confirmed Chapman normally wore two brass rings on that finger. The killer had taken the rings as a souvenir, but he had also taken something more personal from Annie Chapman's body.

When Dr. Phillips was pressed to give more details of the condition of the victim's body, he explained "the womb was entirely removed."[2] A police report by Chief Inspector Donald Swanson confirmed this and noted the details of the missing parts: "Part of belly wall including navel; the womb, the upper part of vagina & greater part of bladder."[3] The killer had crossed over into a darker world.

Dr. Phillips also found some items lying at the victim's feet near the fence, which he believed "had been placed there in order or arranged there."[4] The items were a small piece of coarse fabric and a pocket comb in a paper case. These were possessions of the victim which were removed and carefully placed by the murderer as a form of control over his victim. It suggested an organized killer operating in a cool fashion.

There were a few scratches and bruises on Chapman's jaw and cheek,[5] which led Dr. Phillips to the opinion "the person who cut the deceased's throat took hold of her by the chin, and then commenced the incision from left to right."[6] He also believed, based on other injuries to her neck, she was first strangled. He said the injuries "were consistent with partial suffocation, taken in conjunction with the swollen tongue and turgid nails."[7]

In a lengthy summation at the close of the inquest, the coroner backed up this opinion and walked through a possible scenario of how the murderer executed his method on the victim:

> He pressed her throat, and while thus preventing the slightest cry, he at the same time produced insensibility and suffocation. . . . The deceased was then lowered to the ground, and laid on her back . . . . Her throat was then cut in two places with savage determination.[8]

Just as with the previous two murders, there was no cry heard and no eyewitnesses to the crime. However, a few witnesses came forward and provided statements they may have seen the villain before he committed the act, while others also helped to determine a possible timeline.

A woman named Rosetta Anderson, who lived on Pearl Street, which was in the same vicinity as Hanbury Street, stated that on the previous evening she saw a mysterious man on her doorstep who, as *Lloyd's* described, "looked around him, and behaved in such an eccentric manner that she thought he was a maniac. He intently watched every woman as she passed, but, observing that he was himself an object of suspicion, he suddenly darted out of sight up a court near."[9]

Anderson also said the description of the man matched the description a witness had given of a man who was seen talking to the deceased. This witness was Elizabeth Long, and she had deposed that on the morning of the murder, at about 5:30, she was walking to Spitalfields Market down Hanbury Street when she saw a man and woman talking on the pavement in front of number 29.[10] She saw the woman's face, and later, when she visited the mortuary to view the victim, she felt sure it was the same woman. She did not see the man's face, but she said he wore a brown deerstalker hat, a dark coat, was a little taller than the woman and seemed to be over 40 years old. She said he looked like a foreigner, and when questioned for more specifics, she said he looked "shabby-genteel."

Long also noted the couple was talking loudly, and she overheard the man say to the woman, "Will you?" and the woman answered, "Yes." She went on her way and didn't take much notice of the couple because it was common to see men and women together in that area at that hour.

Another witness may have been in the backyard on the other side of the fence at the time of the murder. Albert Cadosh lived next door at number 27 and deposed that at about 5:20 a.m. he was out in his backyard, and when he returned to the door, he heard a voice say, "No," just as he went in. When he came back into the yard three or four minutes later, he stated, "I heard a sort of fall against the fence which divides my yard from that of 29." He added, "Something seemed to touch the fence suddenly." He didn't look to see what it was and went back into his house.

A girl walking in the garden behind her house at 25 Hanbury Street, two houses down from the scene of the murder, discovered some peculiar marks on a wall and on a garden path a few days after the murder.[11] Detective Inspector Joseph Chandler called at the house to make inquiries and was shown the marks. *Lloyd's* reported he searched the yard further "with the result that a bloody trail was found." It was concluded "further investigation left no doubt that the trail was that of the murderer."

The fencing dividing the yards was said to be about 5'6" high. It was believed the murderer vaulted over the fences of number 29 and then number 27, landing in the garden of number 25, where the curious marks were found. The mark on the wall was described as being "between a smear and a sprinkle," and it was surmised the murderer removed his blood-soaked coat and "knocked it against the wall."

In the yard behind number 25's yard, the police found some crumpled paper saturated with blood.[12] It was believed the murderer found the paper and used it to wipe his bloody hands and then threw it over the back wall. It was alleged that the stains were "subjected to analysis, and . . . proved to be those of human blood." But in an about-face, Dr. Phillips stated the paper had not been examined and the stains on the wall were not human blood.[13]

After mentioning Dr. Phillips' strong stance against the bloodstains being human blood, *Reynolds's* noted the doctor had "withheld information from reporters upon conscientious grounds." They seemed to think he was intentionally withholding, and possibly even denying, the truth of evidence which had been previously released, and they were likely correct.

During the inquest, Dr. Phillips and the coroner, Wynne E. Baxter, had a disagreement over whether the doctor should provide additional particulars about the wounds to the victim.[14] It seemed Dr. Phillips was concerned about the information being reported in the papers. After being forced by the coroner to give the details, the doctor thought in the interests of justice "it would be better not to give more details." The coroner disagreed and believed they had "a right to hear all particulars."

The doctor continued but then stopped and expressed himself more strongly to the coroner, stating, "In giving these details to the public I believe you are thwarting the ends of justice."[15] The coroner responded he had "never before heard of any evidence requested being kept back." Dr. Phillips was then again forced to continue.

It appears Dr. Phillips was onto something which had not yet been considered—that providing too much information to the public could hurt the case. He was attempting to keep control in the hands of the police and not give it over to the public, and more importantly, keep it out of the hands of the murderer.

✳ ✳ ✳

Knowing every detail of the murder, inside and out, Vincent didn't need to rely on the doctor's testimony for his information. After committing the messy crime, at least his hands would have been covered in blood with all that digging around in the intestines. However, it was noted by the landlady "there was an earthenware pan containing water in the yard."[16] So, he may have used this to give his hands and face a quick rinse before he left. It was also noted by Inspector Chandler there was even a water tap in the backyard, so he also had that as another option for washing up.[17]

In the coroner's summation, he concluded, perhaps with just a touch of animosity in his voice, the time of death which Dr. Phillips proposed of 4:30 a.m. could be incorrect because, as the doctor had admitted, "the coldness of the morning and the great loss of blood might affect his opinion."[18]

If the accuracy of the testimony of the witnesses was instead to be believed, then it could be determined that Annie Chapman was murdered at approximately 5:30 a.m. The sunrise that morning was at 5:23, so Vincent would have had to work quickly to get out of there before daylight fully revealed what he was up to. But he didn't seem to be in a hurry. Arranging the comb and the piece of fabric at Chapman's feet showed patience.

Another piece of evidence seemed to emphasize he took his time after the murder. It was reported a message written in chalk was discovered on a wall in the yard. It read: "FIVE; 15 MORE, AND THEN I GIVE MYSELF UP."[19]

Even in the heat of the moment, with the light of the sun beginning to dissolve the night and after strangling Chapman, cutting her throat, ripping open her belly, removing her guts and slicing free her womb, Vincent still had the presence of mind to arrange the comb and piece of fabric, rinse his hands, and pull out a piece of chalk and write a message.

Related to this, Vincent had met the artist A.S. Hartrick when they both lived in Paris in 1886. Years later, Hartrick reflected back and gave an account which included a useful detail about Vincent and chalk:

> Now Vincent had a habit of carrying a thick stick of
> red and one of blue chalk in each pocket of his coat.
> With these he used to illustrate his latest
> impressions or theories of art. As he would start
> work on the wall or anything that was handy, I
> immediately placed a newspaper or two on the
> table, where he would at once begin to set-out his
> latest 'motif' in lines a quarter to half an inch thick.[20]

As Vincent paused in the backyard and watched sunlight slowly paint the dead woman's body into visibility, he must have been filled with a sense of enormous power. He was becoming something great. He could kill whomever he chose and there wasn't a thing the people of London could do about it—not the people, the police, or the detectives. Operating under his new persona, he was too clever for them and possessed too much intelligence and cunning to ever be caught. He could do as he pleased.

And in this state of exuberant confidence, Vincent wanted all of London to know what was on his mind and what they could expect, and he pulled a piece of chalk from his coat pocket and wrote the message that included the threat of more murders to come when he wrote "15 MORE." The obvious intent was to deliver fear to the hearts of all those who read it.

Satisfied with what he had written with the chalk and what he had cut with the knife, Vincent reached above the stone steps to open the door, but a noise stopped him. He heard someone approaching through the passage and quickly reverted to his backup escape route and swung his body over the wooden fence and landed in the backyard of number 27. He then likely stood quietly and watched through the fence as an elderly man, John Davis, who had just finished his morning cup of tea, opened the back door at just before 6:00 a.m. and received a shock from the ghastly sight of a woman's mutilated body at the foot of the steps.[21] Mr. Davis didn't continue into the yard. Instead, he immediately turned back into the passageway and hurried to the front of the house to seek help.

Vincent then crossed the yard of number 27 and peered over the next fence. Seeing it was clear, he jumped over and into the garden of number 25 and possibly bumped against the back wall leaving behind some blood from the edge of his coat in the spot where the little girl found the curious markings on her garden wall. He then scaled the back wall and dropped over into the back of a packing case business[22] where he found some paper and used it to wipe the blood off his coat.

He may have had to climb or jump over more fences to get out of the immediate area and make it to a safe exit onto a street. There was a brewery behind the houses to the north on the same block, and he likely worked his way into this area and then onto a short east-west street named Black Eagle. He could have then headed west to Wilkes Street, turned right and headed north to Quaker Street, then west to Wholer Street, and then a short distance south to the much more congested Commercial Street, where he could get lost in the morning crowd (figure 7.3, escape route).

Of course, he may have taken other shortcuts or gone in other directions to get out of the area, but a remarkable piece of evidence suggests this was the direction he headed, and Vincent's path of escape can be further trailed.

As Vincent made his escape, the heightened sense of confidence he experienced just after the murder advanced into an overconfidence that almost got him captured. The evidence suggests, like the back-and-forth battle that plagued Dr. Jekyll in his struggle to win control over Mr. Hyde, Vincent also fought with his new persona for control. If he had stayed in character as the cunning and cautious Jack the Reaper, he would have headed north on Commercial Street and continued to distance himself from the crime scene, but his Vincent side had a weakness which was difficult to conquer.

Brimming with confidence, Vincent brushed aside the concerns of Jack the Reaper and turned south on Commercial Street in search of a stiff drink. He felt safe on a major road and easily blended in with the rough crowds heading off to their hard jobs or to Spitalfields Market. But he was taking a risk heading south. This brought him back into the vicinity of the murder, and he even passed by where Hanbury Street dead-ended into Commercial Street. But then more wisely, he kept moving south, and a few blocks later, he turned west on Brushfield Street and headed for the safety of more crowds on Bishopsgate Street. He was now smartly moving further away from the crime scene.

However, before reaching Bishopsgate Street, Vincent's weakness called his attention to the Prince Albert pub, and just a half-a-mile from the crime scene on the corner of Brushfield and Stewart Street, he abandoned caution and turned into the pub for a quick drink.

The wife of the proprietor, Mrs. Fiddymont, was tending bar and talking with her friend, Mary Chappell, when, according to an interview she gave later that day, she saw a man enter the pub at 7:00 a.m. "whose rough appearance frightened her, . . . with his hat down over his eyes, and with his face partly concealed."[23]

There were partitions that divided the bar, and the man stepped up to the middle compartment and asked for "half a pint of four ale." As Mrs. Fiddymont drew the ale, she watched the man through the mirror on the back of the bar.

She saw the stranger had noticed Mrs. Chappell watching him, and she noted he then "turned his back, and got the partition between himself and her." It was then she also noticed "blood spots on the back of his right hand," and "that his shirt was torn."

Mrs. Fiddymont turned and served the stranger his ale, which he swallowed in a single gulp. The man then immediately turned and left the pub. Mrs. Chappell followed him to the door, apparently drawn by curiosity. She remarked later that when he came in the bar "the expression of his eyes caught her attention, his look was so startling and terrifying."

As Mrs. Chappell watched from the front door, Mrs. Fiddymont slipped out a side door and watched the man cross Stewart Street and continue west on Brushfield, heading towards Bishopsgate. A builder named Joseph Taylor was working on Stewart Street, and Mrs. Fiddymont called his attention to the stranger. Mr. Taylor saw who she was referring to, stopped working and followed the man. Walking rapidly, he caught up to the stranger but didn't speak to him. The stranger glanced at him, and the look startled Mr. Taylor. He later commented, "His eyes were as wild as a hawk's."

The man with the wild eyes turned left onto Bishopsgate Street and headed south, holding his coat together at the top. Mr. Taylor continued to follow him through the crowd, noting the man had "a nervous and frightened way about him." He further described him and said he "wore a ginger-coloured moustache and had short sandy hair."

Mr. Taylor eventually stopped following the stranger but continued to watch him walk down Bishopsgate "as far as 'Dirty Dick's,' in Halfmoon Street, where he became lost to view." He further described the man as being "rather thin, about 5ft. 8in. high, and apparently between 40 and 50 years of age. He had a shabby genteel look, pepper and salt trowsers which fitted badly, and dark coat."

Mrs. Fiddymont added to this description, saying he wore "a brown stiff hat, a dark coat and no waistcoat, . . . [and] a light blue check shirt, which was torn badly, into rags in fact, on the right shoulder." She also noticed "a narrow streak of blood under his right ear, parallel with the edge of his shirt. There was also dried blood between the fingers of his hand." She was confident and had no doubt she could recognize the man if she saw him again.[24]

Mrs. Fiddymont, Mrs. Chappell, and Mr. Taylor were right in suspecting the strange man with the torn shirt and blood-stained hands of being up to no good. They saw him at 7:00 a.m., only an hour after Chapman's body was discovered. They were the first witnesses to get a good look at the serial killer, and although he was not yet known by name, I believe they were the first true witnesses to identify Jack the Ripper.

Mr. Taylor's description of the stranger having the unique characteristic of blonde hair but with red facial hair matches all too well to Vincent's own self-portraits and to how others described him, providing a strong indication it was indeed Vincent who entered Prince Albert pub that morning.

Matching Mr. Taylor's wording to describe the stranger's sandy hair color, a former and fellow student of Vincent's described him specifically as being "sandy-haired."[25] Vincent's sister, Elizabeth, confirmed his red facial hair color, noting he had "a straggly, red-brown beard."[26] She also said Vincent's eyes were "oft times inflamed from staring at objects in the sun." Vincent's eyes may have been inflamed from the sun, but they were also inflamed from too much alcohol.

Nevertheless, it's clear Vincent had distinctively penetrating eyes. The stranger in the pub also had a fierce quality about his eyes, which so alarmed the witnesses that they made it a point to describe them. Mrs. Chappell's description that "the expression of his eyes caught her attention, his look was so startling and terrifying," gives a good feel for what it was like to stare into the eyes of a killer and matches in many instances the look of Vincent's gaze in his own self-portraits.

Mr. Taylor added succinctness to the terror Mrs. Chappell saw, when he said, "His eyes were as wild as a hawk's." Vincent's young artist friend, Bernard, once described Vincent in remarkably similarly terms, but he used a different bird, noting Vincent had "an eagle's gaze."[27] Whether hawk or eagle, the message conveyed was the same—the stranger and Vincent shared intense eyes.

Bernard further described Vincent as being "of medium height, stocky without the usual excess, quick gestured, with an abrupt gait." This is also similar to Mr. Taylor's description of the man as "rather thin, about 5ft. 8in. high," and as he observed him walking along the street, he said he had "a nervous and frightened way about him."

The only seemingly contradictory description that Mr. Taylor noted was that the man was "apparently between 40 and 50 years of age." Vincent was 35 at this time, but being an alcoholic and living a self-imposed hard life, it's not a stretch to think he looked older, especially after a long night of murder.

The nervous and frightened man with a red mustache, sandy hair, and eyes as wild as a hawk's, who descended upon Mrs. Fiddymont's Prince Albert pub only an hour after leaving behind the gutted body of Annie Chapman was indeed the psychopathic serial killer and alcoholic, Vincent van Gogh. He had thrown caution into the wind to satisfy his unquenchable thirst by choosing to stop in for a shot of ale at a pub which was only half-a-mile from the crime scene. His craving and carelessness nearly led to his early capture by three observant citizens of London.

* * *

Vincent managed to get lost in the crowd, but after having two ladies eye him suspiciously in the pub and a man act as if he meant to follow him, Vincent must have felt like a fox on the run from a pack of baying hounds. He kept his head lowered, held the top of his coat closed to keep his torn shirt hidden, and continued south on Bishopsgate Street until he found a good side street to duck into and wash his face and neck a little better.

Having been spotted and possibly suspected of something, Vincent pushed his way out of the area towards a train station, likely either at Charing Cross or Cannon Street, where he could catch the 9:40 a.m. train to Folkestone for the steamer over to France.

Vincent must have been exhausted. He had arrived in London after a long journey from Arles just the day before on Friday. That, along with the intensity he had put into murdering Annie Chapman, not to mention the ensuing escape over fences, must have certainly taken something out of him. This took stamina, but he had done even more. Incredibly, Vincent had also used his knife to commit another murder earlier in the night before he used it on Chapman.

On Tuesday, September 11, at about 12:45 p.m., three days after the Chapman murder, another gruesome discovery was made. A deal porter named Frederick Moore, who worked on a wharf on Grosvenor Road near the Grosvenor Railway Bridge on the Pimlico side of the Thames, had his attention drawn by a few workmen looking over the embankment at something lying on the shore in the mud near the sluices of the Millbank Distillery.[28] A ladder was obtained, and as Moore stated later, "I went over and picked it up. I found it was a woman's arm, with a string attached to the part nearest the shoulder." He handed the arm over to the police. They began the search for the rest of the woman but found no other parts.

The arm was taken to the Divisional Surgeon for Pimlico, Dr. Thomas Neville, who upon examination noted it was the right arm of a female from 25 to 30 years of age which had been cut off at the shoulder joint soon after death.[29] It was also his opinion the arm had been in the water two or three days. The *Daily News* then dutifully noted, "The date of the murder would be somewhere about the 8th of September."[30] They didn't take the next step, though, and relate it to the well-publicized Chapman murder of the same date.

Reynolds's noted the river was at low tide when the arm was found on the shore at Pimlico and conjectured the dismembered limb may have floated down from Richmond or nearer from Chelsea.[31]

There is something very familiar about a female body part being found in the mud on the shore of the Thames. Vincent had struck again, but not under the auspices of satisfying his fantasy as his developing alter ego, Jack the Reaper. Chapman had fulfilled that fantasy. This murder he did as Vincent, or as the Torso Killer, and this murder he did for Mother.

More specifically, on September 8, Vincent had murdered another woman for his mother's approaching September 10 birthday, just as he had done for her fifteen years earlier on September 5, 1873, when he lived in London and made his first kill at the age of 20. He would have preferred to travel to London and murder on the 5th to match exactly to his first murder, but he hadn't yet acquired the money from Theo. However, Theo did send the money, and he was able to murder only three days later on September 8 which, most importantly, was before his mother's birthday. In his mind, the gift he had for her would get to her in time.

In 1873, before finding the woman's face floating in the Thames, the police had first found the left section of the woman's torso in the mud on the shore near the Battersea Water Works. Interestingly, the 1888 Pimlico arm was found directly opposite this spot, near the Grosvenor Railway Bridge.

Of course, many other crimes and gruesome murders had been committed in London over those fifteen years, and memories of past atrocities surely faded and were lost among so many other terrible crimes. Therefore, the two murders, so far apart in time but so close in proximity and date went unconnected.

An arm is not much to go on, but the location and the date make it relevant. The only other possible clue to look into was the strangeness of a string tied around the arm. Dr. Neville thought the string was used to carry the arm, but this wasn't a viable conclusion.[32] An arm freed from its body would be very easy to carry. It has a built-in handle, after all. There would be no need to tie a string around it for this purpose. So, there must have been some other reason, and I would suggest the reason can be pulled from the past letter found at the meat market just after the 1873 murder.

In that letter, Vincent had told the romantic story of a couple who had taken a leisurely boat ride on the Thames which had gone terribly wrong. Although he had embellished the story a little for effect, Vincent had revealed how he had made use of a boat to commit the murder and dump the parts. Fifteen years later, Vincent likely chose to use the same method to murder another woman in the same fashion.

After stealing a boat on the night of September 7, 1888, and inviting a prostitute from the Battersea area along for a ride, Vincent may have followed the template of his first murder. As the evidence showed from the bruised temple of the 1873 victim, he would have given the prostitute a knock on the head and cut up her body in the boat. He could have simply tossed the parts over the side as the Meat Market letter had noted and as he had done with his first victim, but Vincent's creative mind had thought of more since 1873. He wanted to stretch out the delight of body parts being found in the river, and so he devised a simple way to do this.

Using the boat, Vincent glided up to the pilings of a bridge or pier and tied off some of his victim's body parts, such as an arm, with a bit of string. Then he frayed the string with his knife to assist the current, which would pull on the arm until the string snapped and freed the body part for its journey downriver.

Vincent may have tied the arm to the Grosvenor Railway Bridge and after it snapped loose it only traveled a short distance before being lassoed in by a side current and taken to the shoreline. Then, low tide stranded it on the foreshore where it was found. This helps explain why Dr. Neville believed it had been in the water for two or three days and why the arm wasn't found until three days after her murder.

Vincent didn't tie all the parts to the bridge, though. He had different plans for some of the other pieces. Because it was his mother's birthday, the murder was a gift for her, but Vincent was a thoughtful serial killer. He also wrapped up and placed part of the woman's body as a gift prepared for the police, but they had not yet found their package.

It takes time to steal a boat, lure a prostitute on board, kill her, cut her up, tie an arm to a bridge, and carry and deposit some of the pieces to another location as a gift for the police. It could have taken a few hours, which accounts for why the second victim, Chapman, was killed so late in the morning.

Martha Tabram's time of death on August 7 was estimated by the medical examiner at around 2:00 a.m. Mary Ann Nichols met her end on August 31 right at 3:30 a.m. But with Annie Chapman on September 8, Vincent didn't get to her until 5:30 a.m. It took longer than expected to dispose of the body parts of the first victim of the night, which pressured him to get in his second murder before the sun came up.

Vincent had planned to commit two murders over that night, and he had succeeded. However, he put himself at risk murdering and mutilating Chapman while the sun was beginning to rise over the horizon. However, his desire to follow through on what he had planned was too great. He had to murder again for his mother, but he also needed to add to his count as Jack the

Reaper, and so he went ahead with the Chapman murder despite the late start. He was one acting as two. His two fantasy threads had woven together and fulfilling both had become necessary.

* * *

After a long night, and then a long trip back from London, for the second time in only eight days, Vincent stepped off the train in Arles on Sunday, September 9. Back in his hotel room, he could finally take off his coat and remove his torn shirt and get some rest from all his weary travels, but first he had to check his mail. He had not responded to Theo's letter before he left for London, in which Theo had included the 300 francs. So, Vincent was a little nervous Theo may have grown suspicious of his lack of a timely response and had written another letter while he was away. But to his relief, there was no letter from Theo waiting for him.

Believing Vincent received Theo's letter with the 300 francs on the 6th and left that day for London and was back in Arles on the 9th, Vincent had succeeded in making his trip a short one. Theo's suspicions had not yet had time to develop. However, because Theo had sent 300 francs, Vincent felt he especially had to get a letter back to Theo quickly. He also wanted to cover for the days he didn't respond, so he came up with a technique that would create the illusion he had been in Arles all along.

He achieved this by writing two letters to Theo on the 9th but acting as if the first was written on the 8th and the second on the 9th and sending both letters together on the 9th.

He opened the first letter thanking Theo for the 300 francs and provided a hidden excuse for why he hadn't written sooner by noting how hard he had been working on a painting called the *Night Café*.[33] He wrote, "For three nights running I sat up to paint and went to bed during the day." Noting he had painted for three nights covered the time he was away. He was simply too busy with the painting, and his schedule was too far off kilter for him to find the time to stop and write Theo a letter.

To make it appear this letter was written on the 8th, he then pinpointed the date by referring to an article he had read from the September 8 issue of the Paris newspaper, *L'Intransigeant*. He wrote, "Today I read something about the suicide of Mr. Bing Levy in the Intransigeant. It can't be the Levy who is Bing's manager, can it? I think it must be someone else."

Siegfried Bing ran a gallery in Paris where Vincent had purchased Japanese prints, and Lévy was one of Bing's managers.[34] Vincent was using the unique combination of the two men's names, who both he and Theo knew, which formed the name of the man in the article who had committed suicide, in order to make it appear he was writing the letter on the 8th. If Theo were to look for the article in the September 8 issue of *L'Intransigeant*, he would find it there and verify in his mind that Vincent had written the letter on the 8th, since he had said he had read the article "today."

In the same letter, Vincent then wanted to set up the writing of his next letter, and he wrote, "Anyhow, very soon, tomorrow or the day after, I'll write you again." He also then ended the letter with, "Till tomorrow."

He had also noted in the first letter he would send a drawing of the *Night Café* to him "tomorrow," and to complete the thought, he opened his second letter, "I have just mailed the sketch of the new picture, the 'Night Café.'"35 This gave the impression Vincent was there in Arles working on the sketch on the 8th, had finished it on the 9th, and was now sending the sketch and the two letters together on the 9th.

Relying on the information in the two letters, Pickvance dated the first letter for the 8th and the second for the 9th. However, I believe Vincent was still in London on the 8th and wrote both letters on the 9th upon his return, including references in the two letters to lead Theo to conclude he was very busy and everything was normal down in Arles.

Vincent added to the illusion he was in Arles on the 8th in his second letter by referring specifically to what he was doing the day before, writing, "Well now, yesterday I was busy furnishing the house." He then also needed to hide about 100 francs to cover for the expense of his trip. He noted he had used part of the 300 francs to buy two beds, 12 chairs, a mirror, and some other small items. He noted the total came to 250 francs, but he avoided breaking down the price for each item and played a game of slight-of-hand to plant in Theo's mind a higher price for the items than he had actually paid.

Before closing the second letter and getting it and the first letter off to the post office, Vincent described the scene in the *Night Café* painting with words which fit closely to his hidden life. He wrote, "I have tried to express the idea that the café is a place where one can ruin oneself, go mad or commit a crime." No doubt he was thinking of his close call at the Prince Albert pub when he wrote this.

8

Bloody Ambition
1873-1874

Back in 1873 when Vincent lived in London and committed his first murder at the age of 20, he may have thought of the murder of the pregnant prostitute as a one-time deal, never to be repeated. The pressures of his life had gotten to him. All those troubling thoughts of his family, especially of Theo, had crowded together in his mind until he had to do something to quiet them. The prostitute he murdered was only a substitute for the real object of his anger. However, the murder had fulfilled his fantasy, and Vincent became contented about the whole matter. He could now continue on at his new lodgings with the Loyers as if none of it had ever happened.

Vincent had hope again. With his rage alleviated, he could go on as before, but even better now, since he had learned the valuable lesson of what could happen if he allowed all those issues with his family and Theo to bother him. He would find a way to succeed. Theo would not immediately overtake him. He had a four-year jump on the boy, after all. He had experience on his side, and when Goupil's opened the new gallery, his stature would be right back where it needed to be.

Even though Vincent was feeling good again, the animosity he felt towards his family for conspiring against him while at the same time coddling Theo had not changed. However, the result of the murder had lifted away the emotional weight which so burdened him. With all that intensity removed from his thoughts, he could focus his energies more directly towards how to stay ahead of Theo by succeeding greatly in business and in English society. At work he would push harder to accelerate the opening of the gallery, while at home he would begin winning over English society by enchanting the widowed Mrs. Loyer and her 19-year-old daughter, Eugenie (figure 8.1, photo of Eugenie).

The social side of success was where Theo had the advantage. Everyone liked Theo. It was easy for him to shake hands and make small talk. For Vincent, this was all nonsense. Better to be abrupt and direct. He preferred getting to the point. However, if necessary, he could turn on the manipulation switch and subdue his normal gruffness, give a wink, flash a smile, and get what he wanted. He simply needed to apply that sort of mode more directly to his work and to his social dealings. Then he would get what he was after—success in business and in society and keep Theo from bypassing him.

With his new bright and cheery outlook on life, Vincent began to nurture his friendship with the Loyers. He quickly won them over, and the three enjoyed spending time together. Vincent had successfully put the nastiness of the past behind him. He was building a new way forward, and the Loyers were to be the cornerstone on which he would construct his future tower of success.

But Vincent had developed something more than a friendship for the Loyers. He believed he was in love with Mrs. Loyer's daughter, Eugenie. For Vincent, all that was required to fall in love was to be in the same proximity with a woman, any woman, for even a short period of time. He had a bad habit of mistaking the social graces of the women of Victorian society as being something more than what they were. If he were speaking with a woman, and she perhaps had a furtive smile as they talked, or her eyes seemed to shine more when she looked into his, then Vincent took it as nothing less than a clear indication of her love for him.

He developed this bad habit of misunderstanding women partly because he didn't understand the difference between like and love, but also because he had accepted the highly idealized view of women as presented in a book he was enthralled with by the French writer M.J. Michelete, entitled, *L'Amour* (*Love*). Vincent's already simplistic idea of love was reinforced by Michelete's romanticized and scientific approach to women and love. The book was presented as something of a guidebook for men on how to understand and handle women, both before and after marriage.

Vincent applied Michelete's philosophy to his own dealings with women as if it were a standardized formula for a chemical compound which could be followed step by step to gain the intended result. Say this or that to a woman and she would be expected to respond in a predictable way. For Vincent, this was the answer to his inability to effectively communicate with women. It provided a method he could easily follow. Based on Michelete, Vincent believed if he loved a woman she would automatically, like some sort of steam-powered robot fitted with a dress and bonnet, love him back. After all, it was her nature and her duty to return his love.

Vincent took to heart lines from Michelete's book such as, "She loves in advance him whom God seems to lead her."[1] Also, "She gives herself up, entirely and irrevocably." For Vincent, who had now fallen madly in love with Eugenie, it was only natural and to be expected that she would return his love.

As he spent weeks and months interacting with the Loyers, Vincent dreamed of the day when he would reveal to Eugenie his love and ask for her hand. She would then, naturally, admit her love for him and agree to be married. After all, he believed Michelete when he commented that women "comply almost always wittingly, in order to fulfill their destiny as woman, to insure the love of the man, and to create a family; they submit from the exalted necessity implanted in them, of sacrificing themselves."[2]

Vincent's blossoming love for Eugenie was becoming more and more an important part of the way in which he would conquer the advancing Theo. He would gain her heart, and when the time was right, he would present and she would accept his offer of marriage, and they would be engaged. He would write home with the glorious news, and his family would be all abuzz about Vincent. The focus would be back on him, and the special news of an English woman accepting him would be received as meaning he had been accepted by English society as a whole. This would be good personally but also good for business. Uncle Cent would be proud.

The new gallery would be opening soon, and he would pour all his energy into being a great hit with the artists and customers. The manager would report back to Uncle Cent, who would report back to Vincent's parents and to Theo with gushing compliments of Vincent's acumen and alacrity for commingling with the English people. Vincent would have success all around, and his family would again be thinking of him as the future head of the family. Theo would be relegated to where he belonged—riding Vincent's coattails, as opposed to wearing them.

It was this burgeoning love for Eugenie and what it could bring him that kept Vincent marching off to work in the mornings to the Goupil's warehouse and marching back home in the evenings to spend time with Eugenie and her mother. He could endure the warehouse work knowing it would soon change. He could also endure the thoughts of Theo advancing ever closer on his heels, since he believed he was following a plan that would secure his seat at the head of the table.

In November of 1873, when Vincent then found out Theo was being transferred from the Goupil's gallery in Brussels to, of all places, Vincent's old gallery in The Hague, Vincent could, for the moment, continue to control his emotional responses and see a brighter future. However, he couldn't avoid feeling the sting of Theo taking over his old position. Theo was even living with the same family Vincent had stayed with, and he wondered aloud to Theo in a letter, "Do you have my room at Roos's?"[3]

Theo was taking over his old life, and this was tearing at Vincent, but because he believed in the near future he would counter all that, he could endure the dark thoughts of envy which wriggled through his mind. A little alcohol would slow down the wriggling and help keep him from obsessing on those particular thoughts, and therefore he wouldn't need to take any extreme action to quiet them.

In her memoirs, Vincent's sister-in-law noted Vincent "celebrated a happy Christmas with the Loyers."[4] Vincent was fully devoted to his quest to be accepted by the Loyers, and especially by Eugenie. He only had to wait for just the right moment. He wanted to be sure she was ready, but he also wanted to have something to present to her to show he was a good bet for the future.

At the beginning of January 1874, he would have something. Just as the year before, he was given a raise. He had hoped to have news of the new gallery opening and to tell her of the big role he would be playing there, but he would have to settle for explaining this would occur in the near future, and for now, emphasize his raise.

He was ready to tell Eugenie of his love and to ask her to marry him, but before he could get up the nerve, his eagerness to tell his family got the better of him, and he wrote to his sister, Anna:

> [Eugenie] Loyer is a girl with whom I have agreed that we should consider ourselves each other's brother and sister. You should consider her as a sister too and write to her, and I think you will then soon find out what kind of a girl she is. I'll say nothing more than that I never heard or dreamed of anything like the love between her and her mother. . . . Old girl, don't think there is more behind it than I wrote just now, but don't tell them at home; I must do that myself. But again: Love her for my sake.[5]

Anna, being a good sister, dutifully ignored Vincent's request to keep it quiet and wrote to Theo quoting Vincent and adding her own observation: "I suppose there will be a love between those two as between Agnes and David Copperfield. Although I must say that I believe there is more than a brother's love between them."

Vincent was ready to run the race, but he needed a push up to the starting line, and Theo indirectly provided the push. Vincent had heard from his former boss at The Hague, and he wrote to Theo about it: "I know that you are doing well at The Hague, for I heard it from Mr. Tersteeg."[6] This was the last thing Vincent wanted to hear, especially so soon after Theo had transferred there.

Vincent was again reminded Theo had taken his place. He even had to hear from his old boss how well the Golden Boy was doing in his old position. The thoughts were crowding in again. Tersteeg had always told Vincent he was doing a good job and had always written home to his parents about his good progress. Now, so soon after Theo had started there, Tersteeg was already saying the same things about him and no doubt writing their parents about Theo's unexpectedly dazzling progress. And, no doubt, his parents and Tersteeg were making exaggerated comparisons between how well Theo was doing to how unwell Vincent had done when he first started.

This was a stark reminder for Vincent he was aiming for something which would assuage the anger and worry he had of Theo replacing him as the eldest son and that he needed to get on with it. So, he gathered up his courage and asked Eugenie to take a walk with him and nervously told her he loved her and asked her to be his wife.

Vincent wrote again to Anna with the result, and again, on February 24, Anna dutifully passed on to Theo what Vincent had said: "Vincent wrote that she was engaged, with a good natured youth who would know to appreciate her."7

Vincent was devastated. This would ruin everything. He had pinned all his hopes on Eugenie returning his love and accepting his proposal. She had kept the engagement a secret from Vincent and from her mother. The man's name was Sam Plowman. He had boarded with the Loyers before Vincent had arrived and, evidently, Eugenie didn't think her mother would approve of her engagement to Sam. Therefore, she hadn't shared this with Vincent either for fear he might slip and tell her mother. But now, with the lovelorn face of Vincent before her unearthing his own secret love, she was forced to give him the hard truth of the matter and reveal her engagement.

Vincent's depression returned, which required medication, and for Vincent that was alcohol. He was sliding back down into a deep pit of envy, hatred and self-pity. But then he must have recalled Michelete's analysis of women and wondered if maybe, just maybe, there was still a chance. After all, she wasn't yet married to the man, and she had only just found out about Vincent's love for her. Perhaps, in her female mind she would now be forced to consider Vincent as an option. After all, he was a man, and he had told her he loved her. This should generate a natural response in her to eventually return his love.

The slide down was averted. He would not give up on Eugenie. There was still a chance. He did, by the way, have an advantage over Sam Plowman—he lived in Eugenie's house. When he saw Eugenie again, she didn't act angry or distant with him. In fact, she continued to be friendly. This was a good sign. The plan to win her hand and send the good news home was still in play. Theo hadn't yet won. The dark clouds receded.

* * *

In March of 1874, a new wrinkle was added to Vincent's plan when he heard his sister, Anna, was thinking of moving to London in May. He wrote to the Haanebeeks, "It might be arranged for me to go and bring her back."[8] This meant Vincent could possibly be going home in May, and he tacked a new hope to that possibility. Not only could he dream of sending home news of an engagement, but he could show up in person and reveal the good news in the midst of his gathered family. Perhaps Eugenie would even consent to taking the trip with him, and then the news and the excitement at home would magnify a hundred-fold.

Though he had hope of prevailing, Vincent's confidence had weak cracks which threatened to crumble him into a heap of gloom. Theo continued to stay on his mind through the letters he sent to Vincent, and Vincent was forced to respond to all the activity that was going on back in Holland with his family. He wrote back to Theo, "I was very glad to hear that Mauve is engaged to Jet Carbentus."[9] Anton Mauve was a Dutch painter, and Jet Carbentus was Vincent's cousin. Vincent had to imagine the reaction of his family at the good news of the engagement—news which was very similar to what he had hoped to deliver.

Theo also mentioned he had visited one of their uncles in Amsterdam, and Vincent responded, "I am glad that you go to see Uncle Cor now and then." Then in April, he again responded to Theo, writing, "Glad you visit the Haanebeeks often."[10] When Vincent lived in The Hague, he had gone to visit Uncle Cor now and then, and the Haanebeeks were his close friends. Theo was taking over every area of his life and, in effect, replacing him.

May was approaching fast, and Vincent was feeling the mounting pressure. He needed more time, and he tried to buy some by pushing his deadline back a little. He wrote in the same letter to Theo he was afraid he would "not be able to go for at least four weeks."

As May began and time was running out, Vincent likely approached Eugenie again and expressed his devotion to her, extolling the value of choosing him over Sam Plowman. However, her response was the same. The engagement was still on. It was another rejection by her, and Vincent postponed taking his trip home.

Vincent's anger and desire for revenge returned. He tried to drown those feelings and thoughts under a river of alcohol, but all that did was allow a demon to paddle in and remind him of what he had done before to exact his revenge and alleviate his raging hatred and anger. He had likely kept the memories of the murder at bay, but now the images of cutting up his victim's body flooded back in. He also must have recalled the words of the letter he had dropped in the meat market a few days after the murder. The words he wrote then were just as appropriate now, even more so, when he had written, "I loved her to adoration, but she did not love me in return, and she loved another instead."

Once again, a woman, this time Eugenie, was to blame. Vincent's anger expanded out from his family to include Eugenie, and he recalled the next line from the Meat Market letter: "When I found that out, I vowed vengeance, and minded firmly to take her life, so that no one else should have her." He fantasized about killing Eugenie, but he had sense enough to know he couldn't get away with it. He would be accused, convicted, and then hanged by the English court system. But he could do as he had done before and kill a worthless prostitute in her place, and it would work as before to discharge his need for vengeance.

✳　✳　✳

On Friday morning, June 5, 1874, Robert Nicholls was out in a boat on the Thames about a quarter mile downriver from Putney Bridge at the Cedars (figure 5.2, London map) when he spotted a woman's body floating in the middle of the river—at least what remained of a woman's body.[11] He rowed over and towed it to shore and then hurried off to fetch the police.

The next day, Dr. E.C. Barnes examined the remains. He couldn't determine the age and could only conclude the woman was fully-grown. He stated about the victim at the inquest, as reported by *Lloyd's*, "The head, shoulders, and arms were absent. The right leg to the knee was absent, also the left foot. . . . The body was divided at the spinal column. Two ribs were attached. . . . The intestines were absent."[12] None of the missing body parts were recovered, and the woman was never identified.

Strangely, it had been nine months to the day since the first piece of the once pregnant woman who was killed on September 5 was found. It would seem logical to believe the London papers would have picked up on this and linked the recent murder back to the September murder immediately dispatching their boys to street corners holding copies high over their heads shouting, "ANOTHER WOMAN FOUND DEAD IN THE THAMES." But this didn't happen. It was barely covered. *Lloyd's* and *The News of the World* were apparently the only two papers to write about it, and only then after the inquest had taken place. They were both weekly papers, so the story didn't hit the stands until Sunday, June 14, nine days after the body was discovered.

The likely reason for the lack of coverage was the location. Putney lies further upriver on the outskirts of London, and the body was found about five miles from where the first part of the previously murdered woman's body was found in Battersea. Also, the police didn't seem to take the Meat Market letter seriously. Had they, there would have been plenty to link the letter to the new murder which would have then by association connected back to the September murder.

Vincent's fantasy of his second murder likely still required a prostitute from the Battersea area. With the promise of more money and a nice boat ride, he would have seduced one to come along with him to somewhere between "Richmond and Mortlake," as he had noted in his Meat Market letter. He had also written in the letter, "I threw the remains overboard, between Putney-bridge and Chelsea new bridge." But for his second murder, I believe Vincent added something new which he had dreamed up from his pre-murder fantasies.

Dr. Barnes noted that the woman's body was naked and made no mention of clothing or of a string being tied around any part of the body, but I think this was the first time Vincent made use of his technique of using string to tie remains to bridges. He may have come up with it because he didn't want to take the body in the boat down into Battersea. He could have just thrown the remains overboard, but his solution was to use some string and tie the remains to Putney Bridge and fray the string. Then perhaps within the next day or two the pull of the current would snap the string and the remains would be on their way—the operative hope being that the remains wouldn't be spotted until they reached the more populated and more traversed area of Battersea.

It was also reported that "the remains were in a shocking state of decomposition." Therefore, the murder hadn't taken place the night before. The body may have been tossed in further upriver and drifted there unnoticed. However, because of the large size of the remains, it's more likely it would have then been spotted earlier. Because it was found in the river in the same spot where the Meat Market letter had noted the September remains were tossed from the boat, it's possible the body had just broken free of its holding area under Putney Bridge and was found only a short ride later floating in the middle of the river.

As with his first murder, the central reason for dismembering the victim was to hide her identity. However, distinctive moles and scars had been found on some of the retrieved parts of the first victim's body and reported on in the papers, increasing the chance of uncovering the woman's identity. She hadn't been identified, but Vincent wanted to avoid this mistake with his second victim. So, with her dead body lying in the bottom of the boat, Vincent removed her clothing, lit a candle, and searched her body for any distinctive moles, scars or birthmarks that might be identifiable. He then made sure to remove those pieces.

After tying what remained to Putney Bridge, Vincent rowed downriver a short way and unloaded the other parts from the boat in a sack. Then, finding a secluded spot, he buried the identifiable parts. The Putney area was not heavily populated. Therefore, he had plenty of natural surroundings and privacy to dig a shallow grave.

I believe Vincent possibly saved at least one of the parts, though, an arm, for a little fun and carried it home with him in a sack to bury in the back garden at 87 Hackford Road. In April, he had spoken of doing some gardening at the Loyers. He had written to Theo, "I am very busy gardening and have sown a little garden full of poppies, sweet peas and mignonette. Now we must wait and see what comes of it."[13] How thrilling to know that planted just behind the house where Eugenie lived was an arm in among his growing poppies, sweet peas and mignonette. It was so appropriate, and so devilishly enjoyable. Much later, he would have some more fun with this buried arm.

With a body part of his victim possibly moldering under the garden earth only a few feet away, the mornings at breakfast with the Loyers on the back patio may have provided Vincent with an added twist of delight. And now that his anger at Eugenie's continued rejections had vanished by way of a murder in her honor, Vincent could politely ask Eugenie to please pass the marmalade and do so without bitterness in his heart. He still loved her, and he still held out hope she would choose him, despite her rejections.

Vincent quietly continued his attempt to win Eugenie's heart, but he had a distraction that kept him from committing fully to his efforts. Many days had passed, and the body of his victim had not yet been found, or at least he didn't know whether or not it had been found since it wasn't reported. He had frayed the string only slightly, and he expected it would only be a day or two before it snapped. It would then glide down the Thames and be spotted as it passed through Battersea. This should have made a big splash in the papers, but nothing.

It wasn't until Vincent unfolded the *Lloyd's* newspaper at the breakfast table on Sunday, June 14, that he learned the remains had been found on the 5th. Just as important, he also learned they hadn't been able to identify the victim, and they seemed to have nothing to go on. He could breathe easier. He was free of suspicion. The police had nothing that would lead them to him.

With that worry out of the way and his anger and hatred reduced, Vincent's hope in life and in love may have returned just as it had after his first murder. On June 16, just two days after being relieved by the news in the paper that his victim's body had been found, Vincent wrote to Theo informing him of his intent to leave there on "Thursday, June 25, or Saturday, June 27, if nothing interferes."[14] He may have been ready to once again ask Eugenie if she would be his and to make the trip home with him. By adding the "if nothing interferes," he may have been leaving open the possibility of adjusting the date further if Eugenie agreed to be his but needed more time.

Whether Vincent tried again or not, the result was the same—Eugenie rejected him. One of Vincent's most respected biographers, Marc Tralbaut, described well this period in Vincent's life with Eugenie:

> All his future plans were in ruins, but he still did not
> intend to give up the happiness that he had dreamt
> of for so long. He tried to persuade her to break off
> her engagement, but all his love was thwarted by her
> categorical refusal to do so. He had already thought
> of her as his bride, and this repulse left an indelible
> impression upon him. He lost all his illusions.[15]

With his illusions shattered, and there no longer being a reason to postpone the trip back home, Vincent left behind the Loyers and traveled to Holland.

Vincent's sister-in-law wrote that after the rejection "he came home in a melancholy mood."[16] She also noted how greatly this affected him, writing, "With this first great sorrow his character changed; when he came home for the holidays he was thin, silent, dejected—a different being. But he drew a great deal."[17] It was in depression and sorrow that Vincent turned to art.

As Tralbaut noted, the depression was not only because of Eugenie's rejection, it was also heightened because Vincent had relied so much on their engagement for his future plans. He had expected her to be his fiancé, and he had expected the engagement to fill his family with great joy and pride. But it was the other layer, the one deeper down, that caused him the most pain. Theo would remain the Golden Boy, and Vincent would remain the poor little Dutch Boy who couldn't seem to amount to anything.

At home, Vincent was able to see with his physical eyes what he had only previously envisioned and feared in his mind's eye. There, in person, with his preacher father, dower mother, his three sisters and youngest brother, and Theo, Vincent could look directly into their faces and see their disappointment in him and their excitement for Theo. Oh, how they all loved Theo and thought so highly of him and, oh, how they congratulated Theo on his position at Goupil's and on how well he was doing for being so new at it. Vincent was Cain, Theo was Abel.

Vincent sulked around the house until it was time to return to London. As planned a few months earlier, Anna would be coming back to London with him. She wished to look for work there. They left Holland and arrived in London some time before July 20, and Anna stayed with him at the Loyers.

Anna's presence at the breakfast and dinner table acted as a buffer during the uncomfortable moments when Vincent and Eugenie were in the same room together. But Vincent remained in a bad mood, and in an August 10 letter to Theo, he snapped back at something Theo had written. He opened the letter quoting scripture: "Ye judge after the flesh; I judge no man. He that is without sin among you, first cast a stone at her."[18] He added defensively, "So keep to your own ideas." He then concluded the matter with a line that so perfectly described how Vincent viewed himself within Christianity, declaring, "Virginity of soul and impurity of body can go together."

The impression was that Theo had admonished Vincent for his sexual practices. Either Vincent had revealed to Theo he visited prostitutes regularly, or Theo had heard from one of Vincent's acquaintances in The Hague of his dalliances. It may have had something to do with the trouble Vincent had gotten himself into when he was in The Hague, and Theo, only just finding out about it, then reprimanded Vincent for his behavior. Regardless, Vincent considered it an insult for, of all people, his younger brother, so pure and innocent, to try and tell him he needed to correct his sinful ways. What nonsense. Since he didn't have a wife, Vincent believed it was quite acceptable for him to make occasional visits to the brothels.

For Vincent, this was one more reminder that Theo was not on his side and that Theo should continue to be viewed as an enemy. He also realized he needed to come up with a different plan for outdoing the impetuous Theo. He had no idea what to do, but he knew one thing—he had to get away from Eugenie. He could no longer think of her as part of his plans. With that, he decided to move, and by August 14, he and Anna moved to some rooms just three-quarters-of-a-mile away to the north (figure 5.2, London map).

Hearing the news, Vincent's father commented about Vincent's situation in an August 15 letter to Theo: "His living at the Loyer's with all those secrets has done him no good, and it was not a family like others, . . . but not realizing his hopes must have been a great disappointment to him."[19] He also noted Anna had already found a job outside of London in Welwyn and would be starting there on August 24.

Anna moved out, and Vincent was left alone to deal with his broken heart and to mull over his failed plans. In the span of a year, everything had come crashing down for him, but for Theo, the Favored One, it had been a year of one success after another. Theo was passing by Vincent on his rise to the top, and there was nothing Vincent could do about it.

Vincent sunk further into a depression, and he brooded over what the future held for him. Even if Goupil's did open the new gallery in London soon, Vincent knew it wouldn't matter. He could put on his best act and become a good art dealer, but he knew deep within his envious soul he could never compete with the talent and abilities of the Golden Boy. Theo was a natural—he was talented and likeable.

Vincent concluded he could not beat Theo on Theo's playing field. He would have to find another way to overcome his brother. But he didn't know what the other way would be, and he began to contemplate his next step. He had to find a way, even if it called for more murder.

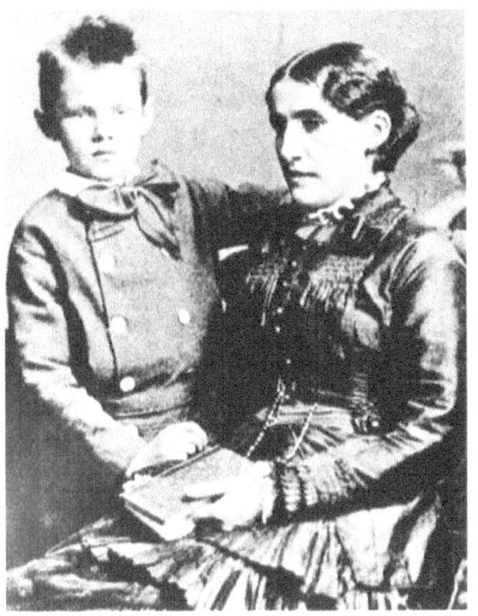

Figure 11.1
Kee Vos-Stricker with Son Photo
Van Gogh Museum, Amsterdam

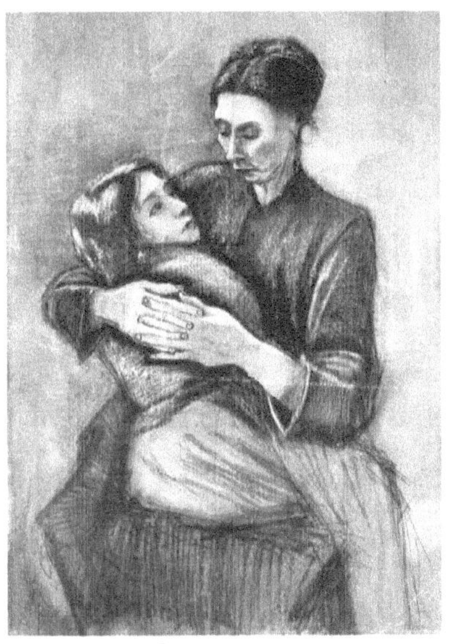

Figure 11.2
Van Gogh Drawing, (Sien) Woman With A
Child On Her Lap, March 1883
Van Gogh Museum, Amsterdam

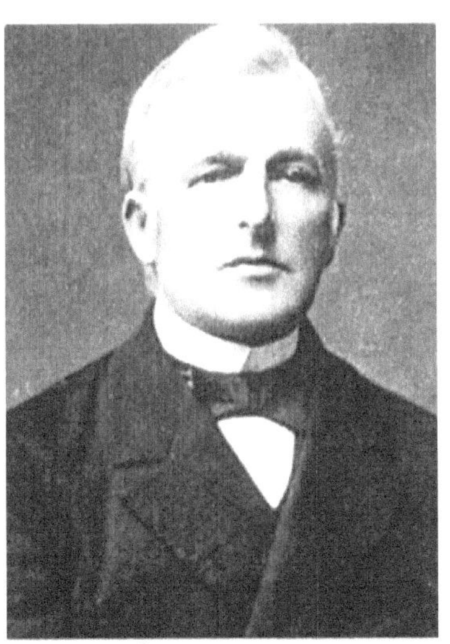

Figure 12.1
Vincent's Father Photo
Van Gogh Museum, Amsterdam

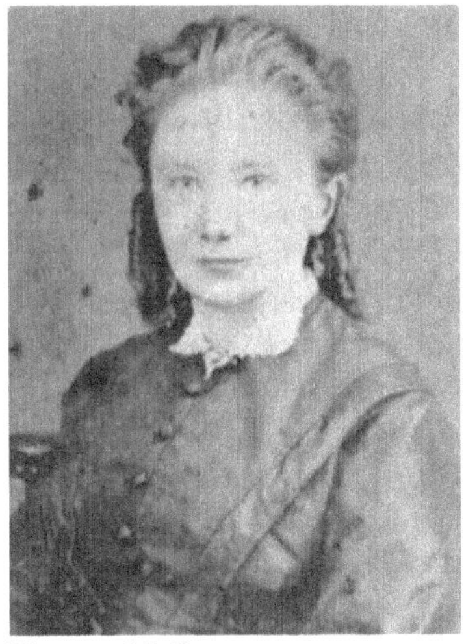

Figure 12.2
Margo Begemann Photo
Van Gogh Museum, Amsterdam

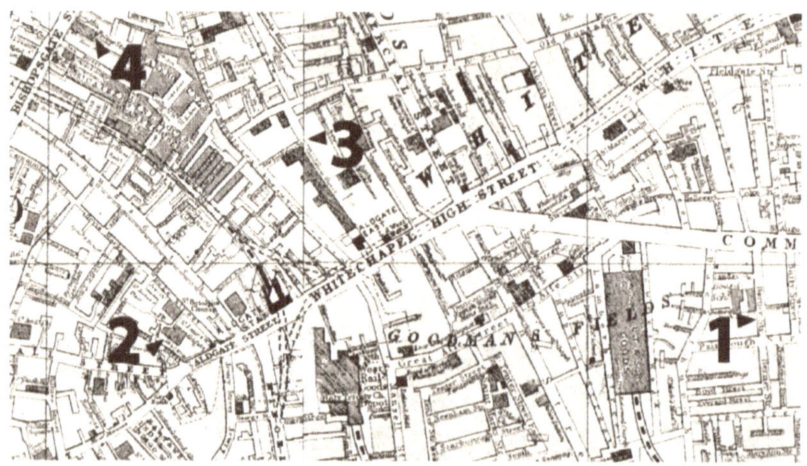

Figure 13.1

Map of Murder Sites, Elizabeth Stride & Catherine Eddowes
New Large-Scale Ordnance Atlas of London & Suburbs, 1888

1. Elizabeth Stride, 40 Berner St
2. Catherine Eddowes, Mitre Square

3. Piece of Eddowes' apron & chalk writing, Goulston St
4. Bishopsgate Street Police Station, Eddowes held & released

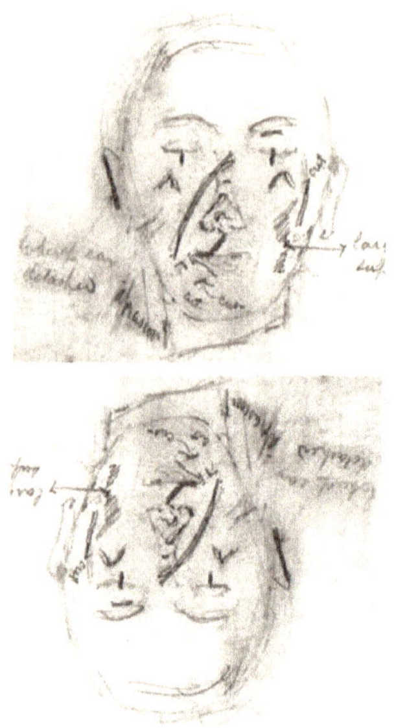

Figure 13.2

Catherine Eddowes Cuts to Face Sketch
The National Archives of the UK (TNA),
MEPO 3/141, sketch prepared by
Frederick W. Foster, City Surveyor

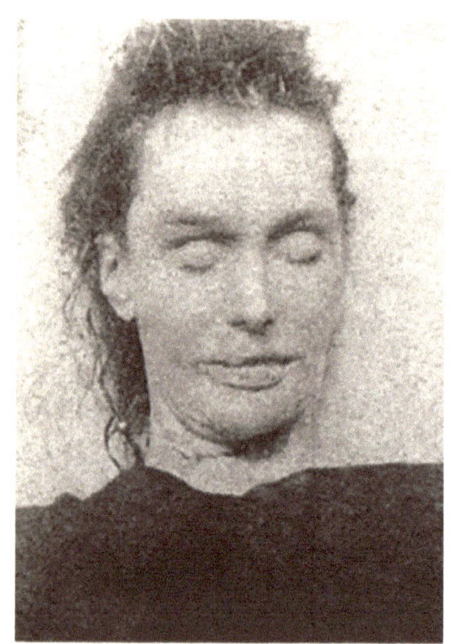

Figure 13.3

Elizabeth Stride Mortuary Photo
The National Archives of the UK (TNA),
MEPO 3/3155

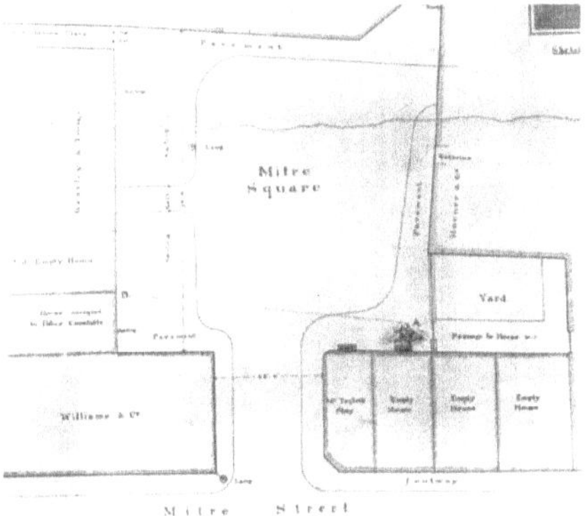

Figure 13.4

Catherine Eddowes Murder Site Police Sketch
The National Archives of the UK (TNA), MEPO 3/141

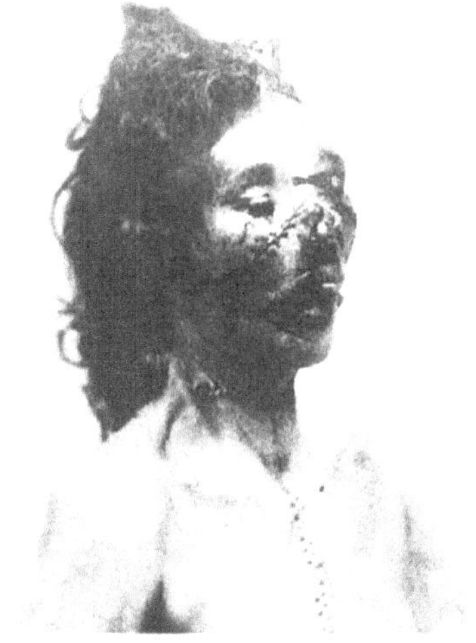

Figure 13.5

Catherine Eddowes Mortuary Photo
The National Archives of the UK (TNA),
MEPO 3/140, f 3B-6

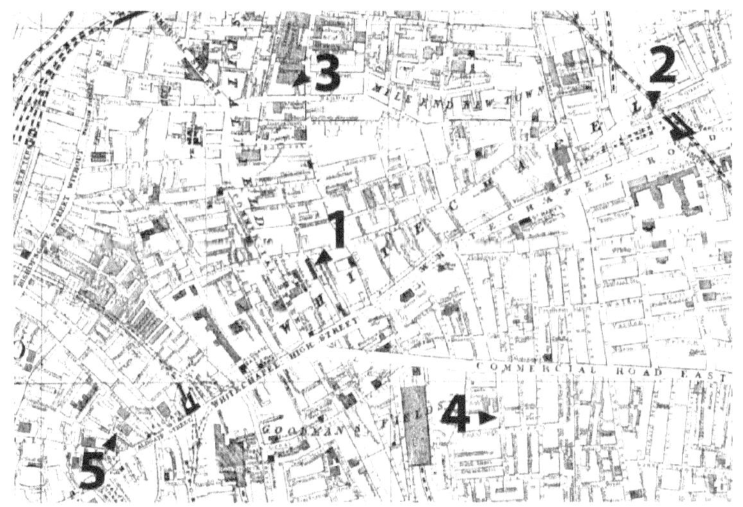

Figure 13.6

Map of Murder Sites, Tabram, Nichols, Chapman, Stride & Eddowes
New Large-Scale Ordnance Atlas of London & Suburbs, 1888

1. Martha Tabram, 47 George Yard
2. Mary Ann Nichols, Bucks Row
3. Annie Chapman, 29 Hanbury St
4. Elizabeth Stride, 40 Berner St
5. Catherine Eddowes, Mitre Square

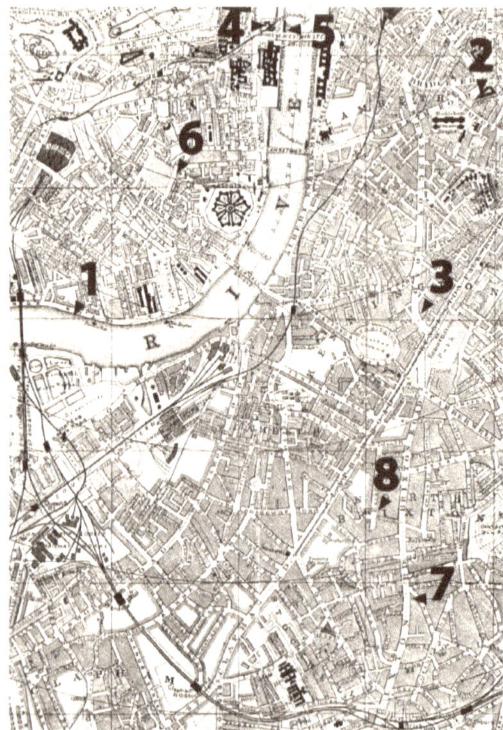

1. Right Arm found in Pimlico near Grosvenor Railway Bridge, Sept 11

2. Left Arm found in Lambeth on Lambeth Rd at the Blind School, Sept 28

3. Vincent lived in 3rd Boardinghouse, Ivy Cottage, 395 Kennington Road, 1874

4. Torso found in Whitehall in cellar of construction site for Metropolitan Police Headquarters, Oct 2

5. Westminster Bridge Steamboat Pier

6. Ripper letter found on street in front of 6 Vincent Square, Oct 4

7. Ripper letter found in pillar box opposite 304 Brixton Rd, Oct 4

8. Vincent lived in 2nd Boardinghouse with Loyers at 87 Hackford Rd, 1873-74

Figure 14.1

Ripper Letters Dropped & Other Relevant Locations
New Large-Scale Ordnance Atlas of London & Suburbs, 1888

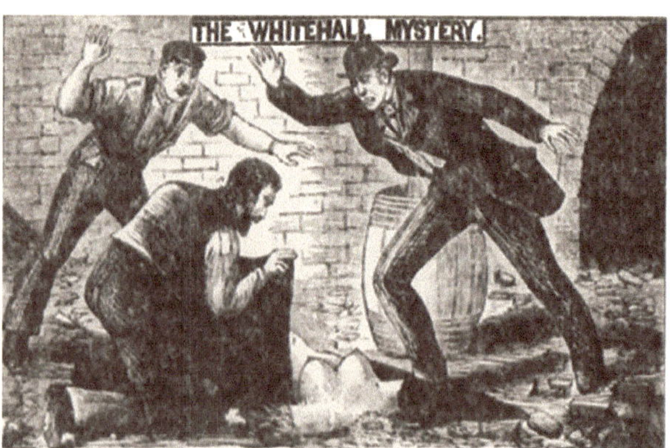

Figure 14.2

Whitehall Torso Illustration
The Illustrated Police News, October 13, 1888

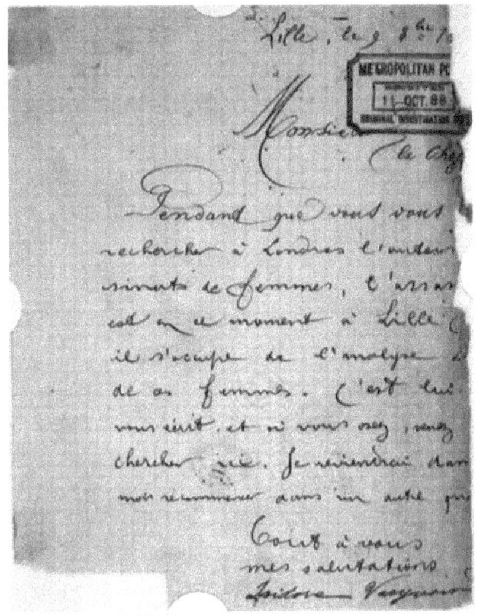

Figure 15.2
Lille Ripper Letter
The National Archives of the UK (TNA),
MEPO3/142, f. 154

Figure 15.4
Vincent Letter, Small Squares Graph Paper,
551, p 3
Vincent van Gogh, Letters of Vincent van Gogh,
1886-1890, A Facsimile Edition

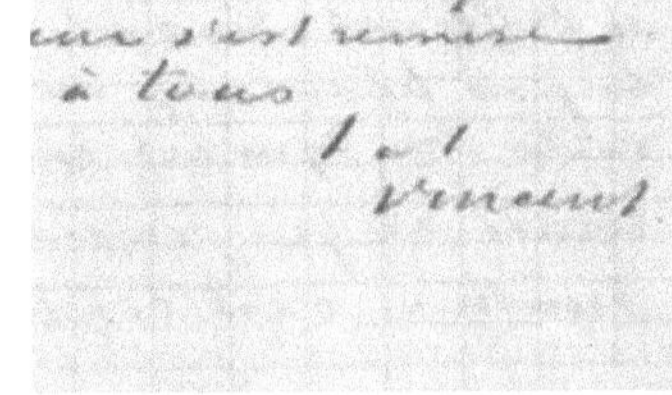

Rectangles, VG 623, p 8

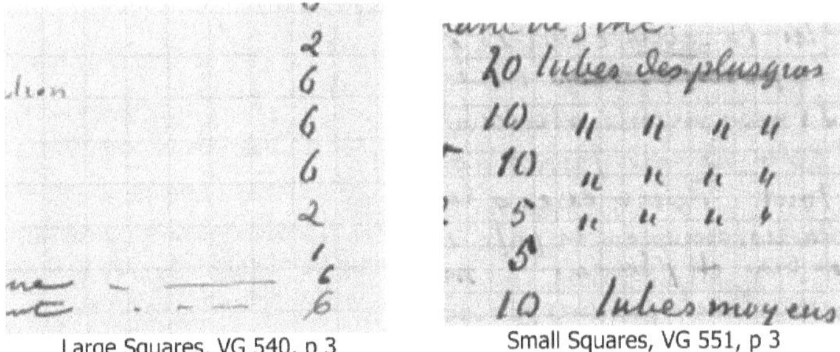

Large Squares, VG 540, p 3

Small Squares, VG 551, p 3

Figure 15.3
Vincent's Graph Paper Types
Vincent van Gogh, Letters of Vincent van Gogh, 1886-1890, A Facsimile Edition

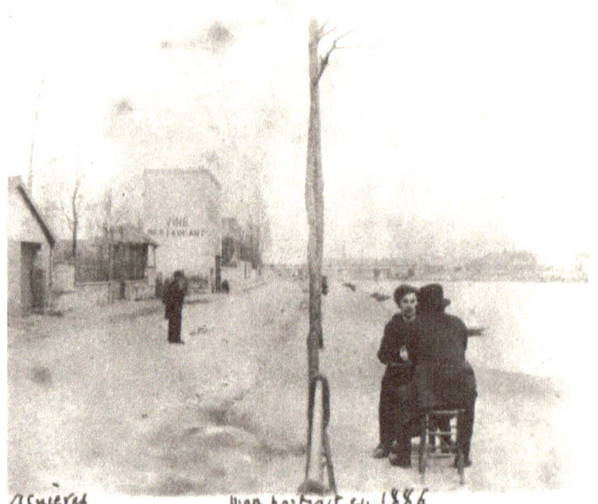

Figure 16.1
Emile Bernard Photo with Vincent (back), Asnières, 1886
Van Gogh Museum, Amsterdam

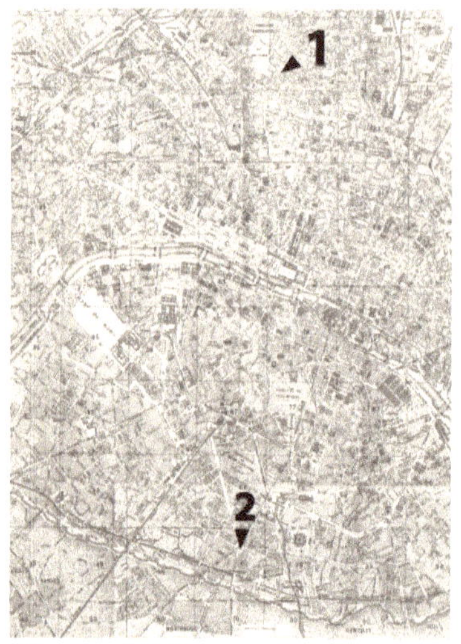

Figure 16.2
1886 Paris Murder Site & Vincent's Address
1887 Nouveau Plan De Paris

1. Theo's Apartment at 54 rue Lepic, Montmartre

2. Area body parts discovered in Montrouge

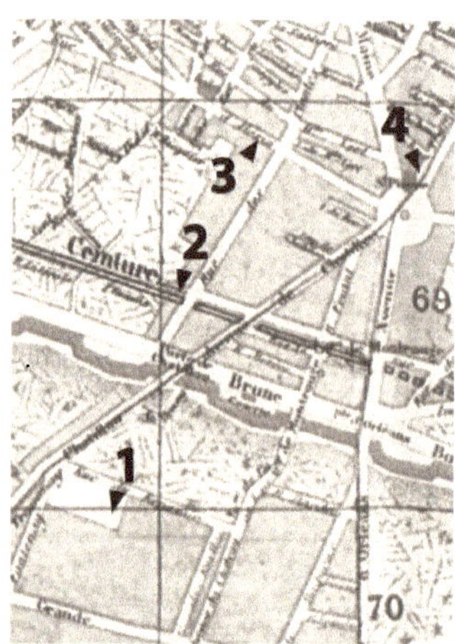

Figure 16.3
Montrouge, Paris, Body Part Drop Locations
1887 Nouveau Plan De Paris

1. Montrouge Cemetery

2. Torso found on embankment at rue Giordano Bruno next to bridge on rue des Plantes

3. Pelvis with Right Thigh found in street urinal in front of 131 rue d'Alesia

4. Arms & Lower Legs found in street urinal next to Saint Pierre de Montrouge Church

9

Jack's Little Helper
September 1888

Still attempting to defeat Theo in 1888, after so many years of failure, Vincent believed he was now finally on the right track. Murdering as Jack the Reaper was giving him the power to paint glorious paintings, and he believed his success at the upcoming World's Fair would bring him victory over Theo. However, as he continued to look for ways to perfect the techniques of his secret persona and push the power he gained from murder even higher, he knew the name of his darker side wasn't quite right.

He may have found the final adjustment needed for the name from a whimsical London magazine called *Fun*. In their August 8, 1888, edition, they reviewed the performance of a politician who had tried his hand at being an actor, and they wrote a little poem about him. Part of it went:

> At parties of late his skill was so great
> That many folk dub him a "ripper,"

Vincent had left London right after the Tabram murder on August 7, the day before the date of this issue. Perhaps it had already hit the newsstands, though, and he bought a copy to read on his long journey back to Arles. If not, it wasn't expensive to have magazines or newspapers sent through the mail, and *Fun* may have been one he liked and was having mailed to himself in Arles.

Vincent's ever-present attraction to London over the years kept him interested in what sort of graphic art was showing up in their magazines and what their artists were up to. He was also an avid reader of newspapers and novels. He regularly quoted from various articles and books he had read, being sure to add his strong opinions. In a long letter to his sister, Wil, in July of 1888, Vincent had revealed to her, "At times, driven by a certain mental voracity, I even read the newspapers with fury."[1] He read for enjoyment and for learning, but he also liked to keep up with current events. But in 1888, his interest in London had shifted more to the daily news, and more specifically to the daily reports of crime in the city. He would have been absolutely fascinated with what was being written about his deeds in London. It would have been unbearable for him not to know what they had to say.

Vincent may have subscribed to one of the widely read daily London papers, such as *The Times* or the *Daily News*, but he may have also chosen a weekly newspaper like *Lloyd's* or the *Illustrated Police News*, both of which summarized the information for the week without leaving out the juicy details of the murders. Also, Arles had a library which may have carried a London newspaper or two. Regardless of how he did it, after beginning his 1888 murders in early August, Vincent would have found a way to obtain London newspapers in Arles.

By whatever means, perhaps Vincent saw the August 8 copy of *Fun* with the poem about the politician turned actor who was referred to as a "ripper." If so, this was where Vincent found the final adjustment needed to complete his name for his burgeoning persona. Seeing the reference to a "ripper," he would have realized there was an additional meaning to the word "rip" that appealed to him. The poem used "ripper" to describe the politician in a context of having the skill to entertain others at parties with whimsical humor and a polite but cutting sarcasm.

Vincent had already begun using the word "RIP" in June when he slipped it into the drawing of the sower in the Russell letter, but he may have only been thinking of its use as the initials for Rest In Peace. But this new use of the word was something that matched well to how Vincent thought of himself. He had previously written something which also captured the same meaning of a ripper as a sarcastic writer when he wrote the tragically romantic Meat Market letter long ago in London in 1873. He wanted more of that. He wanted this to also be part of his new persona. He had already begun to express this sort of literary sarcasm when he wrote in chalk on the wall near Chapman's body: "FIVE; 15 MORE, AND THEN I GIVE MYSELF UP."[2] He meant it as a threat and taunt, not as a signal he would actually give himself up at some point.

But it was the more action-oriented use of the word that attracted Vincent the most. As previously noted, Dr. Llewellyn had used it in this way to describe Mary Ann Nichols at her inquest: "She was ripped open just as you see a dead calf at a butcher's shop."[3] Also, in the *Daily News* of September 10, Annie Chapman was compared back to the Nichols murder and described similarly: "The body had been ripped up."

Since Vincent had switched from stabbing to cutting from the Tabram murder to the Nichols and Chapman murders, this use of the word was certainly appropriate. Combining this use with its representation of having a way with whimsy and sarcasm was just the blend Vincent was looking for. He was no longer Jack the Reaper, the ominous Grim Reaper who wielded his scythe on his victims and brought a somber gravity to the people of London. Instead, he was now Jack the Ripper, a clever devil who first choked with a rope and then ripped with the knife, but always with style and flair.

Vincent was no longer just a painter and a murderer. He would also become like the politician and take up acting. Jack the Ripper would use the streets of London as his stage and give the people what they expected from the performance of any gifted actor—power and realism. His reviews in the papers were sure to reflect the flair with which he enacted his outrageous and shocking performances.

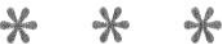

With the murder of Chapman, Vincent's acts were being reviewed much more heavily in the London papers, and the story now spread more widely into Europe and then also across the Atlantic to America. A story that could only crawl after the Tabram murder and had grown some legs after the Nichols murder, now had arms to swim the Atlantic. The *Daily News* noted, "The excitement has been intense."[4]

The whole affair was becoming a spectacle. There was something of entertainment in the air. Spectators gathered around the crime scenes and gawked as if they had only read about the gruesome stage performances of an idolized actor and yearned to be near where he had done his work. Vincent had fans and admirers.

The details of the murders in the newspapers kindled a fascination which set on fire the imaginations of many Londoners. But there were also side stories which heightened the main story and played on the minds of many. These side stories created false images of the murderer and helped to keep his true identity hidden. For instance, a leather apron had been discarded in the backyard where Chapman's body was found. A big stir was kicked up over this because it was known there was a man in the vicinity who went by the nickname of Leather Apron, and therefore the assumption was made that the apron was his calling card.

A reporter from *The Star* gave a description of the man, and this was picked up by the *Pall Mall Gazette*. The reporter said Leather Apron wore "a dark close-fitting cap . . . He is thickset, and has an unusually thick neck. His hair is black, and closely clipped . . . He has a small black moustache."[5] The article added that women described his expression as "sinister," and that they said, "His eyes are small and glittering. His lips are usually parted in a grin which is not only not reassuring, but excessively repellent."

The poor man was later found, questioned and cleared, but the dark and sinister description of the supposed killer had already been formulated in people's minds.

The police followed another black rabbit down a bottomless hole when they telegraphed a description given by a witness to police stations throughout the metropolis and suburbs.[6] The witness reported seeing a man enter the passage at 29 Hanbury Street at 2:00 a.m. This was more than three hours before it was believed the murder occurred. Therefore, it shouldn't have been given such weight, but the police and the papers chose to run with it anyway. The man was described as having a "rather dark beard and moustache, . . . dark jacket, dark vest and trousers, black scarf, and black felt hat."[7]

Neither of these descriptions should have been presented to the public or police as possible suspects. Having done so, they helped create in the minds of the people of London, and more problematic, in the minds of the police and detectives, the false image of a dark-haired sinister man who wore a dark mustache and had a dark scarf tucked into his dark clothing. The description of a sandy-haired man with a ginger mustache, which Mrs. Fiddymont and her friends provided, had quickly been forgotten and supplanted by the darker and more fitting description of a sinister killer.

Attempting to not only develop a physical description of the murderer, a doctor named Forbes Winslow threw his hat into the ring as a speculator to the nature and identity of the villain. The doctor wrote in an editorial, "The murderer of the three victims in Whitechapel is one and the same person I have no doubt."[8] He continued, "The whole affair is that of a lunatic . . . of the upper class of society." He then elaborated on his view of the perpetrator, "[He is] one who, though suffering from the effects of homicidal mania, is apparently sane on the surface . . . and is following out the inclinations of his morbid imaginations by wholesale homicide."

Dr. Winslow was every bit the profiler. He may have been speculative in his views, but something rang true in his commentary. What he described as homicidal mania could be compared to the modern-day description of a psychopathic serial killer.

Just as Vincent had created a persona, the police, the newspapers, and the people of London had indirectly conspired to create their own idea of what such a wretched serial killer should look and act like, creating from the night air a persona of sorts. Unfortunately, their persona inadvertently worked right alongside Vincent's persona to help conceal his identity and sidetrack all who looked for him, allowing him to continue to murder.

✳ ✳ ✳

In the second of the two letters Vincent sent to Theo after returning to Arles on Sunday, September 9, Vincent gave a hint of what was still to come. He wrote, "But I have so many plans in my head, and the autumn promises to give so many magnificent subjects."9 To Theo, he was speaking of art, but to himself he was likely also thinking of the many plans he had in mind for creating magnificent subjects of a murderous sort.

By this time, Vincent's traveling back and forth to London had become routine. He knew what scheduling options were available along his route and which were the most cost effective. He knew what to expect, and he knew within a small margin how long it would take each way.

Free from thinking about travel details, Vincent could focus his attention on what he would next like to do in London. He wanted more, much more, especially now that the newspapers were creating such a fervor. He was doing something great, something larger than himself. The people of London were reading of his messy deeds, and now all of Europe and America were also beginning to see just how powerful he was. But they were having trouble characterizing him, and he wanted to help them along. After all, he wasn't a lunatic, as the good Dr. Winslow had so confidently proclaimed.

Vincent wanted to have some control over how people imagined the fiend who haunted their nightmares. He wanted them to know his completed name, to tell them plainly he was Jack the Ripper. He knew a way, but he wasn't sure yet if it would work. He had to give it a test run first.

In July of 1888, Vincent had met and befriended a postman named Joseph Roulin (figure 9.1, Vincent's painting of Roulin). Roulin was 47, married, and had two children with another one on the way. His wife gave birth to the baby on July 31, and this prompted Vincent to write Theo about Roulin. Vincent noted he was using Roulin as a model and described him as "a postman in a blue uniform trimmed with gold, a big bearded face, very like Socrates."10

On August 4, he also wrote Bernard about Roulin and further described him as "somewhat addicted to liquor and having high color as a result."11 And then in another letter to Theo, he wrote, "The good fellow, as he would not accept money, cost more eating and drinking with me, and I gave him Rochefort's 'The Lantern' besides."12 Vincent continued to use Roulin as a model and painted him several times. He also painted his wife and children. The eating and drinking and the print of *The Lantern* were given as payment for his services.

Vincent then brought up with Theo how Roulin viewed things, noting, "He whole heartedly detests the republic which we now enjoy, and because on the whole he is beginning to doubt, to be a little disillusioned, as to the republican principle itself."[13]

When Vincent first met Roulin in the local café, bending his elbow just as Vincent regularly did, he may have only had in mind a fellow drinking pal and someone interesting to paint. But Vincent never thought in such limited one-dimensional terms. For him, there was always a deeper level to explore with every person and every situation. Meeting a new person was a new opportunity to manipulate for advantage. To a psychopath, a friend is not just a friend, and a postman is not just a postman.

Vincent likely didn't know what other use he could make of Roulin when they first met, but he kept him in mind as he painted his portrait and as they knocked together their glasses of ale and absinthe. Over time, as he found out more about Roulin's situation, he began to see in Roulin's life the area he could use to manipulate him. As they continued to meet and drink together, Vincent built up a trust with Roulin. With the alcohol flowing, and with Roulin possessing a trusting nature, it wasn't long before Roulin's lips loosened and he shared all, allowing Vincent into his life.

But Roulin didn't really seem to have much to offer. What use was a poorly paid French postman with a wife and three children to Vincent?

But then a revelation. One day, Roulin described his job to Vincent. Surprisingly, he was not a postman at all. He worked for the post office, of course, but he was not a country mailman who strolled along the streets of Arles delivering the mail to the locals. He was, instead, as Jan Hulsker noted in his acclaimed biography, *Vincent and Theo Van Gogh, A Dual Biography*, "an *entreposeur des postes* (head of a postal agency)."[14] Pickvance affirmed Hulsker's understanding of Roulin's position, adding that he "handled the mail at the railroad station."[15] Sweetman added more specificity, stating Roulin was a "postal agent at the station, where he was responsible for overseeing the unloading of the mail sacks and their security until transferred either to the post office in Arles or onward to Marseilles or Paris."[16]

Now, this was something Vincent could make use of. He must have secretly rubbed his hands together and contemplated just how he could turn Roulin's postal job into an advantage.

It didn't take long for Vincent-the-psychopath to see how he could put Roulin to work for him. Once he had finalized his name as Jack the Ripper, his attention turned to how best to introduce his new name to his admiring fans in London, and indeed to the world. Not only did he wish to give them his name, but he had a deep desire to define himself. He wished to tell them who he was and what he was about. It had felt so good to tell his story in the Meat Market letter after his first murder way back in 1873. It also felt good to write with a piece of chalk on the wall near Chapman's body. Vincent was an artist, after all, both in painting and in murder. He needed to express himself. He needed to write.

Vincent's many letters to Theo and to others reveal his writing was more than just a way to impart information and ask for money. Many of his letters were crafted with great care, and he expressed his opinions about a wide range of diverse subjects. He often wrote long letters, and even then, many times, he still found it necessary to add a P.S. to finish up. At times he even wrote more than one letter on the same day to add to something he had already written.

Letter writing was a form of expression for Vincent, and even a form of therapy, which worked as an outlet for his views on art and life. He was also developing a very strong need for an outlet to his secret life. He wanted to give his name to the public. Even more so, he wanted to write and tell someone about his other life as Jack the Ripper. Roulin would provide the way.

Because of Roulin's poor financial situation and disgruntled attitude about the government he worked for, and because he had a unique and potentially useful position, Vincent knew he could con and manipulate Roulin in a way which would allow him to beat the postal system. The only way to effectively do this was to find a way to bypass the post office, and Roulin could provide that possibility.

Vincent believed if he handed Roulin a letter with no postage and a London address, Roulin could slip it into a mailbag on the train headed for Paris without the letter being seen or stamped with a postmark by the Arles Post Office, thereby concealing from the recipient where the letter originated.

But there was one worry. If the letter arrived in an international mailbag in Paris, and it was then sorted for England, it would surely be flagged because it had no postage and no postmark. But after a few drinks, Roulin would have assured him this was not a problem. They divided the international mail into regions before loading them on the train, so a letter to London would be placed in a U.K. mailbag. Arriving in Paris, the individual U.K. mailbags would then be quickly combined into a U.K. bin and loaded on a train headed for London for sorting.

After Roulin explained how it worked, Vincent knew he had found a way to express himself to the people of London without them knowing where he was. He could send a letter to London from Arles, bypassing the post office, and thereby bypass a postmark, and now he knew the letter would even bypass Paris. No official in France would ever see the letter. Well, except for Roulin, his trustworthy accomplice. The letter would arrive in London clean. He could leave off postage and feel confident the authorities in London would have no idea of the letter's origin. They would have to assume it was sent from within London and never guess it was coming from somewhere in France.

Vincent knew he could also play around with this some. He was an artist, after all. It was nothing for him to create a phony postmark, and that meant he could further control the deception by making it seem a letter was sent from any location he chose.

The only possible trouble for Vincent in beating the postal system was Roulin, but that wasn't plausible. He had worked on Roulin, treating him like a father until Roulin thought of him as a son. They became bonded by the trust and friendship of two rather mutually poor alcoholics.

But how could Vincent bring up the idea and sell it to Roulin while also keeping the true intention of a letter hidden? Vincent could use his own lack of funds to play on Roulin's sympathies. He likely fabricated some story about friends and situations he remained connected to back in London but couldn't write them very often because of the cost, adding how he didn't want them to know where he currently lived.

As they sipped on their beers one September night, Vincent could have built onto the foundation of deception by using some lightness, saying something like, "You postmen have it easy. You can just slip your letters without postage into the mailbag and throw it on the train, and nobody would know." To which Roulin might have replied, "But it is allowed. I'm allowed to send my letters for free." And then, having spread out the mortar, Vincent could set the bricks in place, saying, "Ah, but I have to pay for mine."

From there Vincent dug his tender claws further into Roulin's trusting and sympathetic heart. Roulin would see how practical it was, and besides, he didn't like the government he worked for, so he wouldn't feel overly conflicted about cheating a little. Vincent would make sure of that. After all, they didn't pay Roulin well, and he had a new baby to support, and Vincent could use the money he saved on postage to buy him more drinks.

It was all so easy for Vincent. He had found a willing accomplice to beat and cheat the postal system. Roulin had no idea the extent to which Vincent would be using him, or that Vincent was making him an accomplice in the goings-on of the murderer, Jack the Ripper.

* * *

As Vincent worked on the unsuspecting and vulnerable Roulin throughout September, he was also pouring the enormous power he had gained from his murders and from the attention they had generated into his paintings. His goal to have a large amount of unique paintings ready for the 1889 World's Fair only grew stronger. He shared this with Theo, writing, "I feel my brain is lucid, and I want as far as possible to make sure of enough pictures to hold my own when the others are making a great show for the year '89."[17]

He also simplified his life and moved into the Yellow House. This reduced his costs by 30 francs a month since he no longer had a hotel room to pay for. But he still expected the same amount of money, and he pressured Theo to send even more. On September 16, he wrote Theo, "You must again send me 100 francs instead of 50."[18]

But Theo had already sent Vincent 50 francs before he received this letter. Vincent then received the 50 francs the day after he requested 100 francs. Even so, Vincent wanted to again make it clear he wanted 100 francs, and so he wrote a letter that day and said, "Thanks for your letter and the 50-franc note . . . In one way or another I'd like to be able to count on getting this month . . . another 100 instead of 50, as I asked you in yesterday's letter."[19]

Theo was sending Vincent plenty of money for his living expenses, and he also paid for and sent him his paint supplies. He had also sent Vincent extra money to buy furniture and have the house freshly painted. So, there really was no need for Vincent to continue to press for additional money, at least for what Theo knew about. But, of course, Vincent had another, hidden reason in mind for requesting more money.

The reason remained the same as it had been since his precious Uncle Cent had given up the ghost and traveled to the great beyond. Vincent wanted to be sure and get what he considered his share of the inheritance from Theo and spend it how he saw fit. And how he saw fit was to put it towards train tickets to Paris and London. He was preparing for his next journey. He wanted to be sure he had his travel money secured in advance and not have to wonder at the last minute if Theo was going to come through for him, as he had done before the Chapman murder.

As always, the ever-reliable Theo fulfilled his request, and Vincent wrote back, "Many thanks for your letter and the 100-fr. note it contained."[20] Shortly after this, Theo even sent him yet another 50 francs.[21]

Vincent had received a total of 200 francs since previously receiving the lump sum of 300 francs and traveling to London to kill Annie Chapman and an unknown woman whose arm was found on the banks of the Thames. He had spent some money furnishing the Yellow House, but he had enough to make another trip. However, he was hoping to have a truly grand time, so he thanked Theo for the 50 francs and then wrote, "Your last letter was dated Friday. It would be rare good luck if I got your next one as early as Wednesday."[22] Why not try for more? He didn't know how much Theo had received from his uncle's inheritance, so to Vincent it was simply prudent to push for more money.

It must be noted I disagree with Pickvance's dating of Vincent's letters during this part of September. Vincent first requested 100 francs on Sunday, September 16. It can then be presumed that Theo received this request the next day on Monday the 17th. Theo had already sent 50 francs when he received Vincent's request for the 100 francs. He could have chosen to send Vincent another 50 francs to make the total 100 francs, but instead, the always-generous Theo sent the full 100 francs which Vincent had first requested, likely that same day, Monday the 17th. So, Vincent then received the 100 francs the next day on Tuesday the 18th, and I believe he wrote Theo back that same day thanking him. Pickvance dated this letter as being sent on September 22. Because I believe this letter was sent four days earlier on the 18th, the dating of subsequent letters have been accordingly adjusted.

On Wednesday the 19th, Theo had then received Vincent's second request for 100 francs. Feeling generous and agreeing Vincent needed the extra money now that he had moved into the Yellow house, I believe Theo sent Vincent yet another 50 francs only a few days later on Friday the 21st. Vincent received this letter the next day and sent his thanks back that same day. Pickvance has this letter dated as Saturday the 29th, whereas I have it for a week earlier on Saturday the 22nd.

The reasoning for Pickvance's dating is understandable. When Vincent had thanked Theo for the second 50 francs, he noted that Theo's last letter was from Friday. Pickvance must have naturally assumed since Theo had sent Vincent 50 and then 100 francs, both within the same week, he would then wait a week to send the next 50 francs. I simply don't believe Theo waited. Vincent had just moved into the Yellow House and wanted more money. Theo was trying to be accommodating and helpful to Vincent's pleading, especially so because he had received the inheritance money.

In this same letter, Vincent also expressed his hope Theo would send him another letter the next week and send even more money, and he specified Wednesday. As previously noted, he had written, "It would be rare good luck if I got your next one as early as Wednesday." He then added, "But there is no hurry and it will be all right whatever happens."

Having sent this letter on Saturday the 22nd, as I believe, he was then referring to the upcoming Wednesday the 26th. He gave this day because he had already planned to leave that day for London. He had enough money to travel, but if he could get more before he left, all the better. His adding, "But there is no hurry and it will be all right whatever happens," reflects this. Vincent had prepared early for this trip, and he was ready to take it.

Vincent was also ready psychologically. Earlier in the month he had expressed to Theo a change had come over him and that he had become surer of himself, writing, "I am beginning to feel that I am quite a different creature from what I was when I came here. I have no doubts, no hesitation in attacking things, and this may increase."[23] Of course, to Theo he was speaking of art, but the extent of his change was in reality much greater. He had become much more confident and efficient as an artist, but also as a serial killer, and he was looking forward to his next kill.

As Vincent made improvements to his painting technique in the comfort of his Yellow House, he likely also dreamed of refining the technique of his maturing persona. He used most of September to contemplate and consider what he would like to do when he again arrived in London. He wanted to do more than he had done on previous trips. He wanted to heighten the experience and heighten the coverage in the papers, which he hoped would also heighten the shock and fear in the hearts of the people of London. He would give them what they seemed to want—more performances and more blood and horror. And now that he had settled on his name, he wanted desperately to give it to them.

As always, Vincent's impatience pushed him into something earlier than he had planned. He knew it would have been much wiser for him to wait until he was in London to reveal his name and to also wait until after he had returned from London to test Roulin. However, his self-confidence and eagerness to do something wicked convinced him to sit down and write a letter to the London police as Jack the Ripper.

On Saturday the 22nd, Vincent wrote the letter and was about to seal it in an envelope. But then, just before giving it to Roulin for him to send the next day, he must have decided it would be best, after all, to wait until he was in London to reveal his new name in person. So, he blackened out where he had written Jack the Ripper in the letter and gave it to Roulin. Roulin then took the letter with him to work on Sunday, the 23rd, no doubt somewhat nervously, and kept it hidden in the pants pocket of his blue uniform until just the right moment. After carrying some packages onto the train, he slipped the letter into the bin designated for U.K. mail. It had no postage, no postmark, and just like that, it was on its way to London.

The very next day, Monday, September 24, the letter arrived in London at the South East District Post Office and was dutifully stamped with the representative S.E. receiving postmark for that date, as seen in figure 9.2. The letter was addressed to the Commissioner of the Metropolitan Police, Sir Charles Warren, whose office was located in the South West district, so the letter was transferred to the South West District Post Office to be delivered.

Upon receipt, the envelope was stamped on the back with the S.W. postmark for the same date, as also seen in figure 9.2. The letter was then delivered either that same day or the next to the police. By Tuesday, it had been opened and stamped with the purple-inked stamp of the Metropolitan Police, which shows the date of Tuesday the 25th, as seen on the letter in figure 9.3.

The letter writer confessed he was the murderer and then teased the police, writing, "My name is," but blackened out the name in the shape of a coffin, writing around it, "So and so." He then said he was a slaughterer and blackened out the address of where he worked and signed the letter with, "I am yours truly," again blackening out the name in the shape of a coffin. But with the second coffin, he didn't completely cover the name, and the last characters are visible, as can be seen in the cut from the letter in figure 9.4. It appears the visible characters are the upper stem and lower stem of a "p," and then possibly the lower curve of the continuation of a cursive "e" that then moves into a more pronounced "r."

Vincent had written Jack the Ripper in both places in the letter, but he had blackened them out, appropriately making the blots look like coffins. He was sure of his skills of manipulation, and he believed Roulin would follow through. He even post-dated the letter for the day it would be received, the 24th. But the cautious nature of his alter ego caused him to play it safe and treat this letter as a test run, and so he blackened out the name. But even then, he couldn't help leaving a little of it showing. He wanted so desperately to give it out.

Full of impatience and adrenaline from the excitement of sending the first letter, Vincent immediately wrote another. After Roulin sent the first letter on Sunday the 23rd, and everything seemed to go well, and Vincent was now sure he had Roulin's complete trust and could therefore rely on him to carry out his wishes, Vincent must have presented the second letter to Roulin later that night over a glass of absinthe. Asking him to send it the next morning and expecting it to arrive in London the day after that on the 25th, he dated it for the 25th. But Roulin was too new at this sort of tomfoolery and too nervous about sending another letter so soon, and he likely asked Vincent to wait until the next weekend to be sure the first letter didn't come back with questions.

Vincent didn't want to wait another week to reveal his name, though. He was planning to leave for London on Wednesday the 26th, so he would have to deliver the letter himself, and he reluctantly tucked it away for later.

Because Vincent had asked Theo to write again by Wednesday, he had to fight off his impatience to leave before then. He was also on edge because, after all this time, Gauguin had still not made it absolutely clear he was coming to Arles. In the early part of September, Vincent's frustration with Gauguin had reached its peak. He wrote Theo about it, "Only you must understand that if I see that he isn't coming, I shall not be the least upset . . . If he comes, he will be very welcome, but I see clearly that counting on him would be just the thing to do us in."[24]

But then Vincent received a letter from Gauguin, and he wrote Theo about Gauguin's plans: "As soon as he has sold something, he will certainly come."[25] Vincent wrote Gauguin back and awaited a more definitive response. He also received a letter from Bernard, who was staying with Gauguin in Pont Aven. Vincent also wrote him back, hinting at having confidence Gauguin was coming, writing, "If Gauguin and I are here together, which will probably happen."[26]

On Wednesday morning, the very day Vincent planned to leave for London, he received a letter from Gauguin which also contained a letter from Bernard. Vincent likely also received a letter from Theo, possibly that same morning or the day before. Theo was reliable, and because Vincent had asked him to respond by Wednesday, Theo would have. Vincent did not want to respond until the day he left so as to stretch out the time he could be away. It was his good fortune that Gauguin and Bernard's letters also arrived before he had left. Their letters brought good news.

If Vincent did receive a letter from Theo with more money, then in the excitement of receiving good news, he forgot to thank him when he wrote him that Wednesday. He began the letter, "Enclosed a very, very remarkable letter from Gauguin."[27] He now knew Gauguin had decided to definitely come, but not immediately. He also found out that Bernard and another artist named Charles Laval, and two other artists, were also interested in coming, but not until February. His dream of beginning an association of artists in the Yellow House appeared to be coming true.

Vincent then noted to Theo he had to write Gauguin and Bernard back that same afternoon, closing with, "I hope I shall get your next letter on Wednesday." Sending his letter on Wednesday the 26th, Theo would likely then receive it in Paris the next day. The week before, Vincent had asked for Theo's letter "by" Wednesday, but now he was back to attempting to control Theo's response more specifically asking to receive his next letter "on" Wednesday, which would be October 3. Vincent was planning on returning from London by that day, and he didn't want Theo writing before then.

Vincent had sent a letter to Theo, Gauguin, and Bernard, all on Wednesday the 26th. After completing this step before leaving, he then took his next step later that afternoon onto a train for Paris with the Jack the Ripper letter Roulin refused to send for him buried deep inside his bag. He was finally on his way, and he was eager to get to London and get to work. He expressed his eagerness in his letter to Gauguin, writing, "These days, I have an extraordinary feverish energy . . . The fervor of my bony carcass is such that it goes straight for its goal."[28] His bony carcass was now on a train heading straight for his goal of mischief and murder.

10

Getting An Arm Up
September 1888

O n the morning of Thursday, September 27, 1888, Vincent arrived in Paris, and by that evening he would once again be rubbing shoulders with the people of London.

Vincent's fantasies and plans for this trip were well envisioned and well thought out. He was a man on a mission, but he was also an alcoholic. He was likely torn between treating the trip as a spree of unbridled drinking, sex, and folly, and between listening to his cautious other self, Jack the Ripper, who continually reminded him he was there for other purposes—such as to provide London with his name, to kill, and to increase fear and panic.

Arriving from the English coast at the Cannon Street station, Vincent hopped off the train and hurried along the streets for half-a-mile to the General Post Office at St. Martin's le Grand. He was eager to give the people of London his name. If he got there before 6:00 p.m., he wouldn't have to pay a late-letter posting fee, and the letter would be delivered that night.[1] He had addressed his devious letter to the Central News Office, London City, which was the Central News Agency. They provided news to the papers and were located at 5 New Bridge Street. This was only a short distance from the General Post Office, which explains why Vincent chose to take it directly there to mail. He wanted to be sure it was delivered and received that same night.

Because of the nearness of the address on the envelope to the post office, Vincent was only required to buy a one-penny stamp instead of the usual two-penny stamp. However, he didn't really need to put a stamp on it at all. He could have dropped it in a pillar box for free. A letter mailed from and to anywhere within London and its suburbs was not required to have a stamp. However, the lack of postage meant another step during the sorting process, and that might slow its delivery. Any London letter not having postage was required to be stamped with the black inked "2d" stamp to represent the government was paying two pennies for its delivery.[2] So, to avoid any delays, since he was there in London and wanted to see the letter quoted in the papers as soon as possible, Vincent took it to the post office where he knew he would have to pay for a stamp. Soon, the people of London would know who they were dealing with.

With his first planned deed of the trip completed, Vincent could ignore his Jack the Ripper side for a bit, and he possibly headed northwest from the post office and made the short walk to the meat market to relive those early years when he lived and murdered in London and wrote a letter to the police for the first time in 1873.

Having those years on his mind, he quickened his step to find the nearest pub for a drink. He was likely drawn towards the east, towards the Whitechapel District, being sure to avoid Mrs. Fiddymont and her friends at the Prince Albert pub on Brushfield Street. He had other plans for the night, but at least for this night he had no plans for murder, so he didn't have to show unreasonable restraint and could get reasonably sloshed.

Later that night, after visiting a few pubs and mingling with the ladies and gents of the East End and feeling comfortably inebriated, Vincent had an idea for some fun. Slipping away from the excitement of the gaslit pubs, he made his way to Bishopsgate Street and headed north to get far enough away from Whitechapel so that what he wanted to do would not cause alarm there and put the Bobbies on their toes. He also didn't want to be seen prowling the area.

Vincent followed Bishopsgate north until it turned into Shoreditch High Street. He kept going further until its name changed again to Kingsland Road in the Dalston area. Being far enough away from Whitechapel and feeling safe, Vincent walked through Dalston searching for a deserted stretch of road. With no one in sight, he took a piece of chalk from his coat pocket, bent down under a streetlamp, and wrote a message on the pavement. He saw it needed something more, so he added a little drawing next to it. The prank done, he stole away into the night wearing a devilish grin.

Another reason for walking so far away from Whitechapel to write a message in chalk was simply because he needed to waste some time. Writing the message might not have been planned, but he had time to do it that night, and with some drink in his belly, he likely wanted to do something spontaneous. But he did have something planned for later that night, and although he could let himself go a little, he still had to keep Jack the Ripper close at hand to prevent him from overdoing it. He wouldn't need to be cold-water-sober to do what he had planned, but he couldn't be stumbling around and bleary-eyed either.

After wandering the streets until later in the night when less police and people were out and about, Vincent worked his way down to the southeast of London into the much quieter Lambeth area into Brixton to do his final deed for the night. This is where he had lived with the Loyers in another time long ago.

After Vincent had murdered not only Annie Chapman but another woman in the early morning hours of September 8, the papers had reported only the right arm of the woman had been found on the foreshore of the Thames at Pimlico. Vincent had expected the police to find another part which he had specifically left for them, but somehow they had not yet stumbled upon their gift. Because they had only found her arm, this triggered an idea in Vincent's stimulated mind when he was in Arles painting feverishly and fantasizing about what he wanted to do the next time he was in London.

Because the woman had been murdered for his mother's birthday, he could reminisce on the first time he had murdered for her birthday back in 1873 and how he had sent that woman's body parts down the river and how her various parts were found.

He was then reminded of his second murder in 1874 and how he had only left a portion of the lower half of her body in the Thames. He had likely carried away the rest of her body and buried her head and the other parts to keep them from being found. But he may have especially recalled how he had buried one of her arms in the garden behind his boardinghouse at the Loyers. Those were treasured days, sitting out on the back patio enjoying breakfast with Eugenie and her mother, knowing the arm was only a few feet away, buried beneath some sweet peas he had planted.

It wasn't very difficult for Vincent to pull together a new fantasy after reminiscing. The arm found at Pimlico was the right arm, and the arm buried in the backyard of the Loyers was a left arm. How perfect. He would wait until late at night, slip into the Loyers' garden, and dig up what was left of the arm he had buried there so long ago in 1874. Then, he would place it at a specially chosen spot for it to be found as a message to the police, if they understood it. They had a right arm, they might as well have a left one too.

And I believe this is what he did later that night in the early morning hours of Friday, September 28. Then he found a cozy place somewhere outside away from the areas of his pranks of the night where he could curl up and get some needed sleep. The darkened corner of a grassy park, or even better, an open spot behind a moss-covered gravestone in a peaceful cemetery among the quiet and the dead would do just fine.

Vincent had sent three messages that night, one by mail, one by chalk, and one by digging up an arm and planting it for the police to find. The anticipation of wanting to read about the discovery of these messages in the papers would have threatened to keep him awake, but he had traveled many miles and had walked many more that night, so sleep must have come easily. He could let his dreams paint pictures in his mind of how each message would be found and how each discovery would add to the uneasiness of the people of London, and he hadn't even spilled a single drop of new blood to do it. All in good time, though.

11

Sweet Revenge
1874-1883

While living in London in 1874, after being rejected by Eugenie and murdering the woman whose arm he buried in the Loyer's garden, and after moving from the Loyer's, the young Vincent brooded over what direction his future would take. He believed the end result of continuing in the field of art dealing would only mean Theo winning, so he had to choose a new road which would provide him the way to conquer Theo.

Sinking into a deep depression, Vincent's work at the Goupil's warehouse began to suffer. His lack of interest was noticed and passed on to Uncle Cent, who decided to take action to help Vincent stay focused on his career. Uncle Cent thought it best if Vincent got away from London. In October, he had him transferred to a Goupil's branch in Paris.[1] But Vincent fought to get back to London, and in December he was sent back.

As Vincent's psychopathic mind ran through the many possible options he could take to defeat Theo, he must have considered that becoming an artist could be the way forward. After all, Theo couldn't outdo him in that area. Drawing was something he had dabbled in since he was a child, and a recent tragedy in his boardinghouse had inspired him to draw. He wrote to Theo, "Enclosed is a little drawing. I made it last Sunday, the morning when my landlady's little daughter died; she was thirteen years old."[2] Death and sorrow put Vincent in the right mood to create.

But at this early time, Vincent didn't have enough confidence in his artistic abilities to think he could ever rise to the greatness he believed was necessary to defeat Theo, so he had to set aside that idea for the moment.

However, the grief he saw in the faces of the dead little girl's parents must have triggered a reminder of his days of visiting sick and grieving villagers with his father the preacher. He likely put on an air of bereavement around the grieving parents and imitated well the role of a caring Christian. He may have even attempted to console them with the familiar Bible verses he had heard his father quote so many times to his suffering Dutch parishioners.

Vincent's psychopathic mind began to sense there might be something useful in what he had learned from his father. Something he could use to gain the respect of his family and rise above the blessed Theo. He had found the way. He would follow in his father's footsteps. He would become a preacher. It was the perfect path to follow. His family would have no choice but to admire and support him for making this honorable choice. No matter how successful Theo became in the world of art dealing, it wouldn't matter since it could never be admired over the sacrificial life of a preacher.

Vincent's focus shifted away from his work at Goupil's and turned obsessively towards religion. His lack of interest at work continued to be noticed and reported on, and in May of 1875, he was permanently transferred back to Paris.[3]

Vincent was making a transition in his life, and he wanted others to view him differently. He wondered aloud to Theo about this in a letter: "I hope and trust that I am not what many people think I am just now."[4] He wanted others, and God, to forget his past and think of him in the new light of being a man who sought to follow after God and no longer see him as a man who sought to follow after ambition.

Vincent had not yet fully transformed into this new image, so he hadn't told his father of his plans to follow him into the clergy. This would explain his father's less than complimentary description of Vincent around this time to Theo. He wrote of Vincent, "There is a kind of naturalness that is blamable. Someone who yields to low passions, follows nature, that is to say bestial nature."[5]

Vincent was working on controlling his bestial nature. He knew he would have to limit and conceal his immoral visits to prostitutes and excessive drinking if he were to hope to gain the acceptance of others as a bona fide man of the cloth. He had discovered, out of his deep desire to overtake Theo, that he possessed the necessary discipline to control himself when he wanted to. So, he was able to keep his low passions in check.

Also, no longer living in the city which so intensified his passions helped him stay in control. He even agreed his transfer from London to Paris was for the best in a letter to Theo, writing, "How much I loved London. Still, I think that it is better for me that I left."[6]

By December of 1875, Vincent felt he was ready to begin his new vocation. But instead of simply making his desires known, he chose to force Goupil's to fire him so that he could, as always, play the victim in the matter. He decided to go home for Christmas and New Year's, which was Goupil's busiest time of the year.[7] When he returned in January, part owner, Léon Boussod, promptly fired him. However, likely out of respect for Vincent's connection to Uncle Cent, Vincent was given two months to find a new job.

He was now fully embracing his new religious posture, but because he was following his ever-plotting and ever-conning psychopathic mind, Vincent was incapable of truly experiencing a religious transformation. He could only play the role of a devoted believer. He had been raised by two devout parents, so he knew the shtick, and he could mimic what he had been taught through years of watching and listening. He also dove into the Bible to make sure he sounded legitimate.

Even though Vincent's Christianity wasn't genuine, he did believe there was a God, and because of his upbringing, he believed God had made him Cain while making Theo Abel in order to punish Vincent for his past sins. This was another reason why he chose to turn to religion as his new profession. He believed if he obsessively committed himself to everything religious God would then show him mercy for the wrongs he had done—those wrongs being the murders of the two women in London in 1873 and 1874.

Because of his strict religious upbringing, I believe Vincent believed God had punished him and would continue to punish him for the murders. He didn't believe the London police had any evidence which could lead back to him, but he believed God would either cause some obscure piece of evidence to come to light that would result in him being captured, or more so, that God would continue to rain down punishment on him for not repenting of his foul deeds. Meanwhile, God would continue to bless Theo and work to have Theo replace him as the eldest and as the future head of the family.

But there was another curse Vincent likely had received while living in London. Syphilis was a prevalent disease among prostitutes and those who visited them. As often as Vincent visited prostitutes in the crowded city of London and in the poorest and filthiest areas like the East End, it is not only likely he had syphilis, but certain.

Tralbaut, and also Ken Wilkie, who wrote *The Van Gogh File*, uncovered good evidence Vincent had syphilis later in life. The only question is at what point he became infected. I believe it was early on and while he lived in London—this being part of the reason for his depression and also part of the reason why he chose the religious route. He hoped God would show him mercy in this area and heal him of the disease. He expressed this hope well when he quoted the Bible to Theo in a letter during this time: "All thy lovers have forgotten thee. . . . I shall restore health unto thee, and take the plagues away from thee."[8]

Vincent's last day of work at Goupil's happened to be on his 23rd birthday, March 30, 1876.[9] He must have believed his plan of redemption was working and God was showing him some favor because he received, that very day, news he had been offered a teaching job he applied for at a school for boys in England.

Vincent left Paris the next day for a short visit in Holland before starting his new position. While at home, he was reminded of who his nemesis was and why he was on the road he had chosen. Theo had been awarded the "trade journey" by Goupil's for the spring.[10] He would be traveling to various towns and making many acquaintances within the art dealing business. This honor was likely initiated behind the scenes by Uncle Cent, who had now washed his hands of the highly disappointing Vincent.[11] Theo was his new protégé and future replacement.

Fully stocked up on his hatred for Theo's good fortune, Vincent set off for his new position on the east coast of England in Ramsgate, seventy-five miles away from London. But this distance would not prevent him from seeing London again, nor would his lack of finances. In June 1876, he showed just how much drive he had for London and how much stamina he possessed. He used some time off from the school to walk the seventy-five miles to London.[12]

Remarkably, later that same month, fate moved in Vincent's life. The school was relocated to just outside London in the town of Isleworth, and Vincent gladly followed. This certainly must have been seen by him as a sign from God he should be back in London and God would restore him.

He now had a chance to look for a different job in the London area. He wrote Theo of his hopes to find a position "between clergyman and missionary among the working people in the suburbs of London."[13]

He didn't get exactly what he was after, but just a month later, Vincent found something close enough with a Reverend Thomas Jones who had a school in Isleworth and preached at a church in Turnham Green.

Working under a preacher, Vincent felt he was truly on his way to respectability, and he doubled his obsessive efforts to be more like his father and to be seen by others as someone who belonged in the pulpit. Vincent's father reached a different impression from his son's letters. He wrote to Theo about Vincent's extreme piety: "If only he learned to remain simple as a child, and would not always go on filling his letter with Bible texts in such an exaggerated and overwrought manner. It makes us worry more and more, and I fear that he becomes altogether unfit for practical life; it is bitterly disappointing."[14]

Seeing the worry caused by Vincent in the faces of her parents, his sister, Elizabeth, expressed the same view as her father, writing to Theo, "He becomes dull with piety, I believe."[15]

Vincent's family, even his own preacher father, believed Vincent was excessive in his religion. They didn't realize the hidden motivation for his turning to such devout religiosity, but it was obvious to them he was pouring it on too thick. However, Vincent believed the more pious he appeared to be to others, the more likely it was he would attain acceptance in this field, so he continued to play his role to the hilt.

Apparently, this strategy worked on Reverend Jones. After only three months, the Reverend decided to give Vincent his first shot at preaching. Feeling his plan was coming together, Vincent had to write to his brother about it, declaring, "Theo, your brother has preached for the first time."[16]

Even though he had been allowed to preach, Vincent's main duty remained something of a gopher for Reverend Jones. He was sent on errands into London to collect money from the parents of the students who attended the Reverend's school. These trips into the city were a delight for Vincent. He painted a picture in words about the trips in his letters to Theo, writing, "I wished you could have seen those London streets when twilight began to fall and the lamps were lit and everybody went home. . . . In the City it was dark, but it was a beautiful walk along the row of churches one has to pass."[17]

Remarkably, his errands even took him into the East End, and he wrote Theo of a planned visit to the area: "Tomorrow I must be in . . . London: in Whitechapel—that very poor part which you have read about in Dickens."[18] And then after the trip, he wrote about it again, adding, "I went to Whitechapel, the poor part of London."[19] He would be drawn back to this area many years later to make different sorts of errands.

It seemed Vincent was in the perfect location to advance in his chosen profession and achieve what he sought, but he was impatient. He wanted to be accepted by others as a preacher, evangelist, or missionary, and especially so by his family, and immediately. When he tried for missionary work in London, he was turned down. He felt the devotion he so openly expressed should convince others he was a special prophet of God who must be put into service in a leadership role immediately. But to most others, his extreme piety was disturbing and offensive.

A trip back to Holland for Christmas in 1876 revealed Vincent's true intentions. He expected his family to shower him with praise for the work he was doing as a man of God, but the positions he had obtained did not grab their attention, and he was not making any money. On the other hand, there was Theo, who continued to be the hope of the future. Nothing had changed. Things were not moving fast enough for Vincent. He was not achieving, and he didn't believe staying with Reverend Jones would get him where he needed to be quick enough. So, he decided not to return to England. Instead, he chose to follow advice from his father and accepted a job in a bookstore in Dordrecht until his father could decide what to do with him. Vincent wrote Theo about his change in direction: "Then the salary would certainly be better than at Mr. Jones's, and it is one's duty to think of that because later in life a man needs more."[20]

At least for the moment, Vincent had set aside his piety and replaced it with, of all things, a higher salary. Such a quick swing in extremes exposes Vincent's hidden agenda. He was only using religion and playing the role of a pious devotee in order to reach his unrelenting goal of rising above Theo. He now believed following his father's advice would lead to an acceptance by him and by the rest of the family. He could show himself to be the devoted son who followed his preacher father's words of wisdom.

Vincent only worked at the bookstore for about four months before his father came through and arranged for him to move to Amsterdam to live with another of Vincent's uncles, Uncle Jan, who was the director of a navy shipyard. Vincent was sent there to study with tutors who would teach him such things as Latin, Greek, and Mathematics to prepare for taking the entrance exam to be accepted into a university to study theology.

It looked as if Vincent was finally on the right track and headed towards gaining his family's respect. If he were to put in the hard work of study, he could gain entrance to a university, obtain a degree in theology, and be placed in a church somewhere preaching to the poor and needy.

It seemed Vincent had even accepted he had syphilis and that he would simply have to live with it. God hadn't healed him, so he would have to apply his increasing piety to this area also and accept God's judgment. He wrote to Theo, "What cannot be cured must be endured."[21]

But then he showed he was the same old Vincent when he added, "One must use the weapons within one's reach and the means at one's disposal to make the most of one's powers and gain advantage." Vincent was always looking for ways to gain advantage, and he would use anyone and anything to get what he wanted.

Vincent made it nearly a year before he determined going the scholarly route would be too much trouble and take far too long for him to get what he was after. He was ready to give up his studies and move on to a quicker way.

Like always, there was something which triggered Vincent to make a change, and like always, it had something to do with Theo. Theo had received wonderful news. Paris was hosting the 1878 World's Fair and Goupil's was sending him temporarily from The Hague to Paris to help with their exhibition of artwork.[22]

Even though Vincent was no longer directly competing with Theo at Goupil's, and therefore it shouldn't have mattered what good things came Theo's way, Vincent's intense envy and hatred of Theo had not changed. The thought of the Golden Boy receiving another honor and knowing Theo's name would again be mentioned in his family's household with such praise and reverence was too much for Vincent to take. He couldn't go on patiently studying to obtain his goal. It would take years, and he wanted something now.

Vincent wrote to Theo on April 3, 1878, and expressed his dismay at having chosen the school route: "Can it be my zeal has deceived me, that I have taken the wrong road and have not planned it well?"[23]

Vincent was again showing his true nature. His real motives for why he had chosen the area of religion were not clear to his family, but his continual choice of changing his course when good news came to Theo should have signaled that Vincent was reacting to Theo's life.

Nevertheless, Vincent's parents were well-aware Vincent was continuing to disappoint them while Theo remained their hope. Their father made this clear in a letter to Theo, writing, "Dear Theo, do remain the crown for us old ones, which is shaken so often."[24] Vincent was the one doing the shaking. Hulsker noted of this time, "Theo's star was rising at the same rate that Vincent's was descending."[25] Vincent was Cain and Theo was Abel.

Everything Vincent should have had, Theo was obtaining instead, and now it was clear he was also obtaining Uncle Cent's support. Uncle Cent certainly must have been responsible for having Theo sent to the World's Fair exhibit, and their parents knew this. Their mother made it clear who they believed in and who Uncle Cent was now supporting when she wrote, "Theo, Uncle loves you so much, I believe that after the disappointment with Vincent, the thought that you may succeed in his old favourite trade gives him a hope in life, something that is so important to him."[26] Vincent's parents were growing tired of hoping in Vincent only to be disappointed, whereas with Theo their expectations were always met.

After giving up on his studies, Vincent's father arranged for Vincent to be accepted in the Training School for Evangelists in Brussels, Belgium for a three-month trial period. Vincent continued his piety, and at the end of the three months, his father wrote to Theo that Vincent was "weak and thin. . . . He cannot sleep and seems to be in a nervous condition."[27] His mother added to the letter the decision reached by those in charge: "Mr. Plugge asked us to come and take him home." His father went and got him. Vincent had failed again.

But his father still persisted in attempting to help his eldest son, and he was able to convince others in Belgium to allow Vincent to try his hand at being an evangelist in the Borinage area in Wasmes for a six-month trial period. But again, the committee that determined if Vincent would continue didn't approve of his religious depravity, and they decided not to keep him on.

Vincent's father wrote Theo that Vincent "does not comply with the wishes of the Committee."[28]

This was also basically the same reason Vincent was dismissed from the Evangelist School. A fellow student there noted later that Vincent "did not know what submission was."[29] A Reverend in Brussels, Mr. Pietersen, who knew Vincent, summed it up best, stating, "Vincent impresses me as somebody who stands in his own light."[30] Vincent could not and would not conform to any other way than his own.

Vincent then moved to the nearby town of Cuesmes to work on his own as a minister until he could decide on his next move. However, he was losing faith in his pursuit of becoming a preacher as the way that would lead him to overcoming Theo. But he struggled along, living a meager life for nearly another year before he was jolted out of his depressed circumstances and forced to think again about what direction his life needed to take.

Once again, it was Theo's good fortune which provided the jolt Vincent needed to make a change in his life. Goupil's had decided it was time to move Theo on to bigger things, and they transferred him permanently to Paris.[31] This brought things full circle for Vincent. Theo had first taken his place at the branch in The Hague where Vincent had begun, and now Theo was being sent to Paris where Vincent's time with Goupil's had come to an abrupt and difficult end. Theo was again taking his place, and Vincent could again feel the burn of envy stirring hot within him. He believed *he* should be in Paris, not Theo. Instead, he was living on dry toast and cold coffee in the middle of nowhere. In his mind, his family and Theo were responsible for him being knocked off course. Otherwise, he would be in Paris or back in London, and by now he would be a great success.

Vincent gave voice to his sense of defeat in a letter to Theo in July 1880: "I am a man of passions, capable of and subject to doing more or less foolish things, which I happen to repent, more or less, afterward. Now and then I speak and act too hastily, when it would have been better to wait patiently. . . . Must I consider myself a dangerous man, incapable of anything?"[32]

Later in the same letter to his secret nemesis, Vincent admitted defeat and declared, "If I have come down in the world, you, on the contrary, have risen." He knew he had failed at becoming a respectable preacher and that Theo's latest advancement had placed Theo too high up in the minds of their family for Vincent to ever rise above him any time soon.

Vincent was too impatient to take the long road the clergy wanted him to travel in order to gain a respectable position. It would be many years before he could acquire success, far too long to satisfy his hunger for immediate satisfaction. He knew he had to give this up as the way to overcome Theo. It would never work. He had to find another way. And he did.

A month later, in August of 1880, Vincent had fully made up his mind to abandon the religious route and begin the path he would doggedly stay on for the rest of his life. He would become an artist.

Vincent had been drawing while in the Borinage. The poor miners he was ministering to provided interesting subjects, and his confidence in his abilities increased. By the time he found out about Theo's transfer to Paris, he felt sure he could make something out of his raw abilities. But he knew he needed to be taught more and practice more, and so he set out on foot from Cuesmes to Brussels to attend the Art Academy.

Arriving in Brussels, Vincent enrolled in the Art Academy and started to work on cultivating his drawing skills with a focus on human and animal anatomy. His father sent him the money to pay for his expenses, but actually, Theo was secretly sending the money to their father to support Vincent. Ever since Theo's transfer to Paris and when Vincent first voiced his desire to pursue art in July of 1880, Theo had begun to support Vincent.

In January of 1881, Theo was promoted at Goupil's while other employees were let go.[33] Vincent did not immediately react to more good news for Theo, but it set him to work harder, and when he found out months later in April that Theo was traveling home to Etten, Holland for a holiday, he decided he would also take a trip home, not for a holiday, but to stay.

Vincent had discovered Theo had been secretly financing him, and he understood the value of this. He realized if he went home, he could have room and board for free while still receiving Theo's money for his artwork and have some left over for other, baser needs, which were returning.

At the age of 28, Vincent was now back at home living under the roof of his mother and father with no intent of searching for another option for how he could become a preacher. In fact, he had no intent of searching for a job of any kind. He was fine with living off his parents and off what Theo was sending. He even believed it was his family's responsibility to support him financially while he now worked at becoming a great artist.

All of the obsessive energy he had put into becoming a pious member of the clergy was now channeled into his art. He was now convinced that becoming an artist was the way to conquer Theo, and he abruptly dumped everything associated with becoming a preacher.

Because of the importance Vincent placed on his art, he developed a stringent resolve and determined not to allow anyone or anything to stand in his way. He was driven by his continued envy for Theo and his growing bitterness towards his family. He would use all of his powers and abilities to succeed at art and undo all he believed they had previously done to him. He would make use of other people and circumstances to achieve his goals of success and restitution, being sure to also exact some revenge along the way.

* * *

Only a few months after moving back home in the spring of 1881, a situation came Vincent's way which he could make use of. His 35-year-old widowed cousin, Kee Vos-Stricker (figure 11.1, photo of Kee), had accepted an invitation from the Van Gogh's for her and her 8-year-old son to come and live with them over the summer. She may have been expecting a peaceful stay out in the country, but she got Vincent instead.

For Vincent, he saw Kee's arrival as a new opportunity to make use of a woman to achieve his purposes in life. Just as with Eugenie in London, he concluded Kee would be the perfect addition to his plan to generate the success he needed in all areas of his life to defeat Theo.

Vincent befriended his widowed cousin, and they spent time together on walks in the countryside of Etten. And just as with Eugenie, Vincent believed he could win over Kee and make her his wife, believing the news of this would make his family proud of him. He would then be showered with praise and respect for providing a widow with a husband and her boy with a father.

So, just as with Eugenie, the day arrived when Vincent felt the time was right to ask for Kee's hand. He had begun reading Michelete again, which he had given up on previously in favor of the Bible during his religious years. He felt the old hope of love returning and believed Kee would, of course, say yes. After all, she was programmed to do so.

In a letter to Theo afterwards, Vincent described how he had handled the scene: "And then I began—at first crudely, awkwardly, but still firmly—and I ended with the words, Kee, I love you as myself. . . . Then she said, 'No, never never.'"[34]

Just as with Eugenie, he had again been rejected, but also as with Eugenie, Vincent did not give up. He didn't take the "no, never never" to be as harsh as it sounded. He believed he would win her heart in time, and unlike with Eugenie, he was determined to fight to the end for her hand. He told Theo, "I must be resolute and firm, like a steel blade." This was an interesting, but appropriate, choice of wording for a murderer who liked to use the knife.

Vincent continued the use of the knife in a more sinister way when he then expressed he believed Kee's negative response was only part of an expected back and forth between lovers when he again wrote to Theo about Kee: "But the surgeon laughs up his sleeve and says, 'Touche!' . . . She must not know that I laughed up my sleeve over the result of the knife's thrust. . . . 'Did I hurt you? Oh, how brusque and rough I was! How could I be so?'"[35]

Kee continued to resist, and then she moved back to her parents' home in Amsterdam to flee her overly persistent and more than a little odd cousin. But Vincent didn't lose heart. He advised Theo, "Take care that you do not give all without taking . . . I made that mistake once: I gave up a girl and she married another, and I went away, far from her, but kept her in my thought always. Fatal."[36]

It would appear, and biographers would generally agree, Vincent was referring to Eugenie here. However, there is a possibility he was speaking of a woman before this, a woman in The Hague, where there was likely some trouble which caused Vincent's family to ship him far away from her to London.

This becomes more of a possibility when considering the line, "I gave up a girl and she married another, and I went away, far from her." Eugenie did marry Sam Plowman, but not until 1878, four years after rejecting Vincent.[37] Vincent's wording gives the impression things happened in quick succession, as if he gave her up, then she married another, and then Vincent went away.

Then also, there is a remarkable similarity to Vincent saying, "I gave up a girl and she married another," and to the line the murderer wrote years before in the Meat Market letter a few days after the September 1873 murder. Back then, he had written to the police, "I loved her to adoration, but she did not love me in return, and she loved another instead." Vincent van Gogh wrote that letter and was that murderer, and he was referring back to a woman in The Hague, both in the 1873 Meat Market letter, and now in the letter to Theo.

Another choice of wording Vincent used in the same letter to Theo makes this even more likely. He referred to himself as "the man whose little boat capsized when he was twenty years old, and sank." In the Meat Market letter, Vincent had described how he had borrowed a boat and had killed his victim. After disposing of the body, he had noted about the boat that he had "washed her out and tore a large hole in her side." The boat then sank, and the murderer fled. It is striking that Vincent would use such similar wording and references as those from the Meat Market letter when referring to the past of the same time. But, of course, it wasn't striking to Vincent. He wrote the Meat Market letter, and now he was intentionally, and joyfully, using wording in a letter to Theo which matched that time period.

Vincent noted he was 20 at the time his boat sank. He had turned 20 about a month and a half before leaving The Hague in May 1873. He was also 20 when he then met Eugenie, but he had turned 21 by the time he had received her final and ultimate rejection the next year in June 1874. The conclusion is that Vincent was referring to a woman in The Hague in 1873 whom he had loved but who did not love him back, and who then married someone else. He was then transferred away from her to London, where he murdered a prostitute as a substitute for the girl who had not returned his love.

Then, in 1874, Vincent repeated the scenario when he tried for Eugenie's hand and was rejected and made his second kill of a prostitute, again using his victim as a substitute for the real object of his anger, that time, Eugenie.

Here he was again, seven years later in 1881, after a long period of restraint from his vices and from following the patterns which previously led him to murder, heading down the same path with his cousin, appearing to be destined to repeat the same pattern. He put all of his hopes into Kee, and like before, he was resoundingly rejected. If the pattern were continued, Vincent was about to kill a prostitute as a substitute for the anger he now had for Kee.

This was very likely what came to Vincent's mind, and with his mother's September 10 birthday approaching, the haunting memories of the past and of murder were, no doubt, unavoidable. And now, when he was trying so hard to erase Kee's "no, never never" from his mind and replace it with his own slogan of "she and no other,"[38] his family was again interfering. His parents tried to talk some sense into Vincent. It was obvious Kee wanted nothing to do with him, but he refused to believe this. His hard-headed attitude caused great difficulty for his parents, especially because Kee was their niece and Kee's father was, like Vincent's father, a respected preacher. The unrelenting attitude Vincent had towards Kee was scandalous and an embarrassment to the entire family.

In early September, matching the time period of his first murder and also the time of his mother's birthday, Vincent decided to go away for a few days. He chose to make a visit to, of all places, The Hague.

Vincent was making a point. He was returning to the place from which his family had forced him to leave and where they had forced him to give up a woman he loved back when he was 20. Now that they wanted him to give up on Kee, he wanted to send them a message of his resolve.

Vincent also returned to The Hague to begin again his indulgence in his vices of heavy drinking and prostitutes. He had refrained from going on sprees during his religious period to avoid being judged a heathen, but now that he had put all that behind him, it didn't matter what others thought.

After he returned to Etten, Vincent opened up to Theo about his new and old views on religion and prostitutes. He said of religion, "But I care so very little for all that rubbish about good and evil, morality and immorality."[39] He then expressed agreement with a quote from the Dutch writer, Eduard Dekker, and declared, "O God, there is no God!" Continuing to clarify his turning away from Christianity, he added, "For me that God of the clergymen is as dead as a doornail. But am I an atheist for all that? The clergymen consider me so—so be it."

Making a clean break from his religious past, Vincent was then free to confess how he felt about prostitutes, and he gave Theo some insight into the reason for his trip to The Hague:

> You see, I am not quite an innocent greenhorn or a
> baby in a cradle. It is not the first time I was unable
> to resist that feeling of affection, aye, affection and
> love for those women who are so damned and
> condemned and despised by the clergymen from the
> pulpit. I do not damn or condemn them, neither do
> I despise them.

He then made his case for visiting prostitutes: "I need a woman, I cannot, I may not, I will not live without love. I am a man, and a man with passions: I must go to a woman, otherwise I shall freeze or turn to stone—or, in short, shall be stunned."

Even though Vincent had taken a respite from pushing for Kee's hand and had indulged in a spree with a prostitute, once he returned to Etten he picked right back up where he had left off. He kept his obsession for Kee going and wrote, "Theo, I love her—her, and no other—her, forever. . . . [It] is as if she and I had stopped being two, and were united forever and ever."[40]

He was sounding more and more like an obsessed stalker and stepped out from behind the bushes a bit more when he told Theo, "Do you think Kee knows how terribly she unintentionally thwarts me? Well, she will have to make up for it afterward!!!"[41] He felt she could do this by helping him with his art, but he used some rather serial killer sounding words to admit he was counting on Kee's help before he had secured her hand, writing, "But I am afraid I am busy selling the skins of many bears that I have not yet killed. However there is one bearskin with which I want to speculate."

Vincent's attitude and anger grew. He may have actually thought Kee might come around at some point, but his main purpose for continuing was out of spite towards his family for not supporting him and for forcing his hand in the past. He was exacting a form of revenge on them.

He let some of that revenge leak out in a letter to Kee's father. Vincent sent him a registered letter to make sure he read it, explaining to Theo, "I was afraid unregistered letters would be ignored, but he will be obliged to read this one."[42] He described it to Theo: "It is a very 'undiplomatic' letter, very bold . . . At first it will cause him to use a certain expletive which he certainly would not use in a sermon."

Vincent was enjoying the power he had over the situation with Kee. He could say and do what he liked, and his preacher father and his preacher uncle could do nothing about it. They had to remain proper and work at protecting their reputations, whereas Vincent could be as abrasive and offensive as he wished.

Vincent decided he would act like a psychopathic stalker and travel to Amsterdam and force the issue with Kee face-to-face. He arrived at Uncle Stricker's house and demanded to see Kee, but his aunt and uncle said she didn't wish to see him. He didn't believe them and called on his years of experience of using sympathy to get what he wanted. He described the scene later to Theo: "I put my hand in the flame of the lamp and said, 'Let me see her for as long as I can keep my hand in the flame.'"[43] Kee's father blew out the flame and told him, as Vincent noted to Theo, "Kee left the house as soon as she heard that you were here."[44]

The needed blow had been struck, and a physically and emotionally wounded Vincent sulked back to Etten. He wrote Theo the conclusion of the matter: "But then I felt something like, 'My God, my God, why hast Thou forsaken me,' and everything became a blank. . . . 'O God, there is no God!'"[45]

* * *

With the Kee Vos situation finally settled, Vincent proceeded with a plan he had devised to move back to The Hague to live and work on improving his art. With this in mind, he couldn't simply take his things and quietly remove himself from under his parents' roof. Instead, he needed to make it clear to his parents they were to blame for not supporting him and push this point to the extreme until they were forced to throw him out. He could then continue to play the wounded victim.

In December 1881, Vincent pushed until he got his wish. He was thrown out of the house by his father and moved to The Hague. He wrote Theo, "On Christmas day I had a violent scene with Father, and it went so far that Father told me I had better leave the house."[46]

In a rare look into how well-aware Theo was of Vincent's games, Theo wrote to Vincent, "I hope to be able to help you out as much as I can until you can earn your own money, but what I cannot approve of is the manner in which you contrived to leave Father and Mother. . . . Confound it, what made you so childish and impudent as to embitter and spoil Father's and Mother's life in that way?"[47] Theo knew Vincent well. He knew Vincent had intentionally pushed their father into throwing him out. Theo had also perfectly described and berated Vincent for his unacceptable behavior. Even so, Theo still wanted to help Vincent, and he continued his financial support.

Vincent didn't take Theo's rebuke well, and he used it as an opportunity to attack his father, writing to Theo, "Every time you say something to Father which he hasn't an answer for, . . . he will say, 'You are murdering me.'"[48] Relating to this, he added, "There! For the rest, the murderer has left the house." How true a statement Vincent was making. The murderer had indeed left the house.

After moving to The Hague, Vincent began to voice his opinion more frequently on certain topics in his letters. He was hiding something from Theo, and this was his way of building a defense for his situation. He wrote, "And I tell you frankly that in my opinion one must not hesitate to go to a prostitute occasionally if there is one you can trust and feel something for."[49]

He got closer to what he was hiding when he then made a point he believed an artist's private life should not be judged. He decided to use a very odd comparison, but not so odd to a psychopath, writing, "An artist's work and his private life are like a woman in childbirth and her baby. You may look at her child, but you may not lift her chemise to see if it is bloodstained. That would be very indelicate on the occasion of a post-partum visit."[50]

Vincent suspected his secret had gotten back to Theo, and he asked him, "Do you perhaps know something that I do not?"[51] He knew he had been found out, so he decided to write Theo and come clean. He explained in a very reasonable manner how he had used a prostitute as a model but couldn't pay her, she was in a bad way, and her and her child needed shelter. So, he felt it was his duty to take her and her child in, and they had been living with him ever since.[52]

Naturally enough, after reading this, Theo didn't want anything more to do with Vincent. He demanded Vincent give up the live-in prostitute. But Vincent had ammunition in the ready for this response, and he said he planned to marry the woman. This softened Theo some, but he tried to make clear to him what was obvious to everyone except for Vincent—it was Theo's money Vincent was using to support himself, the prostitute, and her child. Theo told Vincent the prostitute had to go or no more money.

Vincent responded with defiance. He said to Theo, "I risk my head when I contradict you . . . If my head must be cut off, here is my neck. . . . My life or death depends on your help. . . . Well for heaven's sake, off with my head."[53] Vincent's choice of wording befitted someone who had actually cut off heads.

He took his defiance further, adding, "You want me to leave the woman, . . . but I can't and I won't, . . . and now I tell you flatly, No, Theo . . . I shall do what I want . . . You will not be able to force me to renounce her, whatever your financial power . . . I do not wish to accept any money from you."[54]

Just as with Kee, there was something more at play. Vincent created the situation to cause conflict. He was redoing the past. With Kee, he had pursued her relentlessly and had defied his family's advice in order to rectify the similar situation which had taken place when he had first lived in The Hague. He didn't fight then, and he was transferred to London. Also, his resolve was connected to how he believed he hadn't fought hard enough for Eugenie's hand. And now, the new situation in The Hague was simply a continuation of Vincent's desire to redo the past, and to redo it in a more direct and forceful way. He would not give up on the woman he supposedly loved this time.

Clasina Hoornik was the name of the 32-year-old prostitute living with Vincent, but she went by the shorter name Sien (figure 11.2, Vincent's drawing of Sien).[55] Not only did she have a 4-year-old daughter when Vincent met her, but remarkably, Sien was also a few months pregnant. Vincent had given up on his quest for Kee's hand and had moved to The Hague and had sought out a pregnant prostitute to shack up with. This was no coincidence. This was Vincent enacting his spite and vengeance on his family through an attempt to re-create the past situation, but this time he would stand firm and defy what his family wanted.

Sien may have been the same woman who was at the center of the original problem in The Hague back in 1873. She may have even been pregnant with his child back then, leading his family to send him to London to get him away from the situation.

It's very likely Vincent went looking for Sien when he paused from his fight for Kee and had visited The Hague in September of 1881. Finding her, he may have impregnated her at that time. She was only a few months pregnant when Vincent then moved to The Hague in December.

This sort of planning and execution of revenge was not beyond the envious and psychopathic realm of Vincent's twisted yet intelligent mind. His entire being was controlled by his hatred for his family and envy for Theo. This became more so the case after he failed to become the respected preacher he strove to be which he had hoped would put all of this to rest for him.

Further evidence Vincent's current actions were related to when he had first lived in The Hague came out in a letter to Theo. He noted that many years ago he had consulted his boss in The Hague, Tersteeg, about something, and he wrote to Theo, "I have regretted ever since that I spoke to him about the matter. I well remember I was overwhelmed by some sort of panic at the time, and I was afraid of my family. Now, after some ten or twelve years, I have learned to think differently of the obligations to and the relations with my family."[56] This letter was written on June 1, 1882, so ten or twelve years before was the period of 1870 to 1872, when Vincent lived and worked in The Hague and Tersteeg was his manager at Goupil's. Vincent ran into some sort of trouble in The Hague and was sent to London the next year in May of 1873.

Vincent's parents found out he was living with a pregnant prostitute. They knew he was acting out of revenge directed at them for how they had tried to persuade him to forget about Kee and how they pushed for his transfer from The Hague to London in 1873. Emphasizing he recognized how far Vincent's bitterness and vengeance had gone, Vincent's father was considering having him committed to an asylum. He likely feared what Vincent might do next to revenge the past.

His father had tried this once before during Vincent's religious years in Belgium. Back then, he had considered having Vincent sent to an asylum in the town of Gheel.[57]

Hearing of his father's plans, Vincent lashed back. He wrote to Theo, "I am in the full possession of my civil rights as a Netherlander. . . . I shall not suffer myself to be molested or to be put under guardianship."[58] Then in another letter, he said, "The Gheel Asylum, they already tried. . . . Alas, yes—Father is capable of it . . . If he dares, . . . I shall fight him to the limit. Let him think twice before he attacks me."[59]

To make it clear how strongly he felt about his father's possible intrusion, Vincent described a case of a man who tried to put another man into an asylum. The man warned the other man "a few times quietly, as cool as a cucumber . . . After which he knocked his keeper's brains out with a poker, and remained standing as quietly as anything." Vincent noted the man was tried, and because it was determined to be self-defense, he was acquitted.

Vincent-the-serial-killer was actually threatening the murder of his father to Theo by the use of this story. He was strongly implying he would knock his father's brains out if he attempted to have him committed, and he believed the courts would rightly treat this as self-defense. Vincent wanted Theo to pass this on and make it clear to their father how far he would go to protect his rights and his freedom.

Vincent continued his strong stance with Theo and told him, "Adieu, brother, sleep on it again before you strike the blow and cut off my head . . . I repeat, if it must be, 'off with my head'; but preferably not, I need it so much for drawing."[60] That last bit shows Vincent's type of morbid humor, but also that he believed he was in control of the situation. He knew he had developed a power over Theo which allowed him to get his way. He believed Theo cared about his wellbeing and his artwork and desperately wanted to help him. After all, Theo was Abel, and unlike Cain, Abel believed he was his brother's keeper. A good manipulator like Vincent would exploit this as much as possible.

Just at the moment when everything in Vincent's life had mounded up and was ready to erupt, the unseen hand of fate opened a vent tube. The magma receded, and the volcano grew cold and dormant again. On June 14, 1882, Sien was admitted to a hospital in a nearby town to have her baby.[61] Then, strangely on the same day, Vincent was also admitted to a hospital in The Hague. He wrote to Theo, "I am in the hospital . . . suffering from insomnia and low fever, and passing water was painful. And now it seems that I really have what they call the 'clap,' but only a mild case."[62]

Vincent's malady while Sien was also having a baby created the necessary sympathy in Theo and in their father for them to back off. His father would no longer pursue sending Vincent to an asylum, and Theo would continue to send money.

On July 2, Sien gave birth to a boy and named him Willem, which happened to be Vincent's middle name.[63] Counting from early September of 1881, when Vincent visited The Hague before moving there, to July 2, is ten months—therefore, providing a possibility this was Vincent's baby boy. Even more so because she was admitted to the hospital on June 14, which was nine months, the actual birth taking longer than expected. Vincent's parents and Theo may also have realized the possibility this was Vincent's child.

Vincent, Sien, and her baby and young child all returned to live under Vincent's roof which continued to be paid for by Theo. Now that Vincent had won, he attempted to downplay his defiant attitude and revert back to a sympathetic tone, revealing to Theo, "What am I in most people's eyes? A nonentity, or an eccentric and disagreeable man . . . The lowest of the low. . . . Then I should want my work to show what is in the heart of such an eccentric, of such a nobody."[64]

With the success of his latest stand of defiance, Vincent continued on with Sien. But in January 1883, his domestic paradise began to be threatened. Theo had met a young woman.[65] She was sick and homeless, and Theo had put her up in a hotel.[66] Remarkably, it appeared Theo, the highly respected businessman and Golden Boy, was following in Vincent's muddy footsteps and had met a prostitute who was sick and needed help. Her name was Marie, and Theo wasn't just helping her, he was in love with her.[67]

The irony didn't go unnoticed by Vincent, and he made polite comparisons of Marie to Sien. But Vincent viewed Theo having a woman as a threat to his support. Theo would naturally turn his attention more and more towards Marie, and less and less towards Vincent, and Vincent knew he would eventually be left out of the picture all together. This would be bad due to the loss of his income, but also, Vincent had learned the necessity of keeping Theo close in his overall plan to conquer him. As long as Theo was sending money, Vincent had a certain power over him and could therefore continue to influence and manipulate him.

As expected, the money Theo was sending decreased, and Vincent was then ready to abandon Sien and her children so he could spend more money on his art. They had served their purpose. He began talking to Theo of moving to Drenthe to be on his own and to focus on his work. But it took a visit from Theo in August 1883 to push him on his way. This was what Vincent wanted. He could then lay the blame for why he had to leave Sien squarely on Theo's shoulders. Vincent always needed to be seen as the victim.

On September 11, 1883, the day after his mother's birthday, Vincent said goodbye to Sien and her two children, abandoning them at the station, and he rode the train out of their lives.

Arriving in Drenthe and looking back on his time with Sien, Vincent wrote to Theo about her: "Women of her kind are certainly bad, but in the first place they are infinitely—oh, infinitely more to be pitied than condemned."[68] He then referred to there being another type of woman on the other side of the spectrum, of which he said, "I know that there are women absurd enough to be entirely governed by ambition (they do even more harm with it than men). Lady Macbeth is the archetype of such; these women are dangerous and not withstanding their charm, one must avoid them, or one becomes a scoundrel, and in short time finds oneself face to face with a terrible evil one has committed and can never repair."

Vincent's distinction of the two types reveals his split view of women and shows he had pity for those who were unattractive or used up, but for the ambitious and haughty type, he had anger and hatred, and even more, the sharp edge of his knife. He clung to the pitiful type and murdered the ambitious type.

He as much as admitted he had murdered the ambitious type when he said, "One becomes a scoundrel, and in short time finds oneself face to face with a terrible evil one has committed and can never repair." In 1873 and 1874, he had become a scoundrel and had committed the terrible evil of murder, which cannot be repaired.

Vincent didn't stay long in Drenthe. With his money from Theo reduced, he determined he could play the victim once more and move back home and live off his parents again while pursuing his art. Theo had chosen Marie over him.

Because of her, Vincent had to leave Sien and her two children behind and was forced to move back home. This was how he preferred to view the situation, and this was how he would frame why he had to return home and why his parents would have to take him back. He wasn't returning as the prodigal son seeking forgiveness. Instead, he was the poor soul everyone had betrayed, and it was his parents' duty to provide for him.

Holding onto his self-diluted view of the situation, Vincent strengthened his resolve to defeat Theo through art, determining that from now on, any who dared stand in his way would be dealt with severely.

12

Father Has The Money
1883-1885

Upon his return home in November 1883, Vincent was still seeking retribution for all the perceived wrongs of the past his family had caused him, and he immediately rekindled the old arguments with his parents. He expressed his view of the situation in a letter to Theo: "It grieves me that they do not regret what they did at the time."[1] He then began to get personal, adding, "The good within them is wrongly applied, so that it acts like evil—because the light within them is black and spreads darkness."

By December 20, Vincent's father (figure 12.1, photo of Father) had given in to Vincent's relentless attacks, and he wrote to Theo, "We intend to leave him perfectly free in his peculiarities of dress, etc. The people here have seen him anyhow, and . . . we cannot change the fact of his being eccentric."[2] His father also accommodated Vincent's wish of having a studio prepared for him in a room attached to the back of the house. His father referred to this room as the "mangling room"—an appropriate room for a murderer.

But the attempts to appease Vincent by his father had little effect, and Vincent continued his assault. When Theo defended his parents and wrote Vincent, now 30, that he was being childish, Vincent only increased his vengeance. He wrote back, "In short, this is what Father is—he is 'a stupid one.'"[3]

Vincent had learned resistance was the way, and he sought to continue to harass his parents. But before things could reach critical mass, the expected explosion was averted by an indirect mishap to Vincent's mother. In the middle of January 1884, she paid the price to that invisible hand of fate which so often helped Vincent at just the right moment. While stepping off a train, his mother took a hard fall and broke her thighbone.[4]

This accident interrupted the arguing and calmed the situation, and unexpectedly, Vincent turned his attention and energy towards his mother's care.[5] With things quieted down at home, Vincent wanted to get things straight with Theo. Theo didn't like how Vincent was spending the money he sent on his usual vices, prostitutes in particular. Vincent tried to remind Theo of his needs, writing, "I told you then I hated being alone so much that I preferred being with a bad whore to being alone."[6] He then pointed out he had almost always gone to prostitutes, adding, "Except for the few years which I can hardly understand myself, when I was confused by religious ideas—a kind of mysticism—leaving that period out of it, I have always lived with a certain warmth."

In order to get Theo off his back about how he spent his money, Vincent proposed that for the future he would send Theo what he painted and Theo should think of the money he sent as payment for his work.[7] Theo didn't believe Vincent's art was all that good at this time, but he agreed. Vincent got what he wanted, and things were going well, but that's never a good sign for Vincent. Trouble was sure to follow, and it did.

Vincent wasn't the only one who cared for his mother. A neighbor had been dropping by regularly to lend a helping hand. Her name was Margot Begemann (figure 12.2, photo of Margo). She was 42, unmarried, and in the vicinity of Vincent. Therefore, naturally, a relationship began. But this time things were slightly different. It wasn't Vincent who fell desperately in love. Instead, it was Margot who was smitten.

Through the spring and summer of 1884, their love affair became the talk of the village, and not all were pleased. Margot's two older sisters were adamantly opposed to her relationship with Vincent, and Vincent wrote Theo that Margot "believed she had done something frightful. And this without having done anything she ought not to have done."[8] He added, "I have always respected her on a certain point that would have dishonored her socially (though if I had wanted it, I had her in my power)." This last part gives away what this was really about.

Strangely, Vincent didn't exhibit the same obsessive love towards Margot which he had shown in the past towards other women. Something was wrong. Margot was in conflict with her family and willing to fight to the bitter end to be with Vincent, while uncharacteristically, Vincent stood quietly off to the side holding the coats of the participants. Why wasn't Vincent fighting for this new love of his? Was he worn out from the previous fights? No, he was simply using a different tactic.

Margot meant nothing to Vincent. He was using her to create a stir and cause a continued problem for his family. Even though he was playing nurse to his mother and enjoying the attention it brought, Vincent's nature and motives had not changed. He wanted to cause his family pain and suffering, as he believed they had caused him. Margot showing up to help him take care of his mother was simply a new opportunity for an old psychopath. Vincent used the admiration he received from nursing his mother to lure the unsuspecting Margot into an obsession for him. Vincent was playing a game. He had no real intentions other than controlling Margot and disrupting his family. He gave his scheme away when he noted he could have her if he wanted, because, as he had said to Theo, "I had her in my power."

There was talk of marriage which turned up the heat for Margot. Vincent prodded her to resist her family, and this led to what Vincent was after—a calamity. He reported to Theo, "Margot Begemann took poison in a moment of despair; after she had had a discussion with her family and they slandered her and me."[9] Vincent had used his powers of suggestion and manipulation to lead a woman to poison herself out of her love and devotion for him.

Margot survived and was sent to a doctor in Utrecht to recover. Vincent visited her, but the doctor said, "She has *always* had a very frail constitution, and will always have, . . . [and] she is too weak to marry."[10] Vincent responded, "Of course I shall always remain her friend." Their relationship was over. Vincent didn't vow to wait for her to get well or try and take a stand for their right to be together. None of that. It was over. His use of her had ended.

Vincent had toyed with Margot's emotions and had brought her to the brink of death without picking up a club, a knife, or a piece of rope. He had complete control over Margot and the situation. He loved it and forced it to its conclusion at a specified time. The exact date of Margot's suicide attempt is not known. However, interestingly, Hulsker noted it took place in the first half of September 1884. Vincent had pushed Margot to take the final plunge as another gift for his mother's September 10 birthday. He always had Mother in mind.

The whole Margot affair, together with Vincent simply being Vincent, continued to cause his parents, and especially his clergyman father, great difficulty. His sister-in-law noted, "For his parents the consequences were also painful, because the neighbors avoided the vicarage from that time on, not wishing to meet Vincent."[11]

As his mother's broken leg slowly healed and therefore Vincent's nursing skills became less necessary, the old arguments returned along with the new ones about Margot, and Vincent may have crossed the line in one of those arguments with his father. He admitted to Theo, "But I wish that I didn't hit other people, that Father had not been standing right in front of me at times."[12] Vincent may have only been referring to a verbal sort of "hit," as if he had said something harsh, but the wording suggests the possibility Vincent had physically struck his father. At the very least, Vincent's choice of wording hints at what was on his mind.

With the return of the intense arguing, the best solution must have seemed obvious for Mr. Van Gogh—throw Vincent out of the house again. His father may have tried to reason with Vincent about finding another place to live, but

Vincent would have none of it—that would be giving up the fight. He remained defiant and coarse, and he wrote to Theo of his conclusion about his father: "He always called himself 'my friend'. . . but one fine day I told him flatly: Don't call yourself my friend. . . . People who think that way about me are not my friends but my enemies, and as sure as 2x2=4, they are my worst enemies."[13]

Theo didn't like the way things were heading. He suggested Vincent find another place to live.[14] Vincent didn't like that idea. It would mean losing his rent-free room and free meals, and he would then have to use the money Theo sent him for those expenses. He had previously added to Theo's expenses by renting two rooms to use as his studio at the house of a local Catholic priest. He wanted to keep this studio while also keeping his room at home to stay connected to his parents and continue to cause them trouble. But he also wanted to attend the Art Academy in Antwerp, Belgium, and of course, he wanted Theo to pay for everything. But Theo still wanted to control how Vincent spent his money, so Vincent began to ponder other ways to obtain money which would allow him the freedom to do as he liked while he pursued his art at the Art Academy.

Spurring on a developing plan, at the beginning of January 1885, Vincent heard through his parents about more good fortune which had come Theo's way. They were gloating over their Golden Boy, and Vincent wrote Theo about it: "At home I heard you have had a good year, and had an offer of 1000 francs a month, which you refused."[15] He then made the necessary comparison to himself, showing where his thoughts were focused: "I've hardly ever begun a year with a gloomier aspect, in a gloomier mood, nor do I expect any future of success, but a future of strife." Vincent was Cain and Theo was Abel.

Impatience was again stirring Vincent's envy. He needed to move faster towards his goal. He couldn't allow his enemy to control his money and thereby control his pace of advancement. He was Cain. He needed to embrace more fully who he was, and hearing through his parents of this latest blessing of Theo's pushed him forward with his new plan.

Over the next few months, Vincent became uncharacteristically calm and quiet. The topics of his letters shifted away from his usual stubborn stances and hyper-opinionated views to a much-subdued discussion of his artwork. The roaring Vincent had become tame and docile, and on March 25, his father wrote to Theo about it: "He seems to become more and more estranged from us. . . . This morning I talked things over with Vincent; he was in a kind mood and said there was no particular reason for his being depressed."[16]

The very next day, March 26, Vincent's father was found dead on the doorstep of his home.

Vincent's sister-in-law described the pastor's unexpected and sudden demise: "Coming home from a long walk across the heath, he fell down on the threshold at his home and was carried lifeless into the house." [17]

It was believed he had died of a heart attack. Vincent's sister, Elizabeth, later wrote in her book that her father "had been suffering from heart disease without any one's knowledge." [18] The good Reverend was 63 and healthy. [19]

It was a complete shock to the Van Gogh family. A grieving Theo rushed to get home from Paris, while his older brother bowed before his father's dead body as it lay in bed, selfishly declaring, "Dying is hard, but living still harder." [20] Vincent was only thinking of Vincent.

At the time, all three of Vincent's sisters believed Vincent's constant bickering with their father, together with the most recent escapade with Margot, had caused their father a great deal of distress, which then aided in his heart attack and death. Apparently, others held the same notion—Tralbaut noting many in Nuenen blamed Vincent for his father's sudden death. [21]

It was obvious to everyone Vincent had pushed his father to the limit. Drawing the conclusion that his contentious words and actions had led to his death was easy enough, and his sister, Anna, made sure Vincent also understood this conclusion. A letter from Vincent to Theo about her words gives the idea Anna didn't hold back. He wrote, "I still very much deplore the incident with Anna . . . What she told you does not alter anything of what she reproached me with, however absurd these reproaches were." [22]

Anna had reproached Vincent for causing such strain in their father's life, such intentional and irresponsible strain. But Vincent had further gotten under his sister's skin when he asked about his share of the inheritance. He referenced this to Theo, writing that Anna had "unfounded suspicions with regard to certain things of the future." In the same letter, Vincent then shamelessly went on to express his desire to receive some of the inheritance, writing, "Don't you think it would be fair if I reserved for myself a sum of, for instance, 200 guilders as my share in the inheritance, which for the rest I gladly leave to the younger ones."

Because of the way Anna was acting towards him, and also because his mother was thinking of taking on a boarder, Vincent decided to deflate the situation and move into his studio at the Catholic priest's house. [23]

✳ ✳ ✳

When Vincent had returned home in December 1883, his intent was revenge, and his primary focus was his father. After all, it was his father who had tried twice to have him put away in an asylum. His arguments and difficult behavior were meant to bring pain and suffering to his preacher father. But Vincent's desire to inflict pain and suffering went beyond attacking the psychological and social areas of his father's life. Vincent was seeking physical pain. He wanted to hurt his father, and he, no doubt, fantasized about killing him.

When Vincent discovered his father was thinking of sending the men in white coats after him in The Hague, he had written to Theo, as previously mentioned, the story about the man who had killed another man for trying to have him committed. He had said the man had "knocked his keeper's brains out with a poker, and remained standing as quietly as anything."[24] He was telling Theo he would do the same to his father if he tried it on him.

His father had given up on the asylum idea, so Vincent wasn't forced to follow through on his threat. However, I believe Vincent fantasized about knocking his father's brains out, and when the time was right, he took the opportunity to do just that. I believe Vincent van Gogh killed his father. Not indirectly, as Anna and others had thought by way of his endless arguing, but directly, with force, intent and premeditation.

Vincent's original motive was bestial revenge for what his father had tried to do to him, and he was exacting that revenge by staying under his father's roof and seeking out ways to abuse and discredit him. The Margot affair was just another means to further enrage his father and cause him harm. Had his father suffered a heart attack during this time, that would have been just fine with Vincent. But Vincent wanted the more direct approach. He wanted to lay hands on his preacher father. But living under the same roof, he knew getting away with murder would be a tall order, even for someone as clever as he.

But when, in January 1885, Theo had threatened to take away his allowance and Vincent sought a new way to get his hands on some money to continue to advance with his art, his desire to murder his father found a purpose. Believing he would get a portion of the inheritance once he was dead, he began planning how to do the deed. Once he had the money, he could then go to the Art Academy in Antwerp and freely spend his spare money on what he liked—rum and prostitutes.

Once Vincent decided to murder his father and visualized how best to do it, he must have recalled a letter from home when he was living in Drenthe. He had written Theo about its contents at the time, passing on that their Father "had been unwell after having a fall."[25] Vincent then thought how his mother had also had a fall and broke her thigh. The diseased part of his brain saw these falls as an opportunity. If he could make it look as if his father had another fall, then his sudden death would not be considered suspicious.

When his father spoke to him on March 25, the day before his death, he may have spoken to Vincent about finding another place to live. Vincent may have asked to talk about it further with him the next day. Then, on that day, I believe Vincent lured his father into his makeshift studio at the back of the house with the prospect of continuing the discussion. He let his father go on about how Vincent was causing him a great deal of trouble at church and in the community and how it would be best if he moved along. Vincent then may have calmly confessed to his father it had been his intention all along to make him and his wife look like fools, and he swung some blunt object, perhaps even a fireplace poker, at his father's head and knocked him senseless. The first blow either killed him or Vincent had to add another.

Choosing to strike his father in the head matched the M.O. he followed for the woman he murdered in 1873, whose bruised temple revealed the cause of her death. He likely used the same method on his second victim, but her head and face were never found.

Telling the story of the man who had "knocked his keeper's brains out with a poker" as a threat to what he would do to his father was certainly a compelling statement. Had Vincent been suspected and investigated for his father's murder, and if they had obtained the letter to Theo where he had made this threat, it certainly would not have looked good for Vincent.

Having done the deed, Vincent had only a short walk of a few steps from the door of his studio in the mangle room to the back door of the house. He carried his father's dead body to the back porch and placed it there, being sure the wounded side of his father's head rested on the edge of the hard concrete step.

Vincent then returned to the mangle room, scooped up his easel and paints, and calmly escaped into the fields to create his alibi of being far, far away, busily painting when his father was found.

When he had moved back in with his parents, Vincent had referred to himself to Theo as a rough dog, and he had concluded, "The dog might bite— he might become rabid, and the constable would have to come to shoot him."[26] Vincent, the dog, had bitten his father, and he had brought the body to the threshold of the home and left it as a dog might leave a dead squirrel as a gift for the family. The only question for Vincent was whether the police would try and come after him. But they never did, and like his other murders, he got away with killing his father.

Vincent's dormant thrill for the kill was revived after the successful murder of his father, but there was something more Vincent gained, and he made use of it later with his Ripper murders. Accepting that Vincent first killed his father in the mangle room and then carried the body to the back porch placing it on the threshold of the house, a striking pattern of similarity emerges when this same method is compared to the Ripper murders so far discussed.

In early August 1888, Martha Tabram's body was found on the first-floor landing of some stairs. *Lloyd's* of August 12 reported, "The poor woman was on some stone steps, close to the doors of small rooms wherein several separate families resided." Vincent had chosen the spot ahead of time intentionally to match leaving his victim's body on the doorstep of others, just as he had left his father's body on the doorstep of his own house. Vincent thought of himself as a dog in 1885, and his actions in 1888 showed he continued to think this way.

Unlike his father's murder, Vincent left Tabram where he had killed her. But he would adjust that to match his father's murder more precisely when he murdered Mary Ann Nichols at the end of August. With her, he had lured his victim to a pre-chosen area behind a gate, where he then strangled her. Then, just as with his father, he moved her body for placement on a threshold. For Nichols, that was just outside the stable gate.

The gate was an entrance point, just like the back door was of his father's house, and just as the doors to the residents on the landing were with Tabram's murder. He had again acted like a dog bringing home its kill.

Annie Chapman's murder on September 8 had the most striking similarity to his father's murder. Perhaps Vincent matched it more closely because it was partially committed for his mother's birthday, and therefore the reminder of home made him think of his father also. After strangling Chapman in the enclosed passageway between the houses, he carried her body into the backyard placing it to the side of the steps of the back door, on the threshold, before he tore open her throat and belly with his knife.

Each of the first three Ripper murders match back to Vincent's father's dead body being discovered on the threshold of his home—Jack the Ripper similarly depositing his victim's bodies on the thresholds of doors and gates. Vincent van Gogh was Jack the Ripper.

Vincent had moved out of the family house and into his studio, but he still made occasional visits home, likely for free food, but also because he was anticipating news of the inheritance. Finally, a document relating to the inheritance arrived, and he wrote to Theo about it: "Mother seems to want it transferred in her own name."[27] In the end, that was what happened. All of his father's inheritance was turned over to their mother.

This was not at all what Vincent had expected. He would get nothing. It turned out the murder of his father was all for nothing. He was worse off than before. But Vincent's determination to succeed over Theo still burned strong, and he painted and contemplated other ways to obtain some of the inheritance.

In the meantime, Vincent was paying local villagers to act as models for his paintings which led to a conflict between him and a Catholic priest. Vincent presented the conflict to Theo: "A girl I had often painted was with child, and they suspected me, though I was innocent. . . . They cannot, at least for this once, get at me."[28] Tralbaut noted the pregnant girl's name was Gordina de Groot and confirmed it was believed Vincent was the father of her child. [29]

It is amazing how regularly Vincent stirred up trouble and how there was so often a girl at the center of it, but how a pregnancy was at times also involved. This became a situation, but Vincent fought against the priest and went on painting and seeing the girl.

As this new situation moved inevitably towards something bad, Vincent's increased ardor for achieving his goals brought him to a new plan for obtaining his share of the inheritance. It was so simple, and so appropriate. It was his mother who now stood in his way and prevented him from achieving his goals. She now had the money he needed. Eliminate her, and the inheritance comes back into play. Then he only had to deal with his greedy sisters to get his portion.

It seems so crass and unbelievable to think Vincent would plot to murder his mother not so very long after killing his father, but his own words make it clear what he was up to. He was, after all, a psychopathic serial killer, and for him, such things weren't so crass, more like brave. It was simply what was needed to get what he wanted.

Vincent began his scheme by laying the groundwork in Theo's mind. The plan was to make it seem his mother was so grieved from losing her loving husband that her health would deteriorate, and she would succumb to some natural affliction and die suddenly, just as their father.

Later that year in November 1885, Vincent was ready to implement his plan of execution, and he wrote about their mother to Theo: "I do not think it *impossible* that to her too death may come unexpectedly and softly, just as it came to Father, and for a similar reason."[30] He continued, "But if it should be a passing similar to Father's, that is to say, sudden, it is equally possible that it will happen within a few days as within a few years." Vincent then predicted his mother's death: "If lucidity and the calm persist, I personally expect a crisis after the trip, that is, within a short time—and dying without a struggle."

Vincent was ready to go to Antwerp, so he needed to kill her soon and get the money. He watched for the right opportunity.

Vincent's mother and his sister, Wil, were preparing to move to another town in a few months, and Vincent made his plans to match theirs. He wrote in his next letter to Theo, "You see that I wanted to fix my going to Antwerp at about the same time as Mother's trip."[31] He also continued to prepare Theo for their mother's sudden death, adding, "And with old people it is absolutely impossible to predict anything, because often the heart is no longer normal, for instance because of fatty degeneration, and then they may be gone all at once."

Vincent even planned on seeing his mother's doctor, Dr. Van der Loo, to ask him what he thought about her health, and he informed Theo, "After Van der Loo has seen her, it will be the moment for either Wil or me to ask him outright whether he can tell anything about her life expectancy."

His mother saw the doctor, and when Vincent inquired about her health, the doctor told him there was "nothing the matter with her," and that she "may live another ten years or so."[32]

Vincent had missed his opportunity. Not living at home, it was difficult for him to show up at the house at the right moment when his mother was alone. Wil was always there.[33] Vincent had to give up on his plan to murder his mother, and therefore, give up his hopes of receiving part of the inheritance. However, he still planned on moving to Antwerp somehow, and he wrote in the same letter to Theo that he was "longing for Antwerp now."

But as always, Vincent couldn't simply leave a place. He had to be forced out and seen as a victim, and he created the same situation this time. The Catholic priest Vincent rented his studio from sided with the other priest who had joined together to accuse Vincent of wrongdoing with the pregnant Gordina de Groot, and he gave Vincent notice to leave.

Having obtained his sympathetic victim status, Vincent left behind most of his artwork and boarded a train for Antwerp in November 1885. He fully believed Theo would provide him with all he needed to survive and to attend the Academy.[34] He never returned to Holland again, and he never again saw his mother, his sisters, Kee Vos, Margot Begemann, or Gordina de Groot.

Watching through the window of the train as his homeland blurred by, Vincent must have called to mind the words he had written to Theo after his father had previously thrown him out: "The murderer has left the house."[35] How appropriate. And if a murderer leaves one place, he must arrive in another.

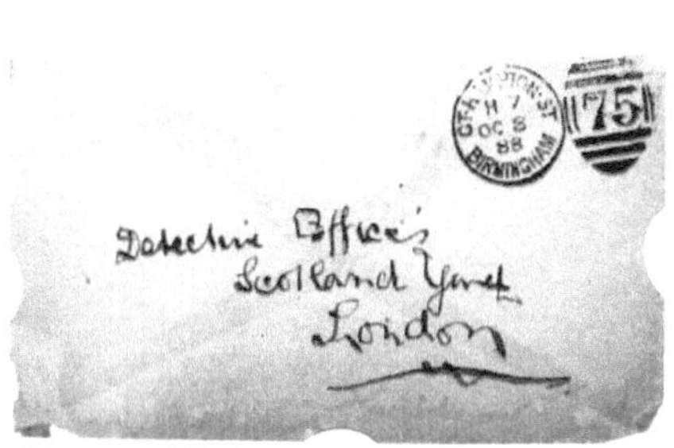

Figure 17.1
Angel of Death Ripper Letter Envelope
The National Archives of the UK (TNA),
MEPO3/142, f. 162

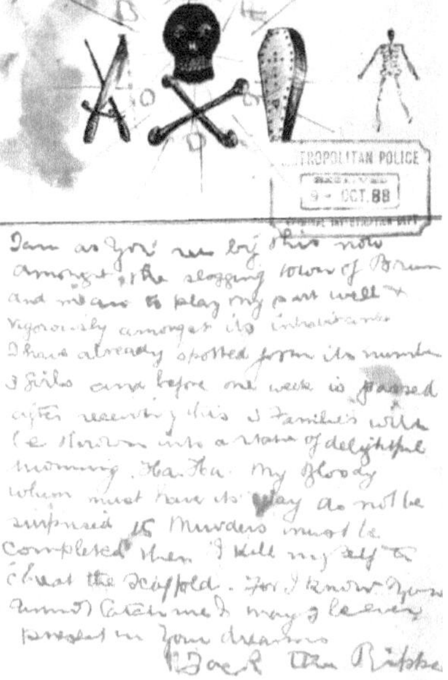

Figure 17.2
Angel of Death Ripper Letter
The National Archives of the UK (TNA),
MEPO3/142, f. 161

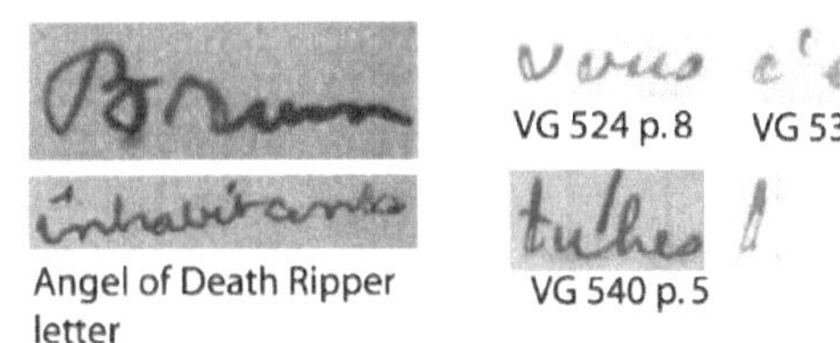

Angel of Death Ripper
letter

VG 524 p. 8

VG 534 p. 4 & p. 5

VG 540 p. 5

VG 546 p. 1

VG letter to Russell
p. 4

Figure 17.4
Angel of Death Ripper Letter Cuts & Russell Letter Cuts & Other Van Gogh Letter Cuts,
Character Comparison, Reed Pen Skip Marks

Angel of Death Ripper Letter: The National Archives of the UK (TNA), MEPO3/142, f. 161

Russell Letter p 4: Solomon R. Guggenheim Museum, New York

Vincent van Gogh, Letters of Vincent van Gogh, 1886-1890, A Facsimile Edition

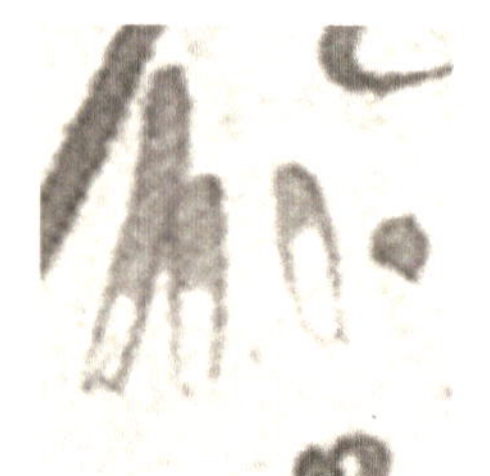

Figure 17.5
Van Gogh Letter to John Russell,
Cut from p 4
Solomon R. Guggenheim Museum,
New York

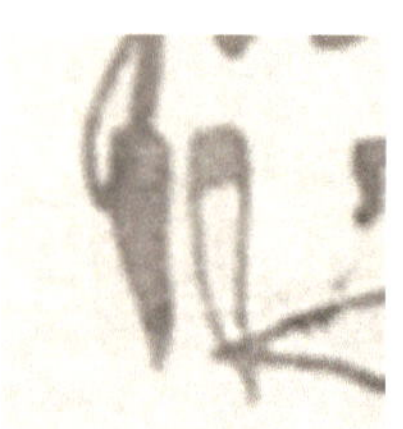

Figure 17.7
Angel of Death Ripper Letter Cut,
Reed Pen Skip Marks
The National Archives of the UK (TNA),
MEPO3/142, f. 161

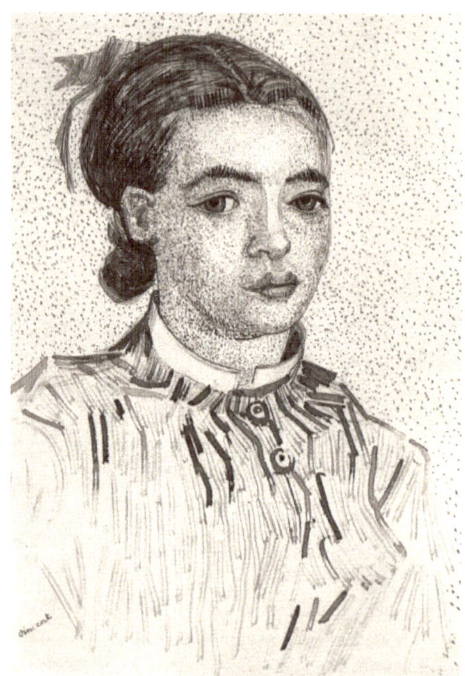

Figure 17.6
Van Gogh Drawing, La Mousmé, 1888, Reed Pen Skip Marks
Sold at auction 2021, Private collection

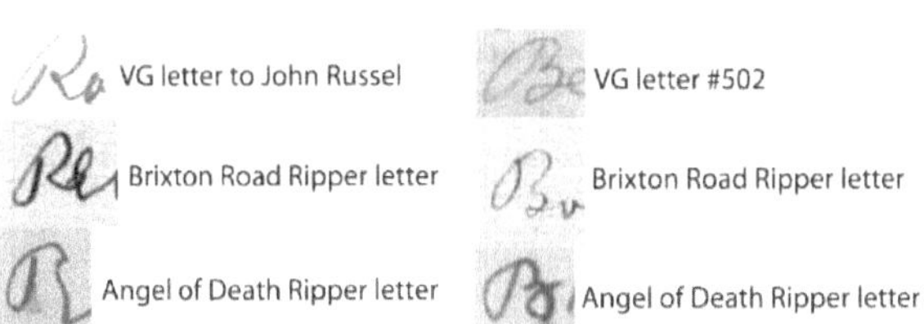

Figure 17.8

Handwriting Comparison, Angel of Death & Brixton Road Ripper Letters to Vincent Letters to Theo 502, p 1, & Russell, p. 4

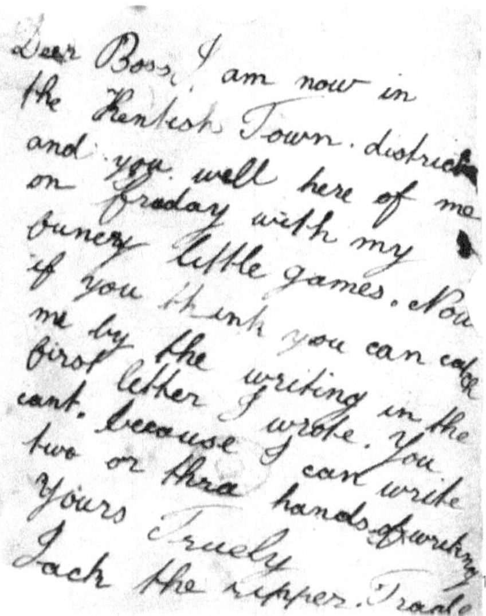

Figure 17.9

Kentish Town Ripper Letter
The National Archives of the UK (TNA),
MEPO3/142, f. 173

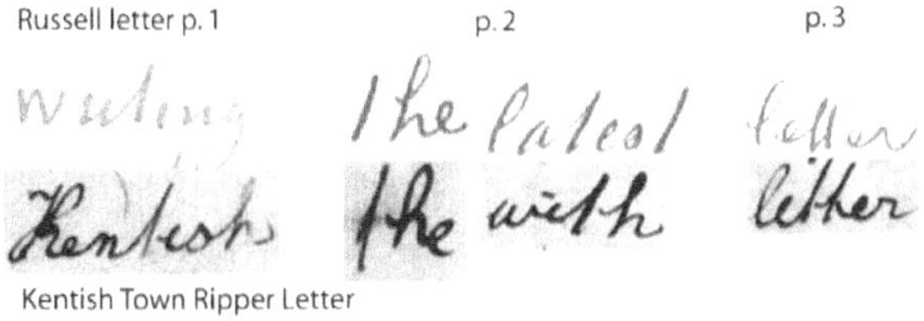

Figure 17.10

Handwriting Comparison, Kentish Town Ripper Letter to Van Gogh letter to John Russell, pp 1-3.

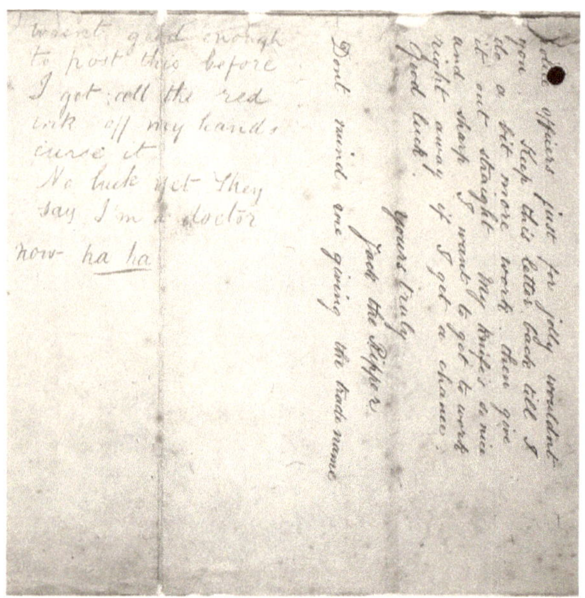

Figure 17.11
Dear Boss Ripper Letter, Cut of Added Paragraph
The National Archives of the UK (TNA), MEPO3/142, f. 3

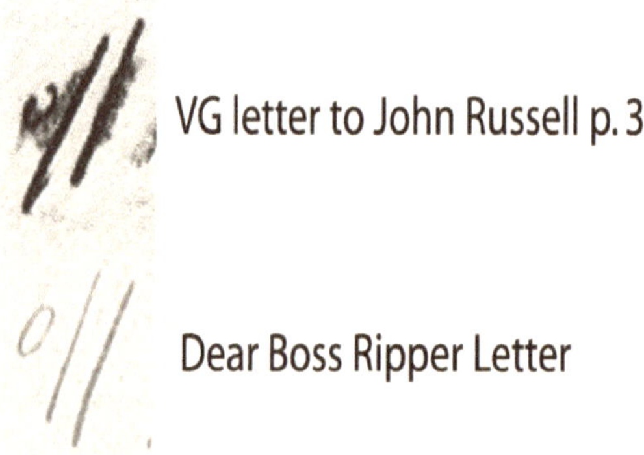

Figure 17.12
Dear Boss Ripper Letter & Van Gogh to John Russell Letter p 3 Character
Comparison to Word "off"
Russell Letter: Solomon R. Guggenheim Museum, New York

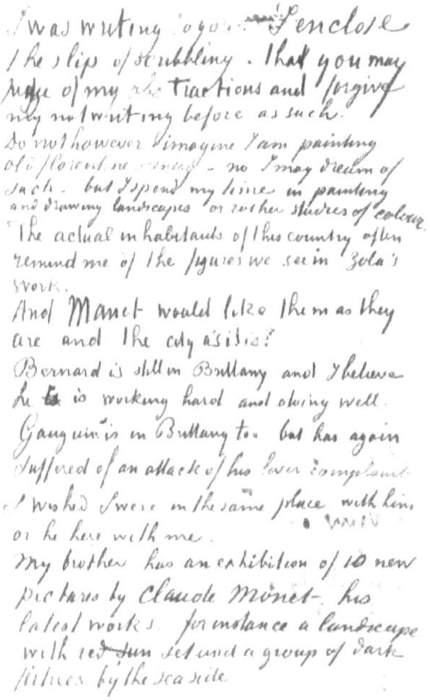

Figure 17.13
Van Gogh Letter to John Russell, p 2
Solomon R. Guggenheim Museum,
New York

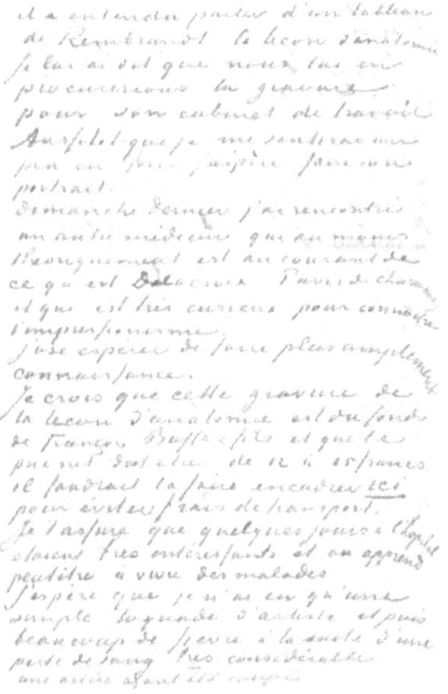

Figure 17.14
Van Gogh Letter, 569, p 3, DAR Examples
Vincent van Gogh, Letters of Vincent van Gogh,
1886-1890, A Facsimile Edition

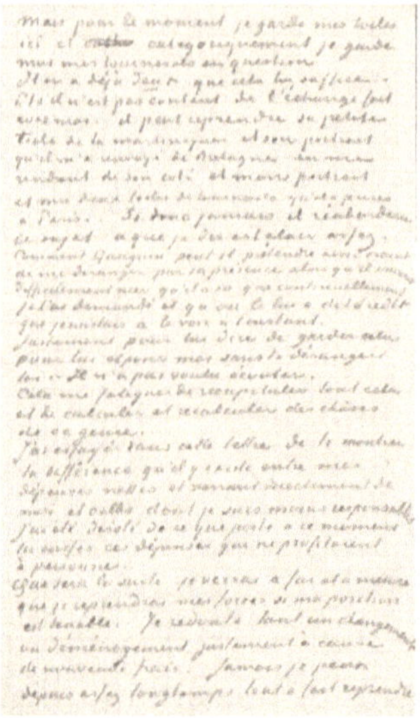

Figure 17.15

Van Gogh Letter, 571, p 6, DAR on word "Changement"

Vincent van Gogh, Letters of Vincent van Gogh, 1886-1890, A Facsimile Edition

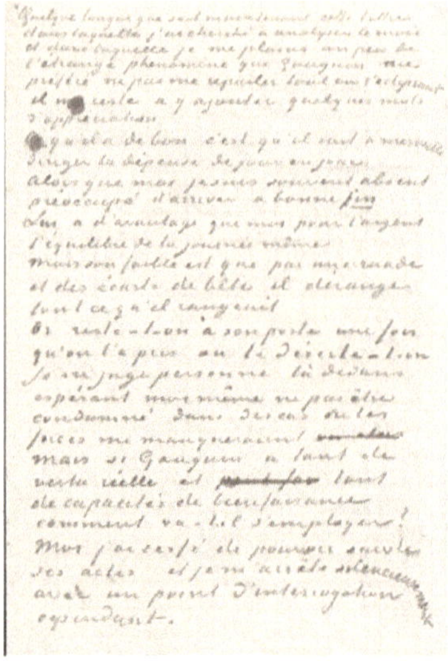

Figure 17.16

Van Gogh Letter, 571, p 9, DAR on word "silencuusement,"

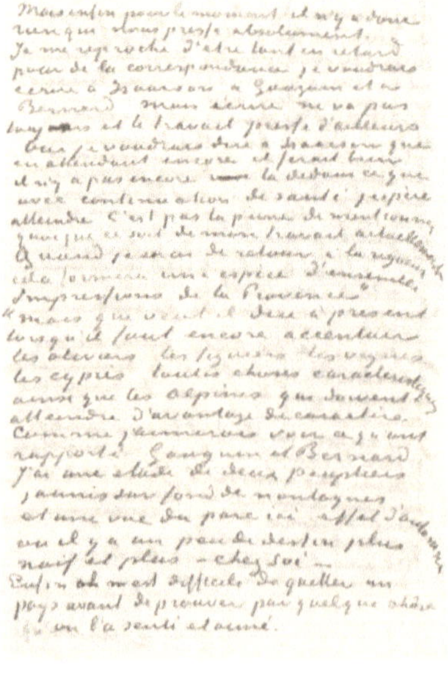

Figure 17.17

Van Gogh Letter, 609, p 3, DAR on Three Words

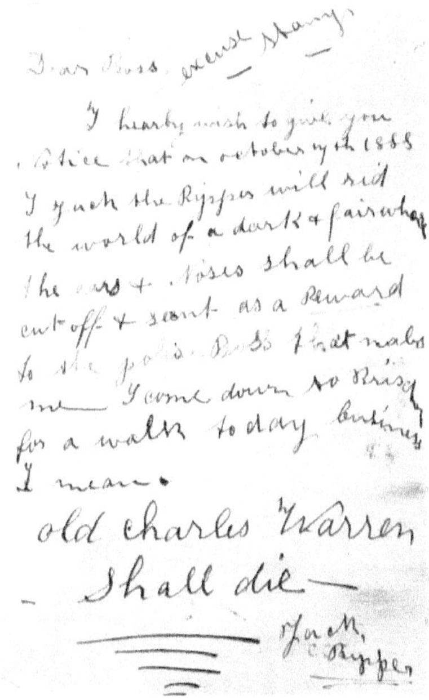

Figure 17.18

Brixton Road Ripper Letter, DAR on Word "whore"

The National Archives of the UK (TNA), MEPO3/142, f. 300

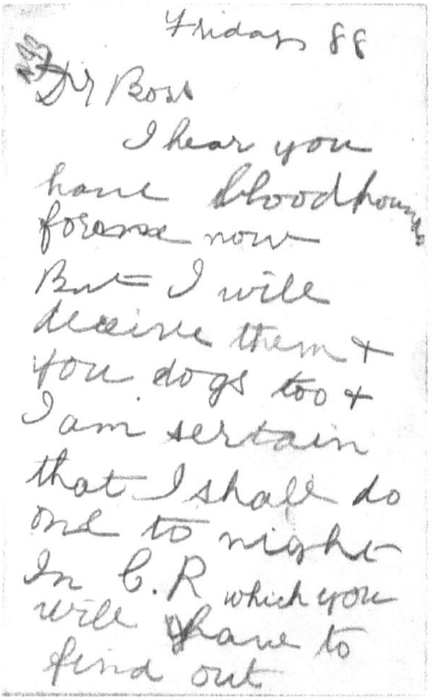

Figure 17.19

You Dogs Ripper Letter, DAR on Word "bloodhounds"

The National Archives of the UK (TNA), MEPO3/142, f. 245

13

Two For Jack
September 1888

With his father's murder now a distant memory, on the morning of Friday, September 28, 1888, Vincent awoke on a hard piece of earth somewhere deep within a London park or cemetery. It was simply another day of business in London. Just beyond the trees and hedge line, almost hidden behind the morning fog, a torrent of rattling cart wheels and trotting horses paraded up and down the cobbled streets. Coal smoke billowed from the morning stove fires. Greasy eggs and bacon were being cooked somewhere nearby and fresh coffee was being boiled. The smells blended together with the fog and smoke to create a uniquely London scent. Vincent was glad to be back.

The previous night of dropping off a letter and writing a message in chalk before digging up an old arm and depositing it had only been a few pranks to get things started—a tease for what was to come. It had been twenty days since he opened up Chapman's belly and pulled out her intestines. He needed a fresh kill. That's why he had returned to London. As the day unfolded, his thoughts turned to scouting locations for murder.

Checking the evening papers, there was no mention of his most recent deeds. However, he saw something that might be useful. The socialist group, the International Working Men's Educational Society,[1] was meeting at their clubhouse in the East End on Saturday night. This sparked an idea for Vincent. As the sky darkened and a coolness settled over London, Vincent became a creature of the night again and followed the familiar streets into Whitechapel searching out the club's address.

He found the club at 40 Berner Street, a side street only a short walk to the south from the heavily traveled Commercial Road, which made it an appealing location. There were streetlamps, but none near the club. Best of all, the club had a side gate, and the area behind it was dark as charcoal. As he walked the length of the street and back again, he also found the street lacked pedestrians, and this was a Friday night in the East End—a good sign. This would make a good spot for a murder.

It also fit the bill for something else he was after. He suspected, because of the area, the club membership was mainly comprised of Jews, many of whom populated the area. He would make use of this assumption.

But Vincent wanted another location, not as a backup, but as a location for a second murder. He had killed two in one night on September 8—first the woman whose arm had been found on the edge of the Thames at Pimlico, and then when he had savaged Chapman later that same morning. But the police and the papers hadn't linked the two together. He wanted to make sure they understood this time he had killed two in one night.

The location of the club was near the center of the district so this would need to be the first murder site. The second site needed to be some distance from the first and towards the direction he wanted to escape. Moving to the west offered the most options to get away. Thinking as Jack the Ripper, Vincent would be sure to plan everything well.

As Vincent headed west on Commercial Road to Whitechapel High Street, and then to Aldgate Street, searching for a second murder site, he may have recalled something from when he had worked for Goupil's in London so long ago. They did some business with a picture framer from that area, and he searched for the familiar streets.[2] Turning onto Mitre Street, he saw the picture framer was still there, but the area in front was too well lit. However, there was a short road to the left of the framer which led into a courtyard named Mitre Square where he found what he was after. There was a streetlamp, but only at the far end of the square. Behind the framer and then a short distance to the right, covered in sweet darkness, there was a fence with a gate. Perfect.

It was time for a few drinks and maybe he would even pick out a prostitute or two and make a few test runs, partly just for the thrill, but also to see how much he was noticed in the chosen areas. There were more constables out and about, so he had to be more careful. Then, a little later, he could return to each location and stake out each spot during the same time he planned to return the next night.

A bakery on the corner of Berner Street and Commercial Road made a good observation point for the first murder site.[3] From there he could watch the Working Men's Club. He could also lean against the wall and watch for when the constables made their rounds. It turned out not to be a street that was patrolled, but constables passed by on Commercial Road regularly.

Heading over to the second location at Mitre Square, he could hide behind the gate in the darkness and watch for a constable. Even though this was also a quiet area, it had businesses, so a constable came through the square on his beat. Waiting for the constable to leave and return again, Vincent found it took him about fifteen minutes to complete his rounds. This would give him just enough time to do his work.

Vincent also had escape routes in mind. At the first location, if all remained calm, he could quickly get to Commercial Road and get lost in the late-night crowds of partiers and hawkers. If there was trouble, he could head south on Berner Street and dart through backstreets towards the west to get out. Even if there was trouble, as long as he safely got out of the first area, he could still make the second kill, since it was far enough away from the first.

The second site was a bit more boxed in. There were two other exit points at the opposite end of Mitre Square, but they were too confining for a safe escape if there was trouble. Fortunately, some of the buildings behind the gate were unoccupied, and he explored and found various paths he could take to escape in a hurry.[4]

Confident he had chosen two good murder sites, Vincent rewarded himself with a few more drinks. Then, perhaps, he walked south to the shore of the Thames and gazed out over its black water and reminisced about the time he rowed a boat to about the same spot and tore a hole in it with his knife and left it to sink. Then he found an unclaimed piece of grassy earth to get some needed sleep.

✳ ✳ ✳

On Saturday night, September 29, after a few drinks early on to steady his nerves and impatience to once again experience the thrill of murder, Vincent likely revisited his chosen locations to make sure Saturday nights weren't much different from Friday nights. They weren't.

The lecture at the Working Men's Club had ended and music and dancing followed. At that moment, there was still too much going on—too many comings and goings for a quiet murder. But Vincent expected things would quiet down later.

At 12:45 a.m., Vincent entered Berner Street from Commercial Road and walked past the club and then turned around and walked by it again (figure 13.1, London map). The earlier rumblings had died down to the chatter of a small group. The time was right. Vincent continued on to Commercial Road, turned right, and went looking for his prey.

Here and there on either side of the street, dark figures of the night sought out their own sorts of prey. But one block away, at the corner of Christian Street, a woman of the night stood alone near the Beehive pub.[5] Vincent made his choice. As he approached, he pulled from his pocket a red rose surrounded by white maidenhair,[6] which he had bought earlier from a street vendor. He thought it would add a nice touch to his work. He presented the rose and asked the woman to come along with him, and she did.

Vincent pulled her along at a quick pace, and to comfort her, he told her he had just come from a meeting at his club and explained there was a good spot there for some privacy. When they turned onto Berner Street, the loneliness of the dark street may have brought to the woman's mind the recent headlines, but when she saw there was indeed a club with lamps blazing and people inside, her fears dissipated. It was just another transaction, with just another customer, on just another Saturday night.

Vincent checked the street for onlookers. There were none, and he marched his catch through the open gate at the side of the club. The passageway was narrow with high walls on either side that made it feel even more restricting. Vincent stopped her just inside the gate and led her behind it, telling her this was the spot. And without hesitation, as the prostitute cinched up her dress with her back to him, Vincent pulled a piece of cord from his coat pocket, wrapped the ends around each hand, and calmly lifted the cord over her head and around her neck. He then crossed over his hands and pulled the ends of the cord in opposite directions with all the angry force he could muster. Her hands went to her throat, but soon after they dropped limp at her sides. Vincent lowered her body backwards behind the gate and laid her to rest next to the wall.

With his victim either dead or possibly only unconscious, but either way, unable to fight for her life, Vincent calmly folded the cord and returned it to his coat pocket and stepped over to the entrance of the gate. Remaining hidden in the darkness, he leaned across the entranceway and checked the street in both directions for signs of life. No one in sight. All was clear. He could now scoop up the woman's body and place her just outside the gate, take the knife to her throat and belly, and then get clear of the place, moving on to location number two.

But just as he began to step backwards, he saw a horse pulling a cart with a man at the reins turning onto Berner Street from Commercial Road. This wasn't good. The driver could be leading the horse right to the club. Vincent had to make a quick decision. He could leave the body and casually walk away and head for Commercial Road with his hat pulled down in front and hope the body wasn't seen until he got further away, or he could stay with the body and hope the man and his horse passed by.

Running out of time, Vincent chose to take a chance and stay with the body, betting the driver would pass by. But he realized if the driver pulled into the passage, he would have to make a run for it past the horse and cart. If he had to do that, he understood he would be leaving the woman behind uncut, and therefore possibly still alive. She could describe him perfectly to the police.

So, Vincent quickly knelt to the right of the woman's head, and with the clopping of the horse growing louder and closer, he pulled out his knife, held his left hand over his victim's mouth, and tilting back her head, he pulled the knife across the left side of her neck, successfully severing her carotid artery. However, the woman was still alive, and her half-conscious mind reacted to the cut, raising her right hand and grabbing at her bleeding throat. She may have even reflexively tried to cry out, but Vincent pressed harder with the knife and cut through her windpipe to make sure she didn't make any noise. The woman stopped struggling, and her hand dropped to her chest. Vincent continued to trail the knife around her throat, but only superficially—he didn't want blood on him from the artery on the right.

As the blood drained from the wound on the left side of the woman's neck, and as the sound of the clopping horse and the rolling wheels of the approaching cart echoed unbearably closer, Vincent stepped over his victim's legs and hid behind the gate and hoped the clopping would keep going. But it didn't. The driver clicked his tongue and the clopping stuttered, and Vincent watched through the gap of the gate as the man pulled on the reins to the right and the horse turned towards the gate entrance. The worst option was happening.

Vincent remained calm and hidden. There was still a chance the driver wouldn't notice the body. She was near the wall, and it was dark. Vincent could hardly make her out looking back at her from behind the gate.

The driver didn't see the body, but the instincts of beasts are more finely tuned to sensing things, and the horse sensed a presence to its right and shied. The driver halted the horse.[7] Vincent still had his knife out, and he readied it for use again.

Because of the darkness, it appeared the driver couldn't make out what had startled the horse. Vincent watched him slide over in his seat on the cart and look down. The driver leaned over and used the backend of his horsewhip to reach down and push at the woman's body. Unsatisfied, the driver stepped down and lit a match. It didn't offer much light and must not have been bright enough for him to see she had a cut throat, since he didn't shy away like his horse. He simply turned and took the bridle and began walking the horse and cart further into the yard. Vincent saw his chance. With the man's back to him, he calmly stepped out from behind the gate and followed behind the cart as it passed. A few more quiet steps, and he was beyond the entrance and heading down Berner Street unnoticed.

Expecting the driver to return with a lamp for a better look and then run up Berner Street to Commercial Road for a constable when he realized the woman wasn't some drunk asleep in the yard of the club, Vincent chose to make his escape in the opposite direction, to the south on Berner Street, and he quickly disappeared along the badly lit backstreets.

Vincent didn't run. That would draw attention. Instead, he walked quickly and was soon out of danger. But he was still close enough to hear the faint sound of constables blowing their whistles. Vincent had guessed right. The man had returned, and a constable had been sought out. They had found the woman's bleeding body, but she couldn't tell them anything.

Things didn't go quite as planned, but Vincent had met his first objective. He checked his hands and clothes for bloodstains and only found some on his right hand where the woman had reached for her neck and had grabbed his hand after getting blood on hers. He found a public pump and rinsed his hands, and to be careful, he dampened his handkerchief and also wiped his face. He couldn't risk having blood on his face when he approached his second victim.

The driver had pulled his cart into the yard at 1:00 a.m., and Vincent made it to the second location in about fifteen minutes. He was there a little earlier than expected, but that was fine. His timing for murder at the second location was to be based on when a constable followed his beat through Mitre Square, which was at fifteen-minute intervals, so he could adjust as needed.

Even after one kill, Vincent was no less impatient for his second, and he strolled along Whitechapel High Street looking for his next victim of the night. As he approached Houndsditch, just the kind of woman he was looking for came stumbling around the corner and practically fell into his arms. She was just the type that needed killing, and he wasted no time leading her to his secret lair.

The woman was a willing sort of prey and a little too drunk to care all that much. Vincent didn't need to concoct a phony story or buy her a pretty flower. She needed money, and she didn't care where he took her.

Vincent turned her onto Mitre Street and led her around the corner of the frame shop and into Mitre Square (figure 13.1, London map). Not a soul had noticed them, and no other souls were within the square. Vincent pointed to the right and told her that looked like a good enough spot over there in that dark corner. When they got to the fence, he tried the gate as if he'd never seen it before and told her it would be even more private behind it. The woman must have laughed at his apparent shyness and followed him behind the gate.

After shutting the gate, like before, Vincent didn't waste any time. Just as he had done only half-an-hour earlier, he had the woman turn her back to him. He had the cord around her neck and was pulling tight before she even had a chance to be afraid of the dark. His prey clawed at the cord and tried to struggle free, but like the other woman, her body soon went limp. However, this time Vincent kept the cord pulled tight a little longer before lowering her to the ground.

Vincent then watched the square through a crack in the boards of the fence. He didn't have long to wait before the expected constable entered from the same direction he and the woman had entered from Mitre Street. The constable immediately turned right and walked directly towards the gate with his lantern. Then he did as he had done on previous occasions, turned, circled around the square and left the way he came in.

It was 1:30 a.m. Vincent knew he had about fifteen minutes to do his dirty work before the constable's beat brought him back around to the square. He was smartly using the reliable regularity of the constables on their beats against them. He removed his hat and coat and dropped them on the ground and opened the gate. He then lifted up the unfortunate woman's body and carried her a few feet outside the gate and laid her down on the pavement with her head near the gate and her feet towards the square.

Although he didn't need to hurry, Vincent performed his work swiftly and efficiently. There was, of course, always the possibility some drunk might stumble into the square looking for a place to sleep, so Vincent remained alert. He left the gate slightly open in the event such a disruption occurred and he needed to flee.

First things first. Vincent knelt by the woman's head on her right side and reached over and cut lightly and then down deep into the left side of her neck. He felt the knife hit bone. There was no movement from her body. The extra holding of the cord must have done it. He pulled the knife around and paused to let the main thrust of blood pour out on the left side. He then continued to drag his knife less deeply the rest of the way around to just under her right ear.

Looking down at his victim's face from above, which was upside down to Vincent, a thought came to mind which he may have fantasized about previously. The work he was doing was like his other work as a painter. He signed his paintings, why not sign his victims? Of course, he couldn't use "Vincent" as he did with his paintings, but why not have a little fun and use his initials? The dimwitted detectives would never figure it out.

With the tip of his knife, Vincent carved a "V" into the woman's left cheek, just below her eye. He added another "V" in the same area on the right cheek. Then, with more force, he carved a large "G" between the two "V's." He started the knife on her right upper lip and brought it up to her nose and around the right side. He then started again with a deep cut to the bridge of her nose and carved a bowed line downward on her right cheek. He made notches on her eyelids to represent the periods for the initials. He added a few quick cuts to her face to help disguise the initials. He finished up with a slash to her right ear, cutting off the lobe. (figure 13.2, drawing of cuts to Eddowes' face)

Remaining at an angle to the entrance of the square, which allowed him to keep an eye on it, Vincent moved down to the woman's right side and pulled up her dress. She was not wearing any undergarments, making his task easier. He made some quick cuts and jabs to her inner thighs and then reached his knife down between his victim's legs and to the right and began a long cut upward. He held the blade firmly and kept it going along the abdomen, dragged it around the left side of the naval, and continued upward while pushing down firmly to separate the tissue and muscles until he hit the sternum and stopped.

Vincent then peeled back the walls of her belly and reached in with both hands and grabbed hold of her intestines and dragged them out and dropped them over her right shoulder, just as he had done with Chapman. Then, to counterbalance his work of art, Vincent cut away a portion of the intestines and placed it neatly stretched out parallel with and between her left arm and body.

With plenty of time remaining before the constable returned, Vincent checked the entrance again and then reached into her belly, found her womb, cut it free and removed it. He then dug his hand around in the dark until he found her left kidney and also cut that free and removed it.

His hands and forearms were drenched in the woman's blood, so he wiped them on her dress and a white apron she wore. He didn't want to get his hands bloody again, so he cut off a piece of the apron and wrapped it around the womb and kidney.

Considering his work done, Vincent retreated back to the gate, gave one last look towards the entrance of the square and at his piece of artwork on the pavement, and then quietly closed the gate grinning. Picking up his hat and coat, he put them on as he swiftly moved through the darkness. Slipping his special package into a coat pocket, he pulled his damp handkerchief from the other pocket and wiped his face, neck and hands.

Without even the slightest bit of panic, Vincent adroitly followed the path he had previously searched out. He passed smoothly and quietly through the vacant buildings until he drifted out the other side like a shadow and walked up High Street, looking very much like any other dark figure passing through the night.

Vincent headed east on High Street which was the wrong direction for escape. In fact, he was moving back into the danger zone of his first kill of the night. But Vincent had one more devious act to perform before he called it a night. Just before reaching the point where High Street splits into Whitechapel Road and Commercial Road, he turned left onto Goulston Street and made his way north. He pulled the apron from his pocket and dumped the contents into some bushes but kept the apron.

After checking over his shoulder, Vincent ducked into the alcove of a stairwell and waited for a moment. All was safe. He dropped the apron next to the wall and fumbled in his coat pocket for a piece of white chalk. The top portion of the wall was painted white and the lower portion black. Vincent-the-artist thought it best to use the black as a background and use white chalk. Above the piece of apron, he wrote a quick message. This was a planned stop, and the message was also predetermined with a purpose.

Possibly again hearing the faint sound of police whistles, Vincent focused on his escape. But he now had nothing incriminating on him to cause suspicion, so he walked along normally with his hands in his pocket, tempted to hum a happy little tune.

He likely chose to turn back and head south on Goulston and return to High Street and Aldgate, and then crossing over to Mansell Street, he could keep going south towards the Thames and away from the two atrocities he had committed. He may have continued on to the river to wash up. Then, listening to the more clever advice of his Jack the Ripper side, Vincent avoided stopping for a drink in a pub and continued his escape out of the area and found a secluded plot of earth to hide and get some sleep.

On Sunday morning, September 30, as the people of London awoke on their day of rest, the newspapers didn't yet carry the news of the night's blood. However, as they made their way to coffee houses and churches, the horrible news was brought their way by word of mouth. The well-known preacher, Charles Spurgeon, delivered a sermon at the Metropolitan Tabernacle that morning. Vincent may have even combed his hair, buttoned his coat, and showed up to hear him preach, not for spiritual enlightenment since those years were long behind him, but for the joyous irony. And if so, Vincent wouldn't have been disappointed.

Spurgeon's prayer that morning was quoted in the *Daily News*: "We hear startling news of abounding sin in this great city. Oh God, put an end to this . . . Let Thy gospel permeate the city, and let not monsters in human shape escape Thee."[8] Vincent would have said amen to that along with the other congregants, but he would have been the only one who said it holding back a snicker.

Because it was Sunday, there wasn't a push to get the story out in the papers that day. However, Vincent checked them anyway, and he found a report on some of his mischief in the weekly paper, *Reynolds's*. The chalk message he had written in Dalston on Thursday night had been discovered that same night. They quoted what he had written: "Look! Look! I am Leather Apron. Five more, and I will give myself up."[9] They also noted a drawing of a man holding a knife to a woman was found next to the writing.

Vincent felt sorry for those people who heard of more murder and were spurred on to buy a paper. They would be disappointed, but at least they would have a story about a chalk writer to read about. This was the second of his chalk writings to be published—the first being near Chapman's dead body. The leather apron which was found near her body had whipped up a frenzy of suspicion for the man nicknamed Leather Apron, and Vincent thought it would be fun to bring up his name again.

There was still no mention of the letter he had sent to the Central News Agency or of the arm he had dug up and put on display, but he still had hope. He was looking forward to the deluge of information that was certain to flood the Monday papers.

His letter to the Central News Agency was meant to be a warning of what was to come and to introduce who he was. Now that the latest murders were behind him, it was only fitting that he should write again with a post-murder letter. So, he bought a London postcard, and later that night, he sat on a park bench under a streetlamp and wrote a little something more to the Central News Agency.

❋   ❋   ❋

On Monday morning, October 1, London rumbled awake with eager anticipation for news of the two latest murders. Its inhabitants were not disappointed. The gruesome details filled the pages of the morning papers, complete with witness interviews and gory particulars provided by the doctors, and the excited citizens of London gorged themselves on all they could consume.

Louis Diemschitz, the man who drove his horse and cart into the yard next to the Working Men's Club, told of how he went into the club and brought out a candle.[10] Seeing that the woman's throat had been cut, he ran up Berner Street to Commercial Road looking for a policeman.

Police Constable Henry Lamb was the first constable on the scene.[11] He touched the woman's face and found it warm. He noted she was lying to the right, just inside the gateway, with her face about six inches from the wall. Her feet were behind the gate so that Lamb was able to close it without disturbing the body.

The woman was identified by her sister as Elizabeth Stride (figure 13.3, mortuary photo of Stride), a 45-year-old widow who made her living as a prostitute.[12] Some witnesses came forward to state they believed they saw Stride with a man at different times and in different places the night before, but in the end, none of their information amounted to any use for tracking down the killer. It was becoming clear that, as the murders became more sensationalized, more witnesses were coming forward with exaggerated and questionable stories looking to get their names in the papers.

One of those witnesses added to the lore of the growing false description of the murderer. Mrs. Mortimer, who lived on Berner Street, said she was standing at her front door between 12:30 and 1:00 a.m., and that the only person she saw was "a young man carrying a black shiny bag."[13] The worried man came forward later and was cleared.[14] However, like previous false images, this was added to the public psyche.

Dr. Phillips and Dr. Frederick Blackwell had been called to the scene. Dr. Blackwell arrived at 1:10 a.m. and later said of the victim, "She could not have been dead more than twenty minutes, the body being perfectly warm."[15] He deposed she was lying on her left side and that "the right hand was lying on the chest, and was smeared inside and out with blood."[16] He found there was no blood on the clothing.

Both doctors attended the post-mortem. The wound to the neck was described as having been made from left to right, cutting nearly completely through the carotid artery on the left side before cutting through the windpipe.[17] The cutting continued around to the right side, leaving a more superficial cut, which did not sever the right carotid artery.

It was noted a handkerchief was pulled tight around the victim's neck, and Dr. Blackwell suggested "her head was dragged back by means of a silk handkerchief she wore round her neck, and her throat was then cut."[18] He concluded her throat was cut while falling or on the ground because "the blood would have spurted about if . . . she was standing up."[19]

Dr. Phillips gave his details of the post-mortem at the inquest but, as he had done at the Chapman inquest, he showed caution in giving out too much information. He said to the coroner, "I will answer any questions put to me, but as there is another case pending I think I had better stop here."[20] They had two murders on their hands, and three previous murders to compare the details. It appears Dr. Phillips was again wisely attempting to not give out all the information to the public.

After Diemschitz discovered Elizabeth Stride's body at 1:00 a.m., the second victim of the night was discovered less than a mile away by City Police Constable Edward Watkins at 1:44.[21] He was walking his usual beat, which he said took him 12 or 14 minutes to complete. He didn't see anything out of the ordinary when he passed through Mitre Square at about 1:30. But when he returned at 1:44 and entered the square from Mitre Street, he turned right and shined his lantern in the darkest corner and discovered a woman's body (figure 13.4, sketch of Eddowes murder site).[22] At the inquest, he stated, "I saw the body of a woman lying on her back with her feet facing the square—the clothes much disarranged—and I saw that her throat was cut and her bowels protruding. The stomach was ripped up, and she was lying in a pool of blood."[23] He at once blew his whistle.[24]

The woman's body was within the limits of the City of London, and therefore the surgeon for the City Police, Dr. Gordon Brown, was called for and arrived on the scene at 2:18 a.m.[25] He described later what he saw: "The intestines were to a large extent drawn out of the abdomen and placed over the right shoulder. A piece of the intestines about two feet long was detached and placed between the left arm and the body, apparently by design."[26] He continued, "The lobe of the right ear was cut completely through." The body was still warm, and he concluded, "Death must have taken place within the half hour."

Having performed the post-mortem, Dr. Brown also described the cuts to the face. Small cuts were made to her eyelids, and there was a deep cut over the bridge of her nose that extended down nearly to the jaw on the right side. The tip of her nose was detached by an oblique cut around the corners of the nostrils and down to the right upper lip. He also noted, "There was on each side of the cheek a cut which peeled up the skin forming a triangular flap."

As for the throat, the doctor said it had been cut all the way around, and that "the large vessels on the left side of the neck were severed to the bone, the knife marking the intervertebral cartilage." The carotid artery on the right side of the neck only had a pinhole sized opening, and he concluded death was from the loss of blood from the left carotid artery. He also noted, "There was no blood on the front of the clothes,"[27] and he therefore believed she was lying on her back when the neck wound was inflicted.[28]

A widow named Eliza Gold came forward and identified the woman in the mortuary as her sister, 43-year-old Catherine Eddowes (figure 13.5, mortuary photo of Eddowes).[29] A man named John Kelly also came forward and identified Eddowes as the woman he had cohabitated with for the past seven years.[30] He stated he had "cautioned her not to stay out late at night on account of the previous murders," but noted that she "was given to drinking." He hadn't seen her since Saturday afternoon and thought she had "got into some trouble and had been locked up."

It turned out this was the case. On Saturday night, at about 8:30, Eddowes was found by police to be drunk and lying on a footway on Whitechapel High Street[31] and taken to the Bishopsgate Police Station. After checking on Eddowes several times, Constable George Hutt felt she was sober enough to be released and discharged her at 1:00 a.m. On her way out, she said, "I shall get a d[amn] fine hiding when I get home."[32] Leaving the station, she turned to the left, towards Houndsditch.[33] Constable Hutt was asked how long it would take to walk from the police station to Mitre Square, and he estimated about eight minutes.[34]

At the same time Eddowes was stepping out of the police station, the murderer was stepping behind Diemschitz's horse and cart to begin his escape. The timing of Eddowes' release and her desire to return to High Street sealed her fate. If the jailer had waited another ten minutes to release her, the murderer would have chosen another victim that night. But her number was up, and Catherine Eddowes arrived at the same spot and at the same time as the murderer, and he arrived ready to make his choice and ready to get to work.

Two different police forces were scrambling to make sense of the night's activities. Constables from both the Metropolitan Police and the City Police searched the streets near the two murder sites looking for suspicious characters, likely focusing only on darkly dressed men with dark mustaches who were covered in blood. They didn't find what they were searching for, but they did find Vincent's last bit of fun for that night.

At 2:55 a.m., Constable Alfred Long found a portion of a bloodstained apron in a passage leading to a staircase on Goulston Street, only a third of a mile from where Catherine Eddowes had been murdered in Mitre Square (figure 13.1, London map).[35] Above the apron, written in white chalk on black bricks, was the message, "The Jews are the men that will not be blamed for nothing."[36]

The piece of apron was taken to Dr. Phillips, who found it perfectly matched an area cut from an apron Eddowes was wearing.[37] The chalk writing was ordered removed by the Metropolitan Police for fear it might cause a riot.[38] Vincent would have loved that reaction.

There was intent behind the chalk writing. Vincent meant to stir things up and cause additional distraction. Both murder sites were heavily occupied by Jewish immigrants,[39] and Vincent chose the locations partly for this reason.

The Working Men's Club was also made up mainly of Jews. The lecture at the Saturday night meeting was "Judaism and Socialism."[40] There was also a synagogue behind Mitre Square.[41]

A discussion ensued over the meaning of the killer's message and over whether or not the police should have rubbed it out. It became a distraction for the police, and the papers covered the controversy to the delight of Vincent.

By design, Vincent van Gogh's paintings exhibit a spontaneous and even sloppy style. His look was intentional, though, and he worked at perfecting the technique of making it appear as if he had dashed off his paintings without much thought or effort. Of course, in actuality, he had put a great deal of thought and effort into his paintings, completing many studies before the final painting was begun. He had written to Theo about this in June: "I must warn you that everyone will think that I work too fast. Don't you believe a word of it."[42]

Vincent was also incorporating his method of painting into his method of murder and had been doing so since he decided to become two. He was a planner. He was organized and in control. His Jack the Ripper murders were not spontaneous acts. He had thought through every step with great care, and this was one of the main reasons he was not captured.

Vincent also continued to follow the practice he had used on his father—kill under concealment and then place the victim on the threshold. Both Stride and Eddowes were found on the threshold of a gate, one behind and one in front. Vincent had now followed that same practice for five Jack the Ripper victims. (figure 13.6, murder sites of Tabram, Nichols, Chapman, Stride & Eddowes)

Additionally, Vincent continued to make use of his developed technique of first incapacitating his victim with strangulation. This possibility was not focused on at the time of the Stride and Eddowes murders, but the evidence suggests it. Both victims had their throats cut, but neither had blood on the front of their clothing. It's easy enough to conclude they were lying on their backs when their throats were cut. However, it was unlikely either would be willing to lie down for their client, especially with Stride, who was found in the mud. And, like the others, no cries were heard beforehand. With both victims having their throats cut, the cause of death seemed obvious. There was no need at the time to consider strangulation was first administered.

Vincent was a painter and, in a way, so was Jack the Ripper. But, as Jack, Vincent preferred to paint using a knife instead of a brush and in flesh and blood rather than on canvas and in paint. For Vincent, the displayed body of

Catherine Eddowes was very close to being a perfect artistic creation, but he still desired something more spectacular. He hadn't yet created the masterpiece in murder he sought. He would have to try again to achieve perfection.

14

I Have A Name
October 1888

With the gory details of the Stride and Eddowes murders splashed across the pages of the London newspapers on Monday, October 1, 1888, Vincent's alter ego was receiving a level of notoriety reserved only for English royalty. He was getting his reward for his work, but there was even more glory given to him that day.

After providing their account of the two murders, the *Daily News* noted the Central News Agency had received an interesting letter on Thursday, September 27.[1] The entire letter was quoted. It began "Dear Boss" and ended with "Yours Truly, Jack the Ripper." Vincent's goal had been achieved. The good people of London now knew what to call him, and the mysterious dark figure who roamed through their nightmares could take on solid form.

It turned out they had received the letter on Thursday night, just as Vincent had hoped when he chose to mail it from the General Post Office earlier that evening. But they didn't give it out to be published until after the Stride and Eddowes murders. Vincent had actually requested this in the Dear Boss Ripper letter. Acting as Jack the Ripper, he had written, "Keep this letter back till I do a bit more work, then give it out straight." Vincent was in control of the media.

At first, they thought the letter was the work of a practical joker, but that opinion quickly changed when two women showed up brutally murdered just two nights later, and especially so when the letter had warned, "You will soon hear of me with my funny little games." And when it was discovered one of Eddowes' ears had been cut off, they must have believed the letter was indeed from the murderer, because he had also written, "The next job I do I shall clip the lady's ears off, and send to the police-officers." Vincent had only partially done what he had said he would do. He didn't send Eddowes' severed ear to the police, but they got it just the same.

Jack the Ripper was a sensation. Vincent was delighted. The name Jack the Ripper was being spread feverishly from mouth to ear, first only here and there in a whisper, but then it was being pushed out of restaurant doors and dropped down from balcony windows until it reverberated and shook all of London.

This was indeed a glorious day for Vincent. He was gaining the attention he so desired for his work. It wasn't attention for his artwork as a painter, though, and he was only receiving it indirectly through the use of a pseudonym, but just the same, he was getting attention.

Vincent had experienced a similar feeling when his words were first published in the *Daily News* back in 1873 when he wrote the Meat Market letter after his first murder. However, back then his work as a murderer and as a writer was largely ignored. Now, his murders and his words were being closely followed. They had significance and meaning, and the name he had chosen for his other self was being reported right alongside his latest deeds. The details were spreading rapidly to other cities and countries. The story which had grown legs after the Tabram and Nichols murders, and which had then grown arms after the Chapman murder, now sprouted feathery wings and took flight, and the legend of Jack the Ripper was born.

Vincent knew there was more to the story, and he scanned the Monday papers for news of his other mischievous deeds of Thursday night. To his great delight, he found a small article at the bottom of page six in *The Times* about a woman's arm being discovered.[2] The article reported the arm had been found wrapped in some canvas on Friday near the Blind School on Lambeth Road (figure 14.1, London map). There had been a stir about the discovery because some thought it was related to the arm previously found on the shore of the Thames at Pimlico. But this idea was quickly quelled when it was noted no flesh remained on the arm. It was described as being "the entire skeleton of an arm from the shoulder-blade to the fingers." It was further made clear the arm had "evidently been dug up after a long interment in the ground."

There's good reason to believe this arm did indeed belong to Vincent's 1874 victim and that he had dug it up and placed it by the Blind School early on Friday morning, September 28. The idea had been triggered by the lone discovery of the Pimlico arm in early September. Throughout the month, he had plenty of time to fantasize about the idea and where to place the arm.

Back in June of 1874, when the lower portion of Vincent's second victim had been discovered floating in the Thames, that was all they had found of the woman's body. She had been cut in half just above her second lower rib. Everything above this, her chest, shoulders, arms and head remained missing. It had been fourteen years since, and therefore it was extremely unlikely any detective would make the link between part of a woman floating in the Thames in 1874 and a skeletal arm found at a Blind School in 1888. They would never tie it back to when Vincent lived in London, and they would never tie it back to him. He chose the location of the Blind School to taunt the police and make his point. The police were blind to who the arm belonged to, and they were blind to who he was. Psychopaths do everything for a reason. But also, by choosing to deposit the arm at the Blind School in Lambeth, Vincent had placed it within close proximity to where he had previously lived.

When Vincent left the Loyers in August of 1874, he had moved only a short distance away to the north onto Kennington Road. Heading further north, Kennington intersects with Lambeth Road where the Blind School was located just a short walk to the east. Having lived in the same area, Vincent knew about the Blind School, and when he thought about doing some mischief by digging up the arm of his past victim and wondered where to place it for the most impact, he recalled the Blind School and made use of it.

No doubt, an enormous power was growing within Vincent after he read about all he had done. What satisfaction! What a day! He was larger than life, much larger than he was in real life, and much larger than Theo. Unfortunately, only he knew this. He couldn't declare his victory over Theo to his family and to the world. It had to remain a silent victory.

After such a glorious day, and after receiving so much hidden acclaim, Vincent couldn't help but stay in London a while longer. He may have stopped in at a pub and joined the enlivened discussions about the fiend now known as Jack the Ripper. He may have even chimed in, giving his theory on the whole matter, even joking that the true murderer could be someone right there in the pub. He wanted so badly to tell someone who he was.

The next day, Tuesday, October 2, the papers carried more details of the two murders. The Elizabeth Stride inquest had begun the day before, and this gave the reporters fresh gore to write about. Of course, Vincent enjoyed reading about his work, but he was also once again rewarded with more of his words being published. The postcard he had written and dropped in a pillar box late Sunday night had been received by the Central News Agency the next morning, and now, just a day later, here were his same words quoted in the *Daily News* and in *The Times*.

As noted, Vincent had requested in the Dear Boss letter, "Keep this letter back till I do a bit more work, then give it out straight." When he wrote the Ripper postcard, he referred back to his previous request and wrote, "Thanks for keeping the last letter back till I got to work again."[3] Interestingly, Vincent had used this same unique wording of "keep this letter back" in a previous letter to Theo. In 1883, he had written, "I am keeping this letter back for a few days."[4] Vincent was simply using phrasing he had used before.

Not only did Vincent thank them for following his instructions to keep the letter back, but he also explained why he didn't follow through on his pledge to "clip the lady's ears off, and send to the police-officers." He explained, "Number One squealed a bit; couldn't finish straight off. Had not time to get ears for police."

Vincent likely planned to cut off his first victim's ears as he had promised, but being interrupted, he didn't get the chance. He must have considered moving that task over to his second victim, but not wanting to deviate from what he had planned for her, he simply gave a quick slash to Eddowes' ear in frustration and continued on as planned. He had carefully calculated all he would do that night, and acting as the efficient and clever Jack the Ripper, he did not want to stray off course. To do so would risk capture.

Because the writer of the Dear Boss letter had followed through on his words, the other details of the letter were then more carefully examined. The main function of providing the public with his name was understood, but then his choice of salutation was also looked at for understanding. What was behind his use of "Dear Boss"? The explanation of this mystery may be less complicated than was thought.

As previously noted, the first Jack the Ripper letter, which Vincent had Roulin send from Arles, had the name of the sender blackened out with coffins.[5] The salutation was "Dear Sir," and the envelope was addressed to "Sir Charles Warren, Commissioner of Police, Scotland Yard." Vincent had chosen to send his first Ripper letter directly to the police, and he knew the title and name of the head man, and therefore he used it on the envelope. When he chose the salutation, he simply followed custom and wrote "Dear Sir."

The Dear Boss letter, on the other hand, was sent to the Central News Agency, but Vincent didn't know the job title or name of who was in charge. Therefore, he wrote on the envelope, "The Boss, Central News Office," and he matched the envelope by using "Dear Boss" as the salutation in the letter. Vincent wanted the letter to get to the man in charge, but he didn't know the man's name or title, so he simply used the slang "Boss."

At the time, the use of "Boss" and other slang in the letter were thought of as Americanisms.[6] Looking into Vincent's life provides a match for this. As previously noted, Vincent had been spending time around the American artist Dodge MacKnight in Arles over the summer of 1888, even right up until MacKnight left in August, so Vincent certainly would have picked up on his use of American phrasing.

MacKnight's Americanisms may have triggered Vincent's use of referring to someone in charge as the "Boss," but Vincent had also been using this sort of slang for a long time. It was noted by Vincent's former roommate, P.C. Görlitz, who had lived with him in Dordrecht in 1877, that they both referred to their landlord, interestingly, as the "boss."[7]

When Vincent wrote the Ripper postcard, he left off "The Boss" but addressed it to the "Central News Office, London City," just as he had addressed the Dear Boss letter, showing a match between the two because he used "Office" instead of the actual name of "Agency." He left off "Dear Boss" to begin the postcard, but shortly after, he referred to the intended reader as "dear old Boss," matching to the Dear Boss letter. And to make sure they knew the postcard was from the same person who wrote the Dear Boss letter, he also signed it Jack the Ripper.

Wanting to keep the fun going, Vincent found a quiet place to sit and write another Ripper letter. The envelope of this letter has not survived, but its police catalogue card shows it was postmarked October 2 in the E.C. District.[8] From this point on, any of the letters thought to be from the murderer could have been written by a hoaxer who was influenced by the Dear Boss letter and the postcard being published in the papers. Based on that, this particular letter of October 2 could be thought of as the first hoax letter received, since it was not signed Jack the Ripper but instead as "George of the High Rip Gang."

However, the contents of the letter reveal it was from the murderer's own hand. Vincent was already mixing things up. He had firmly established Jack the Ripper in the public's mind, so he was already adding a different angle. He had a creative and diabolical mind, after all. He wouldn't be satisfied unless there was variety. In this letter, he wanted to give the impression there was more than one murderer for the police to be looking for, and he wrote in the plural form, stating, "Oh we are masters," and also, "You will hear from me in the west end. My pal will keep on at the east a while yet."

Vincent was adding another layer to his concept of using a persona to murder and write letters by. He was writing as if he were yet another person, "George of the High Rip Gang," and writing as if another member of the gang was Jack the Ripper. Vincent had a lot going on in his head, but his psychopathic mind could handle it just fine.

One of the lines in the letter helps unmask the true identity of the writer. It states, "Oh I am master of the art." The context was murder, but referring to murder as an art is something very fitting for a painter.

This Ripper letter also reveals Vincent's handiwork within the way in which women were referred to. He wrote, "No education like a butchers. No animal like a nice woman. The fat are the best." This relates back to June when Vincent wrote to his artist buddy, Bernard, agreeing with him that prostitutes were like meat in the marketplace. And especially when Vincent had to take it a little further by adding, "The whore is like meat in a butcher's shop."[9] Vincent was continuing that concept, both by butchering women on the streets of London and by referring to them in the same way in Ripper letters he wrote for the newspapers to publish.

✳ ✳ ✳

It seems Vincent's original plan was to return to Arles by Wednesday, October 3. In his letter to Theo, which he had sent on the day he left Arles, Wednesday, September 26, Vincent had written, "I hope I shall get your next letter on Wednesday."[10] Vincent expected to be back on Wednesday the 3rd, so he wanted Theo's letter, with more money enclosed, to arrive that same day. Vincent needed to leave on the 2nd to be back in Arles on the 3rd, but because he was having such fun, he decided to stay a little longer. He was on a devious and murderous spree, and he simply didn't want it to end, especially when things were just beginning to heat up. He wasn't all that worried now about missing Theo's letter by a day or two. He could use his established excuse of being out in the fields painting and being just too exhausted to write letters.

The next day, Wednesday, October 3, the escalation jumped even higher. *The Times* and the *Daily News* reported a woman's torso had been found the day before by some workmen in the basement of a construction site.[11] The construction site had a special significance—it was to be the new headquarters of the Metropolitan Police (figure 14.1, construction site location).

Some of the workers on the site kept their tools hidden in the dark vaults of the basement, and on Tuesday the 2nd, a worker looking for his tools noticed a parcel wrapped in string lying against a brick wall. He told the assistant foreman about it, who then ordered a bricklayer named George Budden to bring it out into the light to be looked at. Budden struck a match and saw the parcel and commented later, "I thought it was old bacon . . . I took hold of the string around it—it being tied up—and dragged it across a trench into a part of the vault where there was light."[12] He cut the string, and opening the parcel, he and the others saw it was part of a woman's body (figure 14.2, illustration of discovery of torso), and they sent for the police.

Dr. Thomas Bond, Divisional Surgeon for Whitehall, was called upon. Examining the torso, he deposed the victim's arms had been removed at the shoulder joints and the neck had been "sawn through below the larynx."[13] The lower portion of the body had been severed just below the naval.[14] The woman's height was estimated at 5'8" and her age at around 25 years. Dr. Bond couldn't determine the cause of death, but he ruled out drowning or suffocation from his examination of the organs. He also mentioned, "Decomposition was very far advanced, and the body was full of maggots."

In an effort to determine the time of death, the area where the parcel was found was further examined. Dr. Bond noted the brick wall was stained black and saturated with decomposition fluids from where the parcel rested against it.[15] He concluded the torso must have lain there for weeks and not days. He estimated it had been about six weeks since death took place, or around the end of August or beginning of September.[16]

There was another important factor which led Dr. Bond to conclude the time of death. *The Times* wrote that when he first saw the headless and limbless body, he exclaimed, "I have an arm which will fit that."[17] They further reported that the arm found in the Thames at Pimlico on September 11 was taken to the Westminster Mortuary where the torso was being kept. The torso was then brought out and placed on a table "and the medical gentleman found that the arm fitted it exactly, the jagged edges of the flesh corresponding in every part."

When the Pimlico arm was discovered on September 11, it was believed it had been separated from its owner two or three days prior. Since the torso belonged to the arm, it can then be more precisely dated to the dating of the arm which placed the time of death at the same time as the September 8 murder of Annie Chapman.

The torso had been wrapped in a richly flowered moiré silk skirt, which was then tied around with stout twine normally used in tying parcels.[18] It was reported that this twine corresponded exactly to that which was found tied around the arm.

Vincent had stolen a rowboat on the Thames in the early hours of September 8, intentionally matching the method he used for his first murder on September 5, back in 1873. After killing his victim and cutting her into pieces, he then tied the arm to a piling of the Grosvenor Railway Bridge, and drifting further downriver to just past Westminster Bridge, he pulled up to the steamboat pier on the Victorian Embankment (figure 14.1, London map). This happened to be the same steamboat pier he had used so long ago when he lived in London and took the steamboat from Battersea to Goupil's each day. He then likely stabbed a hole in the boat to let it sink to match back to his first murder and climbed out onto the pier. He could walk along the pier carrying the woman's torso with no threat of suspicion, since it was disguised as a wrapped package. The pier placed him directly in line with the construction site of the new police headquarters. Hidden by darkness, Vincent carried his gruesome parcel the short distance to the site and deposited it deep inside the cellar.

There was a reason Vincent wrapped the torso up and tied it like a package. It was meant as a gift. He had murdered the woman to match to his first murder fifteen years prior. But also, just as then, he matched it to his mother's September 10 birthday. The murder was for his mother, but his psychopathic fantasizing had given him the idea that he ought to also give the police a gift.

Vincent specifically chose the future site of the police headquarters and placed his gift of a wrapped torso there for discovery to send the police a strong message. He wanted them to feel his power and control over them. He had demonstrated he could walk right into their headquarters undetected, albeit their future headquarters, and deposit a chunk of one of his victims. He was taunting and humiliating them as only a clever psychopathic serial killer could do.

The examination of his first victim back in 1873 revealed she was believed to have been pregnant, and a dead infant was also discovered on the shore of the Thames near the right side of her torso, making it appear obvious the infant had been cut from her belly. There was no way for Dr. Bond to determine if the 1888 victim had also been pregnant. Her uterus and all other parts below her naval were absent.[19] However, the doctor had noted, "There were no indications that she had borne a child, but it was possible that she might have done so."[20]

There was no evidence the woman was pregnant, but Vincent, murdering for the anniversary of his first murder, would have likely found the same type of victim—a pregnant prostitute. However, this time he either didn't want any evidence of the woman's pregnancy discovered or the infant he pulled from her belly floated down the Thames and quietly out to sea unnoticed. Vincent had succeeded in reliving his first murder and killing again for his mother's birthday.

15

Follow The Letters
October 1888

Immensely enjoying how the coverage of his devious deeds kept the whirlwind of news spinning in the London papers, Vincent wanted to keep the funnel turning by generating more to cover. Another murder would be nice, but it was too risky right then—too many constables out and about on their toes. But he could write more Ripper letters, and he wrote one, but that wasn't enough, so he wrote another.

On Wednesday, October 3, 1888, Vincent may have been thinking of leaving the next day and wrote the two letters as a last bit of fun. Later that night, or early the next morning, he dropped one of the letters in front of an address in Westminster for it to be found.[1] He placed the other in a pillar box in Brixton.[2] Vincent dropped both of these letters in areas meant as clues to his identity, but no one picked up on the clues, since the connections weren't known at the time to cause anyone to do so.

There was some significance to a Ripper letter being found in Westminster. The Whitehall torso was discovered less than two miles away. But also, because this letter was left out on the street, as opposed to being mailed, the specific location of where it was left must be considered. For the psychopath, everything has meaning.

Similar to dropping a letter in the meat market after he butchered his first victim back in 1873, Vincent left this letter in a place which also had relevance. The meaning is obvious and astounding and provides a glaring piece of evidence. The letter was found in front of 6 Vincent Square (figure 14.1, London map).

Remarkably, a Jack the Ripper letter had been found outside a London address on Vincent Square. Not only this, to emphasize the meaning, the nearby intersecting road is Vincent Street.

Vincent van Gogh was not in Arles on October 4, 1888. He was in London. He wrote a Jack the Ripper letter and placed it in person on Vincent Square as a secret hint of his identity. He knew the police and detectives of the day would never associate this with him.

Vincent was having some risky fun. Could he be more obvious in giving the police a clue? Wouldn't at least one detective have thought there might be something to a Jack the Ripper letter being found on Vincent Square? Apparently not, but it's likely only a few detectives saw this particular letter, and besides, at the time, the police generally believed most of the Ripper letters were from pranksters, and not from the actual murderer.

Ever toying with the police to direct them onto other trails and relating to how the papers suggested the Dear Boss letter was full of Americanisms, Vincent opened this Ripper letter stating, "I am an American." Before ending the letter and signing it Jack the Ripper, he added to the clues and let them know, "I have been sleeping in Bow cemetery."

Vincent was familiar with sleeping out in the open. Not long after he had left Reverend Jones in the early years and had moved away from Isleworth and London, he had reflected back on his time there in a letter to Theo, writing, "Then there are the London streets in the rain with the lanterns, and the night spent on the steps of a little old gray church—which I did this summer, after that excursion to Ramsgate."[3] Then again later, he had written, "In those years when I was abroad without friends or help, suffering great misery (so that in London I often had to sleep in the open air.)"[4]

This was one of the main reasons Jack the Ripper was never caught. Since he didn't live in London, there was no place of residence to trace him back to. There was no landlord or neighbor or family member to notice the pattern of him being out the same night another murder took place. Even if Vincent were caught out on the streets after a murder had occurred and was taken in for questioning, he could give a false name and present himself as a poor Dutch immigrant who had just arrived in London. Feigning broken English, he could explain he lived out on the street, and there was no one for the police to question to corroborate anything he said. Unless captured red-handed, there was no way for the police to know Vincent was their man.

Whether or not the information found in the Ripper letter was followed up on is not known. Even if the police had, and even if they had found Vincent one morning in Bow Cemetery with his head propped against a gravestone, it wouldn't have mattered. They would have passed him by. They weren't looking for a sandy-haired, red bearded man, only dark-haired men all dressed in black. Because of the falsely created image of Jack the Ripper, Vincent was allowed freedom to play, both in his actions and in his letters. He was, in effect, invisible to the police.

The Vincent Square Ripper letter may have seemed insignificant at the time, but some poor clerk at the police department may have gotten a chill up his spine when he started to write down the next available docket number for this letter—666. Perhaps it was noticed but no meaning was applied to it. It is interesting, though, in a mystical sort of way. Out of all the Jack the Ripper letters, the one with the name Vincent attached to it was assigned the docket number 666. It's either a coincidence, or there's something to it, but who's to say?

The other Jack the Ripper letter discovered on the same day, Thursday, October 4, was noted to have been found in a pillar box at 8:30 a.m. The reason the postman made note of the letter was obvious. Above the address on the front of the envelope was written "From Jack Ripper," and at the top, "Murder."

The letter opened with "Dear Boss" and was signed "Jack the Ripper," but its contents offered little to go on. It was addressed to the police, and the intended message was for them to fear him. However, because the postman saw the letter at the time he collected it from the pillar box, and therefore it is known where the sender dropped it, the letter takes on a greater level of importance. It is noted on the back of the envelope it was collected from "the Pillar Box opposite 304 Brixton Road."

The significance of this is that the pillar box across from 304 Brixton Road was less than a mile from where Vincent had lived with the Loyers and had fallen in love with Eugenie back in 1873 and 1874 on 87 Hackford Road (figure 14.1, London map).

It's highly incriminating evidence against Vincent that on the same day of Thursday, October 4, a Jack the Ripper letter was found on Vincent Square and another was found in a pillar box on Brixton Road, so near to where he had once lived. Because both letters were found where they were dropped, the letter writer was physically in both locations on the 4th. And because both locations relate to Vincent, it's clear he wrote these Ripper letters and was in London on the 4th.

Unfortunately, the London police had no way of knowing the murderer had placed a Ripper letter on Vincent Square because his name was Vincent, or that the murderer had dropped a letter in a pillar box on the same day on Brixton Road because he had once lived nearby. They also had no way to know that the murderer didn't live in the East End or even in London, and not even in England, but instead, lived in a town far away in the south of France. With the exception of Mrs. Fiddymont's description, there was nothing they could go on that would lead them to the true identity of the killer. They were being misdirected and controlled by the misleading testimony of a few witnesses, but also by the killer himself through his chalk and letter writings.

✻   ✻   ✻

Vincent continued to walk the streets of London a free man, and his confidence grew stronger each time he passed a constable who looked right through him. He would have loved to have shown them just how invisible he was by committing another murder right under their noses, no doubt, but Jack the Ripper was too careful a killer to take that risk. He would have to wait before murdering again.

He couldn't murder, but he could continue the fun with more Ripper letters, and he did. Three more were postmarked on October 4, and then on Friday, October 5, another six were received. Vincent was loving all the secret attention he was receiving, and he decided to stretch out his stay even longer and keep the fun going. There was just too much excitement going on right then for him to leave.

Vincent was a prolific writer in his known life, and he also became one in his secret life. A new obsession was blooming, and he couldn't help himself. Writing the Jack the Ripper letters was a wonderfully creative and effective outlet for his manipulative and murderous side. He could write in character and speak his mind. He could freely lie about who he was and where he lived, and he could write to the police or the papers and raise the fear level with threats of committing another murder. The letters gave him control over the police and the public. He could put the police on guard in a certain street because he threatened to commit his next murder there, or he could cause them to search a cemetery or a block of apartments simply by writing he was sleeping in one of these places.

However, just as with Vincent's own letters, the Jack the Ripper letters reveal some of Vincent's own traits, such as when writing both as Vincent and as Jack he referred to women as animals to be butchered. Also, when Vincent-the-artist used an art reference in a Ripper letter by stating he was master of the art of murder. But another strong trait in Vincent's makeup that comes out in his own letters, even though he had turned away from it, was religion, and this theme began to also show in his Ripper letters.

In one of the Ripper letters from October 5, the writer stated, "I'll have a corpse in the churchyard for parson Sunday morning. Glorious fun."[5] Then in another from the same day, he commented about the torso which was found in Whitehall: "If she was a whore God will bless the hand that slew her, for the women of Moab and Midian shall die."[6] He added, "I never harm any others or the Divine power that protects and helps me in my grand work would quit for ever." Clearly, these are the words of someone familiar with religious references. Vincent was making use of a subject he knew well to continue to shape the exaggerated image of the Ripper in the minds of the police. But in doing so, he was also giving away a piece of his true self.

Something else Vincent gave away in his Ripper letters was that he was both Jack the Ripper and the Torso Killer. In another Ripper letter from October 5, the writer confessed, "I have done another one and thrown it in the river."[7] This letter is signed Jack the Ripper. None of the Jack the Ripper murders involved throwing the victim in the river. By using this reference, the writer had tipped his hand a little, showing that the person behind the curtain had not only murdered the five Ripper victims but had also murdered the woman whose arm was found on the shore of the river at Pimlico and whose torso was then found in the cellar in Whitehall.

But then in the Moab and Midian Ripper letter of the same date, the writer, who also signed this letter as Jack the Ripper, stayed in character and pleaded, "In the name of God hear me I swear I did not kill the female whose body was found at Whitehall." Not only was Vincent taking on the Jack the Ripper persona to kill by, but he was also taking on the character of Jack the Ripper to write by. As Jack the Ripper, Vincent could write that he did not kill the female at Whitehall and have it be a true statement. After all, he didn't use the persona of Jack the Ripper to murder her. He was just plain Vincent, or the Torso Killer, when he killed her, just as he was when he killed his first and second victims in 1873 and 1874 and threw their body parts into the Thames.

The *Daily News* had reported about the Whitehall victim: "The authorities do not in any way connect it with the Whitechapel crimes."[8] If the police had given more consideration to the Ripper letters possibly being from the murderer, they could have drawn a different conclusion. But also, if they could have thought to look at some similar past cases of women's body parts being found in the Thames, they would have had some good evidence to look at, and they could have seen that the Torso and Ripper murderers were one in the same. But to be fair, they were kept busy with many other crimes of the day.

Vincent decided to continue his stay in London, and on Saturday, October 6, three more Ripper letters arrived, one of which connected well to Vincent's past. It began, "I don't think I do enough murders so shall not only do them in Whitechapel but in Brixton, Battersea & Clapham."[9] Then towards the end he wrote, "I expect to rip up a woman or two on the Common at Clapham Junction one day next week."

Vincent was in a reflective mood when he wrote this Ripper letter. He was reminiscing about when he had lived in London. Brixton was where he had lived with the Loyers on Hackford Road. The Battersea and Clapham areas were where he had likely lived when he first arrived in London, and also, the area where he had likely chosen his first two victims from. He may have even pinpointed the location of his first boardinghouse by mentioning Clapham Common. This is where Battersea Rise is located—the same area Sweetman estimated Vincent had lived.

To further show his state of mind, Vincent chose to sign this letter, not as Jack the Ripper, but as "The Whore Killer." He was not writing specifically in character this time, but instead, because he was reminiscing on his past murders, he was writing simply as a murderer of prostitutes, or "The Whore Killer."

On Saturday night, October 6, Vincent likely again visited some of the pubs he loved. Then, on Sunday morning, he dropped two more Ripper letters in pillar boxes, one in the E.C. district and another in the S.E. District. Because it was Sunday, the contents of the pillar boxes would not be collected until Monday morning. Vincent knew this, and the delay in delivery may have prompted him to decide it was finally time to end the fun and return to Arles.

I believe he made use of his return ticket to Paris that evening, Sunday, October 7. He may have chosen to take the 6:28 p.m. train to Dover from the Cannon Street station, but just before boarding the train, he dropped another two Ripper letters in pillar boxes.[10] It was his last bit of fun before leaving. It gave him comfort to know that all four letters he sent that day would be delivered on Monday, making it seem to the police he was still there mingling with their populous.

Once again escaping London without being held accountable for his evil deeds, Vincent's train arrived in Dover at 9:25 p.m. He then only had a thirty-five-minute wait for the steamer, and then he was over the Channel and in Calais at 11:45 p.m. Because of the 3rd class ticket, he would then possibly have as much as a five-hour wait for the train to Paris, but I believe Vincent decided to take a slight detour this time, and he left behind a letter trail to prove it.

Just an hour after arriving in Calais, I believe Vincent possibly boarded the 12:44 a.m. train for Lille and arrived there at 3:00 a.m.[11] Arriving so early in the morning, he would have found a vacant spot in a park or a patch of woods to get some sleep. Then, with the new day beginning, he set out to fulfill his purpose for being there.

It wasn't predominately a mischievous intent which brought Vincent to Lille, but instead, it was his artistic hunger. A museum there had some Adolphe Monticelli paintings on display.[12] Valuing the artist's use of bright colors and believing he was Monticelli's replacement, Vincent wanted to have a closer look at more of his paintings. Vincent offered the verification himself that he knew there were Monticelli paintings at this museum in a letter he wrote later to the art critic, Albert Aurier. After noting that Aurier should drop by Theo's place to see a bouquet they owned by Monticelli, he wrote of a Monticelli painting, "In a museum in the north however—the one in Lille I think, there must still be a marvel by him." [13]

After bathing his eyes in Monticelli's paintings, he could no longer ignore the call of Arles. He had been gone a long time, and he needed to get back. But before boarding the train for Paris, he did as he had done in London before leaving, and he dropped a Ripper letter in a French mailbox, giving away to history that Jack the Ripper had been in Lille.

Both the letter and envelope have survived, but the area where the postage should be has been torn away, so there is no stamp or postmark. However, a catalogue card was created when the police received it in London, and it was noted the letter was from Lille and was dated October 8. The letter itself was stamped with a Metropolitan Police ink stamp with the date of October 11, as can be seen in figure 15.2, which provides when the police opened it.

The letter has some unique qualities. For one thing, it is the only Jack the Ripper letter received in London which was written in French and received from France. It was also the only Ripper letter written on graph paper, which reveals a distinct connection to Vincent.

Vincent wrote his letters to Theo and others on a variety of types of paper. He used plain paper, but he also used three different types of graph paper. The different patterns of grid lines consisted of small rectangles, large squares, and small squares (figure 15.3, graph paper samples). The Lille Ripper letter was written on the same small square graph paper Vincent used. Both the Lille letter and Vincent's letters also have the grid lines on both the front and back of the paper. There is also something unique about the pattern of the grid lines on the Lille letter that offers a clue. The left edge is missing a vertical line, so that the space from the edge to the next vertical line is the width of two of the small squares. The length of the letter is eight inches, but the true width of the paper is undeterminable due to the right edge being torn.

In comparing the Lille Ripper letter to Vincent's letters, the best choice would be one with the small square graph paper which was nearest the date of the Lille letter of October 8. This would be a letter which Pickvance dated as October 22,[14] shown in figure 15.4. This letter has the same size small squares, but the length is eight-and-a-quarter inches, a quarter inch longer than the Lille letter. Also, none of the edges have a missing line. It would appear Vincent's small square graph paper was not exactly the same as the Lille letter. But using the attributes of the Lille letter and comparing those to more of Vincent's letters reveals there is indeed a hidden match.

Vincent's October 22 letter was the first letter he had written using the small square graph paper in nearly four months. This was unusual. Before this time, he regularly used the small square paper. This would suggest he was out of this type of graph paper for those four months. Another clue that supports this is found in the letter he last wrote using this paper, which was on June 29.[15] The pattern of small squares of this letter is also uniform to all edges—however, the length of the paper was only eight inches, a quarter inch shorter than his October 22 letter, but exactly matching to the length of the Lille letter!

Vincent's small square letters in the immediate time before the June 29 letter and after the October 22 letter are all eight-and-a-quarter inches in length, so there had to be something unique about the June 29 letter being shorter. Because this was the last small square paper he used before a four-month gap of not using the paper, I believe this was the last page of a packet—the shorter length being an intended result to mark the end of a packet.

So then, what is the significance of Vincent's June 29 letter and the Lille letter being the same length? I believe it is because, not only was a sheet cut shorter to signify the end of a packet, but so too was the sheet at the beginning of a packet cut shorter to signify the beginning of a new packet. I believe Vincent ran out of the small square graph paper with the writing of his June 29 letter. He then went on writing letters for four months using other graph paper and plain paper. He brought plain paper with him to London and used all he had to write Jack the Ripper letters. When he arrived in Lille, he got the clever idea of sending another Ripper letter from there. Why not? There was no way for anyone to trace it to him. But he was out of paper. He still had plain paper and other graph paper back in Arles, so he chose to buy what he was out of—the small square graph paper. He then used the first sheet of a new packet to write the Lille Ripper letter, and therefore it has a shorter length. Then, after he returned to Arles, he used the next sheet of small square paper to write the October 22 letter, and it was the normal length, the longer length.

Not only was the length an indicator of the beginning and end of a packet of graph paper, but I believe the missing vertical line was also intended for this same purpose—signifying that a packet had started and another had ended. If this were the case, then it might be possible to look at Vincent's future letters and see if the end of this new packet showed itself. It does.

Six and seven months later in April and May of 1889, two of Vincent's letters of the small square type have the missing vertical line.[16] But both letters have the longer length of eight-and-a-quarter inches. I believe the reason is because these are warnings that the packet is about empty, because, just a few letters later, the end of the packet shows itself. Two letters then have both indicators—they are both missing a vertical line on the edge, and they are both only eight inches in length, exactly matching to the Lille letter![17] After continuing to regularly use the small squares, his use of this graph paper stopped after these two letters, and he didn't use the small squares again until twelve months later.[18]

Vincent van Gogh wrote the Ripper letter from Lille, and this connection of graph paper shows that he left a silent paper trail as he traveled from England back to France. But his trip wasn't over yet, nor his paper trail. He took the train from Lille to Paris, possibly taking the 1:20 p.m. train, which would put him in Paris at 5:25 p.m.[19] Because he was traveling third-class and likely using the return ticket of his roundtrip ticket to get back to Arles, his best option with the least stops was the 7:15 p.m. train to Tarascon.[20] From there he could catch a quick thirty-minute local train to Arles.

He had less than a two-hour wait in Paris before his train left, and idle hands need something to do, so Vincent found a quiet corner and sat down and wrote another Ripper letter. This time, though, he addressed the letter to the head of the Criminal Investigation Department in Paris, Mr. Goron. The Paris papers were also covering his murders, why not get them in on the fun?

The Paris newspaper, *Le Figaro,* obliged. Mr. Goron had received the letter either on the 9th or 10th, and *Le Figaro* published it in Paris on the 11th. The Parisians could then read the letter and feel they were also part of the Ripper story. The Paris correspondent of the *Daily News* saw the letter and telegraphed its contents back to London, and it was dutifully printed in their paper on the 12th. In their article, it is noted the letter was received by Mr. Goron "yesterday." Since the story was in *Le Figaro* on the 11th, and because the Paris correspondent likely telegraphed his story also on the 11th, then "yesterday" would have been the 10th, or possibly even the 9th.

Dropping the letter in a Paris mailbox before boarding the 7:15 p.m. train on October 8, it wouldn't be picked up and delivered until the next morning, the 9th, and that's when the police likely received it. It was then decided to give it to the papers on the 10th, and they published it in Paris on the 11th. Regardless of the preciseness of the receipt of the letter, the time frame matches to the time frame Vincent was passing through Paris from Lille after leaving London. He had left a letter trail on his path of escape. If the police had considered the murderer might not live in London, they could have at least tracked him to Paris.

In the Paris Ripper letter, Vincent chose to give an explanation for why they were hearing from him in Paris. He wrote, "There are partners, I and another, in this business. One is in England and the other in France." In a way, this was true. Vincent was acting as two.

He also noted, "We are seeking in the human body that which the doctors have never found." Since he was writing this in another role, as a partner, he appropriately didn't sign it Jack the Ripper, but instead wrote the cryptic initials "H.L.P.C."

Vincent caught the train for Tarascon and left behind his trail of letters. He would be back in Arles the next morning. His mind turned to worrying about finding a letter waiting for him from Theo. If it had been there a few days, then Theo would be wondering why he hadn't heard back. Still in a letter-writing mood, Vincent likely began a few draft letters to prepare what he would write Theo. A psychopath must always be prepared.

16

The S. Problem
1885-1886

Fleeing on a train after one of his earlier murders, that of his father, and after failing to do the same to his mother, Vincent left his family behind in Nuenen, Holland at the end of November 1885 and arrived in Antwerp, Belgium. He found a place to stay and applied for and was accepted at the Art Academy, and the ever-reliable Theo came through and sent him enough money to live on.

Vincent began feverishly working to improve his craft. Before this time, he had been painting with a dark and drab pallet. Being exposed to the work of the Impressionists, he began following their technique, and his pallet lightened up and carried more color. He was inspired and excited about his improving abilities. He wanted to learn more about the Impressionists, and to do that, he needed to be in Paris where Theo just happened to reside.

In February of 1886, Vincent began to hint at moving to Paris. But Theo wasn't prepared to handle Vincent living with him in his apartment, and he told Vincent he would have to wait. But Vincent did what he wanted, no matter what others said, and after spending only three months in Antwerp, Vincent boarded a train and arrived in Paris to surprise Theo at the beginning of March.

Vincent arrived ready to work, and Theo got him started by introducing him to the many artists he knew. Vincent had also already planned to attend the well-known Paris art studio of Fernand Cormon. He was allowed to attend, and this was where he first came into contact with other artists such as Émile Bernard, John Russell, and Henri Lautrec.

Bernard described later how the other artists at Cormon's studio viewed Vincent (figure 16.1, photo of Vincent's back). He noted they laughed at him, but Vincent didn't seem to notice.[1] A fellow attending artist, François Gauzi, added that other students were afraid of him, and so they avoided teasing him.[2] Another artist, Archibald Hartrick, also described Vincent later, writing, "In some aspects Van Gogh was personally as simple as a child, expressing pleasure and pain loudly in a childlike manner."[3] Hartrick added, "We thought him 'cracked' but harmless, perhaps not interesting enough to bother much about."

Attending Cormon's Studio and living in Theo's apartment, Vincent used the opportunity to abuse his enemy up close. The aggressive accusations and blame previously directed at his mother and father now turned to Theo, and Theo was immediately faced with the direct assault of Vincent's anger and envy.

Andries Bonger, Theo's close friend and a fellow Dutchman living in Paris, was unaccustomed to Vincent's ways. He described Vincent in a letter at the time: "What a queer life this brother has led. The man hasn't the slightest notion of social conditions. He is always quarreling with everybody. Consequently Theo has a lot of trouble getting along with him."[4]

By June 1886, Vincent's attacks on Theo were in full swing, and Andries wrote in another letter the effect it was having on Theo: "The poor fellow has many cares. Moreover, his brother is making life rather a burden to him, and reproaches him with all kinds of things of which he is quite innocent."[5]

Fortunately for Theo, near the end of July, it was time for his annual trip home to Holland, [6] and he was able to get out from under Vincent's reproaches for a time. But this trip was more than a vacation for Theo. He had a few things planned which he hoped would change the course of his life.

Theo had met Andries' sister, Johanna Bonger, on his trip home the year before. He was now sure he was in love with her, and he wanted to let her know and ask for her hand.[7] Theo was also attempting, with Andries as his partner, to start his own art gallery, and he planned to use his trip home to ask Uncle Cent to invest in his business venture.[8]

Vincent was left behind in Paris, and to keep him company, Andries stayed with him in Theo's apartment while Theo was away. But someone else was also living in Theo's apartment. A girl. Theo had a live-in girlfriend. Her name is not known, but in a letter sent from Vincent and Andries to Theo while he was away in Holland, they mysteriously referred to her only as S.[9]

A problem had developed with S. before Theo had left for Holland, and it persisted while he was away. Theo considered their relationship over, and he wanted S. out of his apartment, but she wouldn't leave. Worried about the continued situation back in his Paris apartment, Theo wrote to Vincent from Holland and said bluntly of his stubborn girlfriend, "Either she gets out or I will."[10]

Vincent wrote back he didn't think Theo's "solution to the S. problem . . . practicable."[11] He agreed Theo and S. were not suited for one another and must part company, but he believed if Theo were harsh with her, it would "drive her to suicide or insanity."

Vincent wasn't truly worried about what might happen to S., but he was worried what affect her downfall might have on Theo, and he added, "The repercussions on you would be sad indeed and leave you a broken man." And if Theo were so distraught, then Vincent would also be negatively impacted. He couldn't allow that to happen when his artistic abilities were improving so well in Paris.

Looking for a solution to the S. problem, Vincent suggested to Theo that he "should try and pass her on to somebody else." He then offered a quirky idea, writing, "An amicable arrangement, which would seem obvious, could be reached by your passing her on to me." He went on, "I am ready to take S. off your hands, i.e. preferably *without* having to marry her, but if the worst comes to the worst *even* agreeing to a mariage de raison [marriage of convenience]."[12]

Incredibly, not only was Vincent prepared to offer himself as a replacement in Theo's failed relationship with S., but he was even willing to go the full measure and marry the girl. To most, this is extreme, but for Vincent-the-psychopath, considering such extreme measures was simply what was needed.

Vincent knew of Theo's plans to reveal his true feelings to Johanna, and he recognized the S. problem was causing Theo distress, so his offer to take S. off his hands was meant to alleviate Theo's concerns. He told Theo of the intended consequence: "You would feel a free man, and your engagement might come off a la vapeur [full steam]."[13]

He then noted that both Andries and S. were sleeping in the apartment and remarked about S., "These are queer days; at times we are very much afraid of her, and at other times we are almighty gay and light-hearted. But S. is seriously deranged, and she is not cured yet by a long shot." S. appeared to be a bit touched. She may have been a good match for Vincent, after all.

Vincent then advised Theo that upon his return he must "talk a lot with her, and try to get her settled down." He added, "aux grands maux les grands remedes [serious diseases demand serious remedies]."[14]

Andries added his comments about S. at the end of this same letter. He agreed with Vincent's assessment, and wrote, "The problem is that S.'s eyes must be opened. She is not the least bit in love with you, but it is as if you have cast a spell on her. Morally she is seriously ill."[15] He continued, "We have been as kind as possible to her. If we hadn't, she would have gone mad." He further added he was optimistic about her recovery because of something she had said which indicated she understood what was the matter with her. He quoted S. as having said, "How stupid I am not to be able to set up a reasoning."

Obviously, S. was wrestling with some sort of psychological issue, but Andries added an assessment which showed there was something more: "The great difficulty is her obstinacy, which we have repeatedly bumped our heads against, as against a stone wall." He then said he thought Vincent's idea was impracticable, and he also revealed that Theo's relationship with S. was more than a fly-by-night one, and he wrote, "During the past year your relations have had no other result than getting her hopelessly muddled." This letter was written around the end of July or beginning of August of 1886, which means S. was living there when Vincent had expressed impatiently back in February that he wanted to move to Paris from Antwerp. This explains, at least in part, why Theo wanted Vincent to wait—he hadn't told him S. was living there.

Andries went on to suggest to Theo about S.: "If she could live a month with somebody else who would be able to satisfy her sensuality and take care of her (for she requires a lot of care) so that she might recover her health, you would be forgotten." He then concluded, "The situation is not at all hopeless, though it is precarious."

It sounded as if Theo had again developed a relationship with a prostitute, as he had previously done with a girl named Marie. References to S.'s strong sensuality and being morally seriously ill, along with her stubbornness to leave his apartment, suggest this may have been the case. Also, Vincent's flippant suggestion to take her off Theo's hands was another indicator. It seemed S. had nowhere to go, and this was likely the reason she refused to leave the apartment.

Theo may have thought it was fun while it lasted, but he wanted a wife, and he hoped Johanna would be this to him. He couldn't have S. hanging around the apartment if Johanna agreed to an engagement. If she found out, it might be enough to scare her off.

Theo had written Vincent in hopes he would pressure S. into leaving before he came back. Theo may have been hoping Johanna would return with him to Paris after she agreed to an engagement to visit with him and her brother. S. couldn't be there.

Vincent understood this, and he took it upon himself to find the solution to the S. problem. However, offering to take her off Theo's hands may have only been an option intended to allow her to stay in the apartment. Then, when Johanna arrived, S. and Vincent would agree to say S. was Vincent's girl. Further evidence this was how Vincent was thinking is found in the same letter. After he offered to take S., he then said this would allow her to keep house for Theo.

There was only one problem with Vincent's proposal—S. was stubborn. She wouldn't go along with it. She was attached to Theo, and she wouldn't let go. Vincent didn't do well when others wouldn't follow his will, especially when their actions threatened to interfere with his advancement as an artist. The S. problem was becoming serious and required a more serious solution, and as he had noted to Theo—serious diseases demand serious remedies. Vincent knew what was needed.

With Theo out of town for about another three weeks, Vincent still had plenty of time to come up with something. But for what he wanted to do, it was better if he did it sooner rather than later. Better to have everything taken care of and out of the way long before Theo returned so there would be less chance of Theo discovering the true method Vincent had used to solve the S. problem.

Being an experienced psychopathic killer, Vincent's demented yet calculating mind only needed to be presented with a problem in order to activate and find the most effective and delightful solution. By Tuesday, August 3, Vincent knew what he would like to do, and he enacted his devious plan to get rid of S.

Vincent likely began being more friendly towards S. a few days earlier. He would have avoided the usual arguments, as he had done before he had murdered his father. Then, on the 3rd, he may have invited her to come along with him on one of his regular excursions to the outskirts of Paris where he sat out in nature and painted. They could make a picnic of it, and he could paint her portrait out in a field of ripening wheat.

Having been worked on for a few days, S. must have set aside any misgivings she normally had of Vincent, and believing he was not attempting to lure her away from Theo's apartment, she agreed to go along. After all, it was a beautiful late summer day in Paris. A picnic would be nice. She may have made some sandwiches and looked for something to carry the food and wine in. Vincent told her he would take care of that, and he asked her to change into the green silk skirt he liked. He may have said it would go well against the golden wheat. Flattered, she did as asked, while Vincent placed the sandwiches and wine on the dining room table and pulled up the corners of the tablecloth and twisted the ends together to form a sack. He then tied a cord around the end to secure it and threw it over his shoulder. He handed S. a blank canvas to carry, took his bag of paint supplies in his other hand, and the two of them left Theo's apartment for a pleasant day in the country, looking very much like two Parisian lovers enthralled with one another and the world around them.

A tram driver named Mr. Pamplume had a problem. It was less serious than the S. problem which Vincent sought to solve for Theo, but pressing all the same—he needed to use the bathroom. His shift had ended just after midnight on Wednesday, August 4, and he was making his way home along Avenue d'Orleans in Montrouge, a suburb in the south of Paris. [16] There were plenty of shops and restaurants along the way where he could pop in and use their toilet, but it was 12:30 a.m.—they had closed hours ago. He needed to find a spot to relieve himself soon.

Fortunately, traveling the same route home every night, Mr. Pamplume knew where the outdoor street urinals were located, and he knew that just up ahead one was located near the side wall of the Saint Pierre de Montrouge Church, and he quickly crossed the road.

This particular urinal had three compartments. He turned into the first, but seeing there was some sort of object sticking out of the bowl of the urinal, he exited that compartment and went to the next. That one was empty, and he relieved himself. Out of curiosity, he returned to the first compartment to investigate the object.

There was little light to see by, but he could make out that the object was wrapped in some fabric, about two feet long, and tied in the middle with a cord. It was some sort of package, but who would leave it in a urinal like that?

Mr. Pamplume apparently considered himself a responsible citizen, and he felt it was his duty to find out what was in this strange package. So, he reached down and peeled back a corner of the fabric. He wasn't expecting to see a woman's hand, but there it was.

Horrified, Mr. Pamplume hastened to notify the police officer stationed at the corner, and they took the macabre package to the police station on Avenue d'Orleans.[17]

The Police Commissioner of District 14, Mr. Percha, was called for, and he sent for a doctor to examine the contents of the package.[18] It contained a woman's arms and lower legs. The arms had been cut off at the shoulders, and the lower legs had been separated at the knees.

The limbs had been wrapped together in two different materials. The outer layer was of white oilcloth and was believed to be a tablecloth.[19] It had recent coffee, grease, and wine stains.[20] Inside this, the arms and legs were wrapped in a section of a green silk skirt. [21] The cord that tied it all together was braided and about six feet long.

A short distance away, and a few hours later, between 3:00 and 3:30 a.m., two workers stopped at a street urinal located in front of 131 Rue d'Alesia and made another discovery of a female body part.[22] The urinal was set in an alcove, and a metal shield provided privacy for the user, but it also provided concealment for the murderer, allowing him to deposit his cargo unseen.[23]

The two men weren't as fortunate as Mr. Pamplume. His find was wrapped and therefore less shocking, at least on first sight. Their find was free of packaging, naked and gruesome.[24] In the urinal bowl, there rested the pelvis of a woman with only the right thigh attached. The body part was taken to the police station and was found to match to the already collected lower legs and arms.[25]

About an hour later, at 4:15 a.m., a young farmer named Mr. Chatenay was walking alongside the railway belt in Montrouge on Rue Giordano Bruno when he noticed something resting on the top of an embankment that dropped down from the street to the railway line—which passed this area in a deep trench.[26] Rue des Plantes intersects Rue Giordano Bruno running north to south and crosses over the trench and tracks via a bridge.

Mr. Chatenay was about sixty-five feet away from the bridge when he caught sight of the object.[27] As he approached, he saw a street sweeper nearby, Mr. Desse, and called him over and pointed through a breach in a lattice fence and said, "Look there, a sheep's back."[28]

Mr. Desse bravely entered through the breach in the lattice to investigate. The object was lying in the midst of some acacia just inside the fence. Mr. Desse quickly realized the piece of meat was not sheep but human. It was a female torso with the left breast cut off. The ribs on the right side were fractured and bone fragments poked through the flesh.[29] The police were called and collected the torso and matched it up with the other parts of the woman.[30]

The police searched the area that morning for the still missing pieces, but to no avail. The head, left breast, left thigh, stomach and intestines, and the internal parts of the pelvis were not found.[31] The pieces that were found were examined and it was reported they were "temporarily enshrined in the freezing apparatus."[32]

The doctors estimated the age of the victim to be anywhere from 18 to 25 years old.[33] Based on her arm hair, they believed she had brown hair, and they estimated her height at about 5'.[34] She had white skin and was small but plump. Her hands and feet were poorly maintained. The index finger of her right hand had needle pricks, but they believed she only used the needle from time to time and was not a dressmaker or seamstress.[35] They suggested she may have had many lovers but for some reason didn't believe she was a prostitute.

The remains were noted to be in a state of rigor mortis.[36] They therefore believed death was recent and estimated she had been murdered no earlier than the afternoon of the day before her body parts were discovered.

The police decided to exhibit the tablecloth, the cord, and the piece of green silk skirt at the morgue for public viewing, believing someone might recognize the items and provide them with the identity of the victim.[37] Unfortunately, the items were not recognized, and the victim's identity remained a mystery.

By choosing to conceal the head, as he had also done with some of the other parts of the woman, the murderer had succeeded in keeping the identity of his victim hidden. *Le Figaro* reported bluntly on August 5 what needed to be found: "We continue to seek the head."[38] In their August 8 issue, it seemed they might have been rewarded. They reported at daybreak of the previous morning they watched as police officers arrived with a team of diggers at a garden in Rue des Plantes near where the torso had been discovered. The diggers were being directed where to dig by an officer who carried a piece of paper. The paper was an anonymous letter received by the Chief of Detectives, Mr. Taylor. The writer had confessed to know where the missing head was buried and instructed Mr. Taylor where to dig for it in a garden. After upturning twenty different areas without finding the head, the digging was called off, and the letter was deemed a hoax.

Continuing their search for more body parts and for the scene of the crime, the police did find a bloodstained newspaper and black silk scarf on the slope of the railway trench near where the torso was found, but neither item was believed to be related to the crime.[39]

The arms and legs which were found in the urinal near the church were the only body parts wrapped. The torso near the railway and the pelvis with the right thigh in the urinal on Rue d'Alesia, were left unwrapped. This offers a good clue to the order the body parts were dropped, and therefore also to the direction the murderer was moving, which could help pinpoint where the victim was killed.

Because the tablecloth and cord were wrapped around the arms and legs, which were already wrapped in a green silk skirt, it can be concluded the tablecloth and cord were used as a makeshift sack to carry all the body parts. After dumping the torso, and then the pelvis, the murderer simply left the arms and legs within the green silk skirt, wrapped them in the tablecloth, and tied the package in the middle with the cord. He continued on to the urinal by the church and dropped the package in one of the urinals—no longer having a need to keep the makeshift sack. With this in mind, the route the murderer took can be determined to be from south to north, moving from the first drop near the railroad tracks to the last drop by the church.

Also validating the direction taken is the logical assumption the murderer would drop the heavier parts first—the torso being the greatest burden and therefore dropped first. The pelvis with the attached right thigh was the next heaviest piece and was dropped second. Lastly, the lighter arms and lower legs were left in the makeshift sack and deposited.

Accepting that the first drop location was the torso on Rue Giordano Bruno near the Rue des Plantes Bridge, and that the murderer was heading north, it can then be presumed the murder site was likely to the south of this—believing the murderer was dropping the pieces as he fled to the north away from the scene of the crime. It so happened, a nice place for a murder was only a short distance to the south at the Montrouge Cemetery.

Vincent enjoyed visiting cemeteries, and he may have previously visited the Montrouge Cemetery, possibly on one of his many excursions. But there was another reason which made the Montrouge area a good place for a murder. Deep below the surface, a maze of dark tunnels had long ago been carved through the bedrock beneath Paris. Limestone had been extracted from these quarries and was used to construct the buildings of Paris. In 1786, a hundred years before Vincent's time, because of overcrowded cemeteries and the dwindling availability of usable land, it was decided the bones of the dead would be transferred from the cemeteries to the tunnels down below.[40] Femur bones and skulls were neatly stacked to the ceiling throughout the tunnels creating eerie sorts of works of art. In the end, the bones of approximately six million Parisians were moved into the catacombs.

A place such as this, with its stench of death and morbid creations, would have certainly attracted both the artistic and murderous sides of Vincent. During his time, guided tours through the catacombs under Montrouge had already been in operation for decades.[41] Visitors were guided down a spiral staircase deep into the earth carrying candles and boxes of matches as they journeyed along the dark and damp underworld. But the tour only explored the main section of the catacombs. Many smaller tunnels also branched off from the main tunnel, and many hidden entrances and vent tubes existed, through which vagrants and criminals could steal away and get lost in the tunnels.

After deciding the best solution to the S. problem was to lure his victim to another part of Paris and kill her, Vincent must have considered other suburbs which were far enough away from Theo's apartment in the north district of Montmartre, but the cemetery and catacombs of Montrouge made it an easy choice (figure 16.2, Paris map).

Naturally, Vincent didn't want to kill S. and leave her pieces in Montmartre where others who knew her in the area might identify her, even if they didn't find her head. He had to convince her to go with him as far away as he could. Luring her with a picnic in the country and the prospect of painting her portrait may have been just the sort of bait Vincent used to pull S. away from Theo's apartment.

S. was in the midst of an emotionally and psychologically draining situation. She knew she was no longer welcome in Theo's apartment, but Vincent didn't treat her harshly and demand she leave. Instead, he likely played the caring and understanding friend who wanted to show her he cared about her. Andries even followed Vincent's lead and did the same, as he had described in the letter to Theo, when he noted, "We have been as kind as possible to her. If we hadn't, she would have gone mad."

But for Vincent-the-psychopath, this was only a ploy. At the first sign of S.'s stubbornness to leave, Vincent knew what had to be done, and he began to put on his act of kindness. Whether she was a prostitute or not, her stubbornness against doing what she was told, and the resulting attitude which caused her to believe she deserved to stay there with Theo, would have triggered within Vincent the anger he had towards the ambitious type of women—those women who he had said were like Lady Macbeth.[42]

Besides despising S. for her similarity to Lady Macbeth, Vincent was willing to take extreme measures to deal with S. because she was threatening to disrupt his progress of becoming a great artist. His progress with his art had been impacted by a girlfriend of Theo's once before when a few years earlier Theo had chosen to support Marie over continuing to send Vincent enough money to support himself, Sien, and her two children. He was forced to move back home and live with his parents and endure all the conflict which then ensued. He couldn't do anything about Marie at that time, but now that he was faced with another girlfriend of Theo's who could cause him trouble, he would not hesitate to make use of his acquired skills to solve the S. problem.

It had been many years since he had murdered and cut up the woman in 1873 and the other in 1874, but it had only been a little over a year since he had murdered his father in March of 1885. Not only had a situation again arisen which called for murder as the solution, but also, Vincent was looking forward to it. And when Theo's annual trip to Holland approached, he knew he would have his opportunity to strike.

With Theo out of town, Vincent's niceties towards S. had likely softened her enough for her to agree to a day in the country in Montrouge. On their way back, Vincent either led her through Montrouge Cemetery to see the interesting monuments or, because he had so completely won over her trust, he convinced her to follow him down a seldom used entrance he knew to enter the catacombs. The catacombs would have been his first choice. If she were too afraid, though, then the cemetery would do just fine.

If S. was in an adventurous mood and was disarmed by Vincent's charm, and she chose to follow him into the catacombs, then Vincent only had to lead her to one of the many small chambers where a quick knock on the head would keep her from echoing a scream through the web of tunnels. Then he could cut and dismember her body at his leisure by the light of a candle.

If she were in a more timid and less trusting mood, the catacombs would be replaced with a quiet walk through the cemetery at night. The monuments offered sufficient cover for Vincent to strike his blow and drag the body into a dark place to take care of the cutting.

If he murdered her in the catacombs, he had the option of throwing the parts behind one of the stacks of ancient bones where eventually her skull and femur would look like the others. If it were the cemetery, he could have slid aside the heavy cover of one of the aboveground tombs and dumped the pieces and guts inside and then returned the cover.

Regardless of how he disposed of the missing parts, he had decided he wanted to display the remaining parts. Murderers generally don't want their victims to be found. However, psychopathic, sexual serial killers tend to want to show their power and control over their victims and over society. In many cases, they choose to leave the body or body parts of their victims on display to create shock. This was a signature of the murder in Montrouge, and it was also the signature of the London murders of 1873 and 1874. Similarly, the same need to display his victim even showed up in the murder of his father, depositing his body on the threshold of his own home.

This characteristic also continued two years later in September of 1888 with the Whitehall torso, which was placed in the cellar on the construction site of police headquarters in London. Also, the bodies of the Jack the Ripper victims Tabram, Nichols, Chapman, Stride and Eddowes, were all placed to be easily discovered.

Vincent was a planner. Not only had he chosen beforehand to entice S. to Montrouge for her death, where he had carefully chosen the possible murder sites, but he had also planned to cut her up, hide the head and some of the parts, then drop the other parts to be found. As with his other murders, Vincent had fantasized about the murder and needed to follow the script of what he desired to happen. Every aspect of what he did was important. The success of luring her into the area to kill her; the committing of the murder itself; the cutting of her body and hiding the parts; and then the carrying away of certain parts and placing them where they could be found, were all necessary to the fulfilling of his fantasies of the crime.

Whether or not he lured S. to Montrouge with the temptation of a scenic picnic in the country, he brought the tablecloth and cord along with him, either using the items to form a makeshift sack to hold the picnic supplies, or he carried them in his art bag for later use. Either way, he had already devised and planned on using the tablecloth and cord as a means to covertly transport and place S.'s body parts in other areas.

The drop points were also likely chosen ahead of time, at least in regard to making use of the two street urinals as cover for placing the body parts. But most definitely he knew ahead of time he wanted to leave some parts in the urinal next to Montrouge Church. That one had religious significance and meaning for him, and he made sure his route would lead to it.

After he cut up S.'s body and hid the head and other parts, he then cut away a section of her green silk skirt and used it to wrap together the arms and lower legs. He did this to keep them together, but mainly he was thinking of minimizing bloodstains on the tablecloth.

He likely placed this package of limbs lengthwise in what would be the bottom of the makeshift sack. Then the other two pieces of the body were placed on top of this in the same order they were when they were attached— the pelvis with the right thigh, and on top of that, the torso. He used a black silk scarf S. was wearing and some sheets of newspaper to cover the cut ends. This also helped prevent staining of the tablecloth that might show through and be noticed. With each of the pieces stacked lengthwise, he then pulled up the corners and twisted and tied them together with the cord. Any blood which remained in the pelvis and torso which happened to drip down to the arms and legs would be absorbed by the skirt before leaking through and showing on the bottom of the sack. Vincent was a careful killer.

With his grizzly package prepared for transport, Vincent grabbed the knotted end of the sack and swung it over his shoulder. Then, tucking his canvas under his arm and carrying his art bag in his free hand, he headed north out of the cemetery, or up and then north out of the catacombs along Rue des Plantes.

It wasn't long before he saw his first opportunity to place a piece of his victim. As he crossed over the bridge above the railway trench, he removed the torso from the sack and tossed it over the side onto the embankment so that it would be seen (figure 16.3, locations of body parts). When he threw the torso, the newspaper and S.'s black scarf, which he used to cover the ends, came loose and floated down into the trench where they were later found.

Having deposited the heavy torso, Vincent's load was much easier to manage, and he continued north and deposited his next piece, the pelvis with right thigh, in the street urinal on Rue d' Alesia. He then rolled the arms and legs up in the tablecloth and quickly tied the package together in the center to hold the limbs together. He tucked his grisly package under his arm and carried it east on Rue d'Alesia until he reached the circle-around where the major roads of Montrouge met and where the tall steeple of Montrouge Church rose up and faced the circle from the north. In this busier area, Vincent knew he had to be a bit more careful in making his last delivery.

As he crossed in front of the church, he must have considered dropping his package on the front steps, on the threshold. He would have loved that. However, it was too risky a move, and he stuck to his plan and turned onto Rue d'Orleans and walked a short way to the north until he reached the three-compartment street urinal located near the side wall of the church.

Seeing the first urinal vacant, he stepped in and removed the package from under his arm and placed it upright in the bowl and then continued north on Rue d'Orleans. He was soon clear of the area and clear of possible suspicion.

Vincent continued on a direct route to the north, and in no time, he was on Boulevard Saint Michel crossing over the River Seine. He may have hesitated on the bridge to look upriver and appreciate the ominous Notre Dame Cathedral. The shimmering yellow light on the water from a few streetlamps must have tempted him to stop and paint the scene, but he knew on this night it was best to keep moving. He continued north to Montmartre and to Theo's apartment, where he was safe, and where there was no longer an S. problem.

To Vincent's great delight, on Thursday, August 5, a day after the early morning discoveries of his gruesome deliveries and his retreat back to Theo's apartment, the Paris newspapers began reporting the shocking details of the severed pieces of a woman's body being discovered out on the streets of Montrouge. It had been many years since he felt the thrill of reading about his work in the papers, and just as he had wanted more of it back in 1873 after his first murder, he wanted more now. He wanted to keep the story going, keep the fun alive, and on August 6, he repeated what he had done after his 1873 murder—he wrote a letter to the police.

This was the letter which was received by the Chief of Detectives, Mr. Taylor, where the writer confessed to being the murderer and directed him to a garden where the head was supposedly buried. Not finding the head, it was thought the letter was a hoax, but Vincent knew better, and again he was pleased to see one of his letters published in a newspaper—especially so because the police had followed his directions and had wasted their time looking for the head.

With Theo's return to Paris still a few weeks away, Vincent had no worries of his brother reading the Paris accounts of a butchered young girl in Montrouge and connecting it to why S. was no longer inhabiting his apartment. Andries had a chance to put it together, though, but Vincent took care of his suspicion before it could get started with some well-crafted lie about where S. was. Something about visiting her sick mother in Lyon ought to do.

With so much time remaining before Theo's return, Vincent's psychopathic mind wondered why he should be limited to only sending one letter to the police. There was no reason why he couldn't send another, so he did.

His deviant brain was not only thinking of the joy another letter would bring but, just as with the Meat Market letter in 1873 and the recent Find the Head letter to Mr. Taylor, he had a purpose in mind. He wanted to continue to mislead and misdirect the police. It was unlikely anyone in Montmartre who knew S. would suspect it was her body parts that were found at the opposite end of Paris in Montrouge, so Vincent didn't really have much to worry about. But murder causes paranoia, and Vincent wanted to help keep the Paris police off his trail. Besides, he enjoyed it.

On August 10, *Le Petite* reported a letter had been received the previous day by Commissioner Percha. They described the writer of the letter as "a joker who has demonstrated bad taste." The letter bore the postmark of the city of Tours, and the writer announced, apparently due to the guilt he felt over the murder, he planned to throw himself into the River Loire, which runs through Tours.

It was noted the writer had made an effort to conceal the writing, and they described the letter as being "designed in a style of an unbridled romance." Additional details of the contents of the letter were not given, but it seems Vincent gave another romantic account of how he had so sweetly murdered and cut up his victim, as he had done in the Meat Market letter. This is too remarkable and unusually similar a style between the two letters to conclude it's only a coincidence.

As for the letter being postmarked from Tours and the contents relating to the river in Tours, these were only diversionary tactics from a maturing psychopathic artist. Vincent didn't need to travel to Tours to send a letter back to Paris. With his artistic skills and creative mind, it was not difficult for him to create a realistic postmark from any location he desired. Tracing around a coin on the envelope with black or red ink, adding the city name, a date, and a few other numbers, all made to look slightly messy as an inked stamp would look, was easy enough, especially if he had a sample postmark to go by. A letter to Theo from an acquaintance from Tours would fit the bill. He would put this skill of creating phony postmarks to use again in a few years to much greater effect in 1888.

Vincent must have felt some satisfaction when he saw this letter covered in *Le Petite*. However, it didn't appear the police were taking it seriously, so just a few days later, he decided to write another letter to try again to divert the attention of the police. His always creative mind provided him with a unique method of delivery. He rolled up the letter and stuck it in a bottle and threw it into the Seine.

The bottle was fished out of the river near Notre Dame at the au Double Bridge by a boater named Martin. Martin handed the bottle and letter it contained over to the police. *Le Figaro* then got their hands on it and reported on August 13 that the letter described a confession and gave the name of the murderer of the young woman in Montrouge. The letter writer was then quoted: "I throw myself into the Seine, at the de Charenton Bridge, because of family business." The letter was signed Louis de Bréville and included the Montrouge address of Avenue d'Italie, at either number 36 or 76. *Le Figaro* sent someone to check both addresses. At number 36, the occupants had never heard of a Mr. Bréville, and number 76 was a church. Knowing Vincent, the address was for the church.

The purpose of including a name and address in the letter was for leading the police to believe the murderer lived in the Montrouge area. They would be forced to waste time visiting the address and asking around for Louis de Bréville. Never finding this person, they were to then believe the letter writer's claim—that he had thrown himself into the Seine and drowned and therefore give up looking for the murderer all together.

In both the Tours letter and in this letter in the bottle, Vincent suggested the murderer had caused his own demise by throwing himself in a river. The Paris police could ignore the Tours letter, but they would, at the very least, be inclined to be on the lookout for a man's body floating in the Seine.

Vincent had control. He knew he could go on writing letters to the police and keep them off balance, and most importantly, keep them from ever considering that the victim and the murderer had lived together somewhere outside of Montrouge, and most definitely not to the north in Montmartre. But with Theo returning soon, Vincent chose to stop writing letters, and this must have been part of why he wanted the police to think he had killed himself. They could conclude they hadn't received additional letters because the murderer had indeed drowned himself.

False information and misdirection were the main purposes of the letters. However, just as with the 1873 Meat Market letter, some truth was mixed in with the exaggerations. In the letter in the bottle, the writer provided his reason for suicide as being "because of family business." It must have also been the intended conclusion to be drawn for his motive to murder the woman. This was the same motive Vincent had for murdering his brother's stubborn girlfriend—for the sake of the family business. S. was threatening to disrupt Theo's life and work, and this would disrupt Vincent's life and work.

With no other letters received from the murderer, and no other body parts or evidence being discovered, the story of the young woman cut to pieces in Montrouge disappeared from the pages of the Paris newspapers. By the time Theo returned to Paris from Holland on August 26,[43] there was nothing left for him to read about. Unless someone happened to update him on what he had missed while away, Theo would have no inclination to suspect the reason why S. was no longer living in his apartment was because she was no longer living. And, of course, Vincent would have continued the contrived story with Theo which he had begun with Andries about where S. had gone.

As much as Theo wanted S. out of his life before, he may have hoped she was still in his apartment when he returned. Things hadn't gone well for Theo on his trip home. Uncle Cent had previously promised to help Theo finance his business, but when he asked, his once supportive uncle firmly turned him down.[44]

Most certainly, the main reason Uncle Cent turned Theo down was because of Vincent's involvement. He considered Vincent poison, and with Vincent living off Theo, he knew if he gave money to Theo some of it would be wasted on his undeserving nephew who refused to provide for himself.

Theo had left on his trip to Holland with great expectations. Fully expecting Uncle Cent to keep his promise and finance him, he intended to visit Johanna to reveal his love for her believing he would have a much better chance of success with her because of his newly financed future. However, as Theo would confess to Johanna later, being bitterly disappointed after Uncle Cent reneged on his promise, and because he tied the two together, he did not go through with asking her to be his wife at the time.

Vincent would have also felt bitterly disappointed upon hearing from Theo about Uncle Cent's refusal to provide the financing. But the news had a bittersweet taste for him. Bitter, since he was hoping Theo would get the financing and start his own art gallery—which Vincent would benefit from. Sweet, because Theo had experienced disappointment and failure, and especially sweet because it was by Uncle Cent's hand.

Vincent may have also had a similar reaction after learning there would be no engagement to Johanna. Expecting Theo to procure the financing, he could have accepted Theo getting married. Fully expecting to share in the rewards of Theo's business, a wife would not have threatened him. But with no business, he was glad there would be no wife. In that situation, Theo having a wife would threaten his continuation of receiving Theo's financial support, as had happened with Theo's previous girlfriend, Marie.

Because there would be no business and no wife, and therefore things would remain the same as they were before Theo left on his trip, it must have struck Vincent as ironic that he had killed S. for no reason. It turned out it wouldn't have made any difference if he had allowed her to go on living. She could have even continued to live in Theo's apartment. Her threat to Theo's engagement or to him owning his own business no longer existed.

Vincent would have seen the irony, but being a psychopath, his emotions would have quickly turned to anger and blame directed at others—the targets being Uncle Cent, Theo, Johanna, and even S. It was their actions and involvement in his life, after all, which had forced him into a situation where murder was necessary. And if S. hadn't been so stubborn, she would still be alive. Her murder was her own fault. They had all forced his hand.

Having accepted Vincent's story of S. going off to visit her sick mother, or some other such concoction, would have been crafted so that Theo and Andries were expecting S. to return at some point. That would give more life to her dead corpse and give them no reason to suspect Vincent had actually killed her. However, after a sufficient amount of time had passed and S. hadn't returned, Andries apparently began to wonder what might have happened to S.

In his delightful book, *The Van Gogh File*, Ken Wilkie was on a journey in 1972 to uncover additional details about Vincent's life. Amazingly, he found Andries' 86-year-old second wife still alive and well and traveled to her home to interview her. He wanted to know if her husband had spoken about his time with Vincent in Paris and if he had said anything about the mysterious woman who was living in Theo's apartment. Mrs. Bonger knew about the letter Vincent and her husband had written to Theo about S. She said she had spoken to Andries about the girl and noted that when Andries "asked the brothers later what had happened to her, the question was evaded by both Vincent and Theo."

Having very likely read the reports of the Montrouge murder and noting that stubborn S. was no longer coming to the apartment, while at the same time Vincent was telling him S. had gone on a trip somewhere, Andries may have been putting the pieces together. As time passed and S. didn't return, either out of suspicion or curiosity, Andries had unwittingly asked her murderer what had happened to her. It must have only been curiosity, because if it were suspicion of Vincent, Andries would have found out the hard way, just as Vincent's father and S. had found out, that you don't threaten Vincent's future. Andries would go on to live a full life, but there were to be many others who would cross Vincent's path who would not.

17

Down At Right
October 1888

No doubt reminiscing on his murder of S. as he passed through Paris in October 1888 and caught his train south for Tarascon, Vincent then arrived in Arles at 10:10 on the morning of Tuesday the 9th.[1] He had returned after a long stay in London which included a side trip to Lille on his way back. As he walked from the train station to the Yellow House, all that must have been on his train-weary mind was checking his mail to see if and when Theo had sent him a letter.

Once again attempting to avoid a large gap in his response to a letter from Theo, Vincent had requested Theo not send his next letter until the date Vincent believed he would return from his latest trip to London on Wednesday, October 3. Vincent knew he would be low on funds after traveling and wanted the money Theo would send to arrive just when he needed it.

However, due to all the excitement in London, Vincent chose to extend his stay. If Theo followed his request, his letter sat in Arles unanswered for nearly a week. But Vincent's psychopathic mind had plenty of time on the train ride home to derive the best method for calming any suspicion that was sure to be building in Theo's mind as the days ticked by without an expected response from Vincent.

Arriving at the Yellow House, Vincent found Theo had written but had not followed his request to have it there by Wednesday the 3rd. The postmark must have revealed it wasn't sent until either Saturday the 6th or Sunday the 7th, so it either arrived in Arles on Sunday the 7th or on Monday the 8th. What a relief. He only missed it by a day or two. He could easily deal with that.

Vincent could have simply used his previous excuse of being out in the fields painting furiously and just didn't have time to write. But Vincent wanted to be sure it was firmly in Theo's mind he had been in Arles all along, so he worked at the best way to create the illusion.

Theo only sent 20 francs along with his letter. Vincent was most certainly broke after his long stay in London and his side trip to Lille. He would need more to live on, and his first action after returning on Tuesday the 9th showed his desperation. He quickly sent Theo a telegram requesting another 20 francs.[2] He was desperate for money, but mainly this was his first step in establishing the illusion for Theo that he was not only in Arles that day but had never left. This was an obvious attempt to get a quick response to Theo in order to stop any suspicion that might be growing. If he hadn't sent it, it would be another day before Theo heard from him.

Vincent then employed a tactic that would have been hard for Theo to see through at the time, which was the same tactic he had used after the Chapman murder. Returning from that murder, he had written two letters to make it look as if one was written the day before. However, this time, he expanded on the deception and wrote three different letters as if he had been writing them over the last few days, enclosing them in the same envelope and sending them all together on Tuesday, October 9.

Vincent wrote the first as if it were before he had received Theo's latest letter. He wrote, "I hope you will write soon, I am very hard up because of the stretchers and frames that I ordered."[3] Not only was he attempting to show he was asking for money before Theo sent it, but he was also establishing a reason for his request—because he had spent money on stretchers and frames.

The second letter was written to appear as if he wrote it as soon as he had received Theo's letter with the money on Monday, and he went to great pains to establish this was true. He wrote, "Thanks for your letter, but I have had a very thin time of it these days, as my money ran out on Thursday, so it was a damnably long time till Monday noon."[4]

By specifically noting he had received Theo's letter on Monday at noon, Vincent was tipping his hand and showing his deception by trying too hard. Vincent didn't think so, and later in the same letter, he reinforced the idea he was there on Monday and had written this letter on Monday. He wrote, "It is Monday, the very day I received your letter."

Besides sending more money, Vincent's other objective was to get Theo to believe not only that he had been there on Monday but had been there from the previous Thursday to that Monday. This was why he wrote, "My money ran out on Thursday, so it was a damnably long time till Monday noon." The reason he chose to try and cover that time period, even though he had been out of town much longer, was because of his previous request to have Theo send a letter which he would receive on Wednesday, October 3. Because Theo's expected letter with money didn't arrive until Monday, October 8, Vincent knew he needed to focus on that timeframe and establish he was in Arles. He was also attempting to turn the tables on Theo. He was diverting attention away from his own lack of response and putting it towards Theo's slackness for not sending him money on Wednesday, as he had previously requested.

Vincent continued the con, noting the time period: "These four days I have lived mainly on 23 cups of coffee, with bread which I still have to pay for." He then used his lack of money to again establish the missed days, noting, "Do you know what I have left today for the week, and that after four days of strict fasting? Just 6 francs." But Vincent didn't feel he had yet made the illusion concrete, so he further noted the Thursday through Monday time period, writing, "I have been so hard up since Thursday that from Thursday to Monday I only had two meals"

Vincent also noted in this letter he was including the supposedly previously written letter, stating, "Herewith another letter that I wrote about Gauguin's portrait during the last few days."

In his third letter for the day, Vincent continued the same themes and the same objectives. He returned again to requesting money and attempting to anchor his whereabouts of the last few days, but with an added twist. He wrote, "Do you know what I have left today out of the money you sent this very day? Well, I have 6 francs. I asked you to send it to me on Friday, and I only received your letter four days later, on Monday noon."[5] Again he felt it necessary to mention it was Monday and that it was noon. But the twist was he said he asked Theo to send the money for Friday, when he had actually asked to have it on Wednesday. This was no error on Vincent's part. He meant to note Friday for good reason.

Vincent already had a long history with Theo of continuously and relentlessly asking him for money and for more of it. There was no way Vincent would have allowed himself to run out of money without sending Theo multiple letters pressuring him to send more. He knew Theo would expect this. By stating he was expecting the money on Friday instead of Wednesday, Vincent was attempting to lessen the perceived amount of time he was expecting money from Theo. There was absolutely no way Vincent would not have repeatedly written Theo from Wednesday until he received the money on Monday. In fact, based on his normal practice, he would have written Theo again before Wednesday, and when no letter arrived on Wednesday, he would have sent one that day to say how hard up he was and so on for each day until Theo sent more money, always escalating his needs. Vincent didn't follow his usual desperate pattern, and his expected desperation didn't show itself until the following Tuesday when he sent a telegram and three letters which were written to look as if they were from Monday and before. The reason for this was because Vincent wasn't in Arles. He was in London.

After doing all he could to make sure the third letter and the second letter both appeared to have been written on Monday, Vincent slipped up and provided the clue he was actually writing this third letter on Tuesday and not

Monday. He wrote, "Herewith yesterday's letter which I am sending you, such as it is." He's referring to the second letter as "yesterday's letter," which he clearly defined as being written on Monday, therefore revealing he wrote this letter on Tuesday.

Vincent was attempting to have his cake and eat it too. He had already presented the third letter as being written on Monday, but because he had sent Theo the telegram on Tuesday, and because there would be a Tuesday postmark on the envelope when he sent the three letters together, he knew he had to show some admission he was sending the letters on Tuesday. The conclusion Theo was to draw was that the third letter was written on Monday but then continued on Tuesday when it was then completed and sent. This was how Pickvance also took this letter, and he dated it accordingly as October 8 and 9.

The next day, Wednesday the 10th, Vincent sent yet another letter reminding Theo he had sent a telegram requesting money the day before, writing, "Yesterday I sent you a wire asking you for another 20 francs, I shall have nothing but that for my food all the week."[6]

Vincent's obvious attempt to create the impression he had written but had not yet sent three letters to Theo over the course of a few days and was then sending them all together on Tuesday, and that he also sent a telegraph the same day, shows a communication overload and a desperation for money he should have had the previous week. This provides a clear indication Vincent was not in Arles during this time and was attempting to cover not being there. But also, in a letter a few days later to Theo, and in a letter to Wil, Vincent provided a clue to his whereabouts during that time.

The letter to Wil was originally estimated to be written from somewhere between September and the first half of October. Pickvance thought it was earlier and changed it to August 27. I believe the original dating was closer to being correct and the subject matter suggests this is the case. Vincent wrote, "I think of Monticelli terribly often here. . . . I am sure that I am continuing his work here, as if I were his son or his brother."[7] Remarkably, Vincent is writing his sister about Monticelli because he had just returned from his trip to London where he made a side trip to Lille on his way back so he could visit the museum where some of Monticelli's work was on display.

A letter to Theo, which Pickvance dated October 10, backs up the original dating of the letter to Wil, because in it Vincent wrote the same thing about Monticelli: "I so often think of Monticelli."[8] He further noted that the panels on a chest of drawers were "exactly like those on which Monticelli painted." Monticelli was on Vincent's mind at this time because he had just visited his work in Lille where he had sent one of his Jack the Ripper letters from while passing through.

Another person on Vincent's mind at this time was his friend Roulin. In the same letter to Theo, Vincent compared Monticelli's known drinking habits to Roulin's: "My friend the postman, for instance, lives a great deal in cafés, and is certainly more or less of a drinker, and has been so all his life."

Now that Vincent was settling back into his life in Arles, he picked up where he had left off with Roulin. The two were back to being drinking buddies, and Vincent was back to paying for Roulin's rounds of beer. Of course, Vincent was doing this with a purpose in mind. He had tested Roulin in September with his first Ripper letter in which he had blackened out his alter ego's name with shapes of coffins. Roulin had passed the test, proving he could be trusted. Roulin was now an accomplice who couldn't turn on his drinking pal—partly because he liked having his drinks paid for, but also because he was in on it with Vincent and therefore culpable. He could never tattle. He would be exposing his own crime of misusing his postal position.

Knowing he could implicitly trust Roulin, and even after just returning from a long journey and writing all those letters to Theo, the obsessive Vincent wanted to write even more, and he wrote more Ripper letters. After filling Roulin to the brim of his postal cap with beer at their favorite café, I believe Vincent slid envelopes with Ripper letters tucked inside across the table to Roulin with a grin. Roulin, so full of appreciation at having his friend who bought him drinks back in town, shared Vincent's grin and pocketed the letters. Roulin was now fully his. Vincent had secured his means of cheating the postal system, and having obtained such a unique ability, he would want to continue to make good use of it.

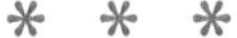

* * *

Another person on Vincent's mind after his return to Arles from his latest trip to London was Gauguin. Vincent mentioned this in his October 9 trio of letters to Theo, writing, "My whole mind, like yours, is set on Gauguin now. And like you, I hope that he will come right away."[9] Only a day or two later, he heard from Gauguin. He informed Theo of Gauguin's response: "He will not be coming till the end of the month."[10]

Vincent wanted Gauguin to come right away and busied himself with preparing the Yellow House for his arrival. A chest of drawers he bought with Theo's money was for Gauguin's room, and he had gas installed in the studio and kitchen on the ground floor.[11] He also wanted to impress Gauguin, so he poured his energy into completing paintings of sunflowers to hang in his room.

Even though Vincent was hard at work again on his paintings and looking forward to Gauguin's arrival, he also had a growing anxiety and frustration which needed an outlet. He had made kills in London at the end of August and September and, no doubt, he desperately wanted to continue the pattern with another kill at the end of October. But with Gauguin planning to arrive at the same time, Vincent would be hard-pressed to complete his goal.

However, Vincent was not ready to give up so easily. Gauguin had stated his reason for delaying his departure as poor health. Vincent wrote back and tried to convince him he would be just fine and to come right away. He wrote, "But is it absolutely true that the journey to Arles is as exhausting as you say? Nonsense, since the worst lung cases make it. You well know that the P.L.M. exists for that."[12] The P.L.M. stood for the Paris, Lyon, Marseille express. Vincent knew the route well, and he likely got the idea of mentioning lung cases from someone he shared a train car with on one of his recent train rides between Paris and Arles.

As he waited for Gauguin's response, hoping his powers of persuasion were strong enough to convince Gauguin to depart sooner, Vincent's fear and anxiety of not being allowed to continue to escalate the mayhem in London drove him harder towards the only means he could use to remain engaged in the affairs of Londoners—he wrote more Jack the Ripper letters.

With anything Vincent set his mind to, his tendency was to spiral into obsession. Whether it was painting, alcohol, prostitutes, or even killing, Vincent's nature was to take all things to excess, which he also did with writing Ripper letters. He had already become obsessive about it while in London, and the obsession was so strong he had to write two more on his trip back to Arles— one in Lille and another in Paris.

With the added anxiety of possibly not being allowed to return to London at the end of October because of Gauguin, Vincent's obsession only increased. After reconnecting with Roulin, he continued to have him send additional Ripper letters from Arles. Since he was now certain he could fully trust Roulin, he felt no need to be cautious with him, and instead of handing him a Ripper letter to send now and then, he gave him handfuls to mail each day. On October 10, at least seven Ripper letters were received in London. One then arrived on the 11th and another on the 12th, and then at least another five came in on the 13th.

Not all of these were Vincent's. Other individuals had been inspired by the creativeness of the published Ripper letters, and they wrote their own versions. At least four hoax letter writers were tracked down and prosecuted. Two of these sent Ripper letters to their local police, one far away from London in Bradford in Northern England, and the other even further away in Glasgow,

Scotland.[13] The other two sent Ripper letters to individuals they had disputes with as a threat, one in London and the other in Wales.[14]

However, of the Ripper letters received in London by the police and papers, I believe the evidence shows the hoax letters and hoax letter writers were very few, and that Vincent wrote nearly all of the Jack the Ripper letters—his obsessive nature working hard and showing itself in this area.

Vincent's creativity was also hard at work in the Ripper letters. At times he created phony postmarks, as he had previously found useful when he wrote the letter from Tours two years prior while living in Paris just after he murdered Theo's stubborn girlfriend, S. Being an obsessive artist, he was also compelled to view the Ripper letters as artistic creations, often including drawings as he did regularly in letters to Theo, Bernard, Russell and others.

One of the best examples of Vincent's artistic touch is found in one of the two Ripper letters he sent before he left London on Sunday night, October 7. It would seem at first glance this Ripper letter could not be from Vincent and must be considered a hoax since it was postmarked from Birmingham which is a hundred miles to the northwest of London. But knowing Vincent's clever tendencies and artistic abilities, a closer look is needed, and it then becomes clear he wrote this letter and created the postmark.

Possibly finding a discarded envelope stamped with a Birmingham postmark, Vincent re-created the postmark on a fresh envelope and dropped the letter in a London pillar box. The main motivation for this was the same as always—to divert the police while having some creative fun. The day he was leaving London for his destination to the east and to the south in France, he was leaving behind a Ripper letter supposedly sent by the murderer from the west and to the north in England in the opposite direction.

It's not only intuitive reasoning which leads to this conclusion. The evidence is there. The envelope has survived intact, and it's clear from the postmark the writer of the letter was up to some funny business. The clue is not found in what is there but what is not there.

It was true no postage was required if a letter mailed from within London was sent to a London address, but a letter sent to London from as far away as Birmingham would have certainly required postage. It would not have been delivered to London without it. As can be seen on this Ripper letter envelope in figure 17.1, the postage is missing. The first obvious inclination would be to consider the postage fell off over time or was stolen, but if that were the case, the area where the postmark covered the postage would also be missing from the envelope, but the postmark is complete.

The next inclination would be to suggest the postal worker in Birmingham missed hitting the postage with the postmark stamp. What makes this very unlikely is this postmark is more than a postmark. It's a combination postmark and cancellation, or obliterator, stamp, which was a standard inked stamp which included the postmark on the left and the cancellation stamp on the right. The postmark served to show the date and location of when and where the letter came through the originating post office, but the purpose of the cancellation portion of the stamp was specifically designed to "cancel-out" the postage and therefore prevent the postage from being reused. So, because this was a cancellation stamp which was meant to be stamped over the postage and mark it, and because it covers fully the area where postage should be, it's clear there was no postage on the envelope. Therefore, it can be concluded the postmark and cancellation stamp were mischievously created.

The supporting evidence of this derives from something else that is missing. If the letter was sent from Birmingham and then received in London, it would have been stamped with at least one receiving postmark to show when and where it had been received at a London post office. As can be seen, there is no London postmark on the envelope.

The conclusion—the letter was dropped in a London pillar box with a phony Birmingham postmark. When the letter was picked up and brought to the post office for sorting, a postal worker noticed something strange about the envelope which had a Birmingham postmark with no postage. He therefore didn't stamp it with a London postmark and instead flagged it for further inspection. Because there was no return address on the envelope, the common practice was to open the envelope to try and determine who the sender was. It would have then been discovered to be a Jack the Ripper letter and handed over to the police. In the excitement, no London postmark or official post office stamp was applied.

As for the letter, shown in figure 17.2, it is highly artistic. The drawings across the top are crudely constructed but were clearly created by at least a somewhat skilled hand. The shading of the objects and the three-dimensional aspect of the knife handle and coffin give this away.

The skull and crossbones with the halo is an obvious symbol of the Angel of Death, and each of the items are related to death. There are what appear to be individual characters written on either side of the skull and three more around the crossbones. The character to the left of the skull looks like a capital "B," but the character to the right isn't so clearly defined. It appears to be a capital "A" turned counterclockwise onto its side. The character to the left of the crossbones is an "O," the lower character is a capital "D," and I believe the character to the right is a capital "G" turned clockwise on its side. Keeping with the religious theme of the Angel of Death, these three characters spell out GOD.

The "B" and "A" on either side of the skull don't have as clear a meaning, but it seems they may stand for BEFORE and AFTER. My interpretation of the drawings and characters is the writer was saying: BEFORE the Angel of Death of GOD there is the knife, and AFTER the Angel of Death of GOD there is the coffin and the skeleton.

The significance of this is the writer thinks of himself as acting as the Angel of Death of God. The Christian cross on the coffin provides the symbol of which religion the writer is operating under. Vincent's Christian upbringing as the son of a preacher and his years of pursuing the path of a preacher himself certainly fit well the profile of someone with a religious, and specifically Christian, background. It was how Vincent was so overzealous during his religious years, and how it all ended so badly, and afterwards how he turned against the clergy, his father, and Christianity itself, that fits so well with the attitude of the creator of this Ripper letter.

As for the written portion of the letter, some of Vincent's characteristics show themselves. The most notable is what writing instrument was used. There's a certain sloppy style to the handwriting, and its line is thicker than the common fountain pen of the day. Like most, Vincent mainly used a fountain pen to write his letters, but he also liked to occasionally use a reed pen which he had discovered worked well for making sketches and drawings. As previously noted, he used a reed pen to write the letter to John Russell where he had drawn a picture of a sower with "Ha, ha" and "Rip's" hidden in the strokes. Since the Russell letter was written in English, it offers a good standard for comparison between Vincent's writing characteristics and those of Jack the Ripper.

Looking at a comparison of the Angel of Death Ripper letter in figure 17.2 and page four of the Russell letter in figure 2.2, the general similarity in writing style can be seen. Both letters show the thicker and sloppier flow of a reed pen. Also, the reed pen leaves behind a distinct skipping pattern which can be found in the Ripper letter, Russell letter, and also throughout some of Vincent's other letters.

Figure 17.4 provides a comparison of this skipping pattern. The skipping shows in the Ripper letter in the words "Brum" on the first line and "inhabitants" on the fourth line. In "Brum," the ink is missing from the middle of the downward stroke on the right side of the cursive "r," and with "inhabitants," the second "t" shows the same missing ink from the middle of the downward stroke.

Matching this skipping characteristic in the Russell letter is the "y" at the end of the word "very" on the first line below the drawing. Then two more lines down, the skip mark is also on the "y" at the end of the word "kindly" and on the "t" of "to." Other examples of this distinctive skipping characteristic are found in other Van Gogh letters, as shown.

This skipping can be attributed partly to the reservoir of the reed pen running out of ink. The middle gap of the reed pen is no longer holding the ink, but the edges are, so the outer lines of the characters continue while little or no ink is applied in the middle. As each of the examples show, the skipping generally only occurs on a downward stroke, and this can be attributed to the angle of the reed pen as it contacts the paper at a downward angle. The resulting skipping would then occur in an accidental manner as words were formed. However, Vincent was aware of this skipping attribute of the reed pen and made use of it in his drawings intentionally.

An example of this is found in the sketch of the sower in the Russell letter. There are three very distinct downward strokes in the lower left corner that show how the skipping action of the reed pen can be used for effect. As figure 17.5 shows, the three strokes have their outer lines intact but the ink filling the middle begins but then abruptly ends and is missing. This intentional use of this style of stroke can be seen in many drawings Vincent made using the reed pen. The most exaggerated example being a sketch of a girl in *La Mousmé*, as seen in figure 17.6, where the female sitter's blouse is filled with the empty strokes of the reed pen.

Vincent unintentionally made his reed pen skip marks in the writing of the Angel of Death Ripper letter, but he also added an intentional mark. Down at the bottom of the letter where he signed it Jack the Ripper, just to the left of Jack, he made two marks. The intent of the marks must have been as opening quotes, but he couldn't add the closing quotes to the end of "Ripper" because he ran out of room on the page.

Taking a closer look at the two marks in figure 17.7, it becomes apparent the mark to the right looks very similar to the intentional mark Vincent liked to make using the reed pen. It has the same characteristic of the middle filled at the top but the ink stopping in the middle while the outline continues. It is also similar to the marks in the sower sketch in the Russell letter in figure 17.5.

As for comparing the writing characteristics in Vincent's handwriting to the Jack the Ripper letters, there are many matches. However, Vincent used various writing styles in his letters, even at times shifting styles within the same letter. The Jack the Ripper letters were also written in many different hands to disguise the writer's true identity. Therefore, to layout an exhaustive comparison of handwriting would be unproductive. Even so, as an example of the likenesses, figure 17.8 shows the similarities in the creation of capital "B's" and capital "R's" between Vincent's handwriting from the Russell letter, another of his letters, and the Angel of Death and Brixton Road Ripper letters.

What is most similar about how Vincent and Jack made their "B's" and "R's" was how in both cases each character begins with a downward stroke that loops around to the left and then up.

Fortunately, though, it's not necessary to focus too much on the comparison of Vincent and Jack's alphabetic characteristics. This is because Vincent's handwriting habits provide some very distinct traits by which his letters can be effectively identified and compared to the Ripper letters. The first of these is Vincent's habit of not crossing his lower cased "t's" and "f's," which was so pronounced a habit at times that if a reader was not familiar with his habit, it would be difficult to decipher what he was writing.

Using the Russell letter again as a standard, a quick look at page four in figure 2.2 shows how easy it is to see this habit of Vincent's. Looking at the third line down where it reads, "I have been to the seaside for a," shows the uncrossed "t's" of "to" and "the," and the uncrossed "f" of "for." Three lines down from this, the crossbars are again left off the "f's" and "t's" on the words "fine," "figures," and "there." The next line down, line seven, also shows more uncrossed cursive "t's" in the words "straight" and "stylish."

The Angel of Death Ripper letter was written in cursive and, as figure 17.2 shows, in comparing uncrossed cursive "t's" from the Russell letter, some of the cursive "t's" from the Ripper letter are also missing their crossbars. This habit also shows itself on the envelope in the words "Detective" and "Scotland," as seen in figure 17.1.

This habit continued in a more pronounced way in the other Ripper letter which Vincent mailed the same day he left London on Sunday, October 7. The writer purported to be writing it from an area in Northern London named Kentish Town. Comparing the "t's" in this letter in figure 17.9 to the Russell letter exhibits the same habit of leaving "t's" uncrossed, as shown in figure 17.10.

The comparisons of the uncrossed "t's" and "f's" from the Russell letter to the Ripper letters are very similar, but Vincent had another habit which also shows itself in Ripper letters. He had a regular habit of mixing cursive and plain text. This can be seen in the Russell letter, and it shows itself in the Kentish Town Ripper letter where he wrote the word "the" in cursive, but not the letter "t," and he didn't cross it. The comparison of the same word in the Russell letter in figure 17.10 is strikingly similar.

This matching similarity in writing habits can then also be traced back to the most notable Ripper letter, the Dear Boss letter, where the killer first provided his name and also opened the letter with a reference to the "Boss." The letter was written in a controlled and neat cursive style, with the "t's" being crossed, so it seems there is not a match. However, as often happened at the end of Vincent's letters, he had to add something more, and he did so when he wrote the Dear Boss Ripper letter. After he completed the letter and signed it Jack the Ripper, writing very carefully to keep his identity hidden, he then turned the page sideways and added a quick paragraph to note he couldn't get the red ink off his hands and to state how some thought he was a doctor. The writing is less neat and less controlled. Vincent may have added this after he had a few drinks and wasn't being as careful, because the writing style and habits of this paragraph reveal it was Vincent who wrote the Dear Boss Ripper letter.

Looking at the added paragraph in figure 17.11, it is noticeable the writing style is mainly cursive but also has a plain text style mixed in at times, just as Vincent had a habit of doing. Vincent was being careless, but he hadn't had too many drinks to forget to go back through and add crossbars to the "t's," as he had done in the rest of the letter. However, he forgot to add crossbars to the "f's" in the word "off" on the fourth line down, and comparing this to the same word found in the Russell letter in figure 17.12 provides a stark match.

Vincent also wrote "ha ha" in the Dear Boss letter, just as he had written in the Russell letter in June, but in that letter he had to hide it in the drawing of the sower whereas in the Ripper letter he didn't have to hide his fun. He could openly write this expression of his mocking and sarcastic humor and not worry about being judged for it. Feeling the freedom this brought, he added another "ha ha" to the end of the extra paragraph.

Vincent's unique use of a reed pen, distinctive habit of not crossing his "t's" and "f's," and mixing plain text with cursive are excellent indicators and provide good comparison matches to the Jack the Ripper letters. However, Vincent had an even more unique and distinctive writing habit which clearly defined his writing. If it was also found in the Ripper letters, it would be distinct and compelling evidence Vincent van Gogh wrote Jack the Ripper letters.

At many times in Vincent's life, he started things without considering where his decisions would lead or what the consequences would be. He always had higher expectations for what he was doing, but it seemed his efforts always turned out bad for him in the end. This same habit of beginning something without considering the end also showed up as a habit in his writing. He sometimes found himself writing more than he expected in a letter and would have to add a P.S. or write smaller as he neared the end of the page so it would fit. Sometimes he continued to write up the side of the page to complete his thought and fit it on the page. But the writing habit which most reflects both Vincent's life and his writing is how he would regularly begin a sentence and continue it seemingly without the ability to judge how much space remained before he reached the edge of the page and how he dealt with that.

Of course, it is a common occurrence for letter writers who find they have a word that's too long for the end of a line to choose from a variety of ways to deal with the problem. One way is to leave some empty space at the end of the line and begin the next line with the word. Another way is to scrunch up the word to make it fit, or write it smaller. Some may choose to write the word just above or below the line. Then, of course, the more formal method of hyphenating the word may be employed. Some writers may consistently use only one method, while others may use different methods at different times.

Vincent was a person of obsessive extremes, though. He couldn't be a mere casual drinker—he had to be a hardcore alcoholic. He didn't visit prostitutes only occasionally—he sought their company frequently. Also, the quantity of his many drawings and paintings and his rapidly applied brushstrokes express visually his artistic obsession. So, it was no surprise to find he was also obsessive about something in his writing habits.

Vincent regularly and almost exclusively used the same method to deal with running out of space at the end of a line in his letters. It wasn't simply his choice of method which reflected his obsessive nature. It was also how often he ran into the problem and had to make use of the method. Additionally, it was the extreme exaggeration of how he employed the method which made this habit so uniquely Vincent's. In other words, his obsessive nature shows through distinctly in this particular writing habit.

Vincent's choice of dealing with more word than space at the end of a line was to bend the word downwards. This habit didn't show in every letter, but it showed in many of his letters, and it was a common writing habit throughout his life. Sometimes it was only a single word on a page, other times a few, but at other times it seemed almost as if he were suffering from a disease which blocked his ability to anticipate the edge of the page and he would have many within the pages of a letter, and even many on the same page.

Continuing to use the Russell letter as the standard, an example of a down-at-right (DAR) word can be seen. In figure 17.13, which is page two of the Russell letter, about a quarter of the way down the page the word "colour" takes a turn downwards even though it appears there's enough room to write it without the downward turn. But this is only an example of a slight bend downwards. Vincent's other letters show more severe examples.

Vincent's letter in figure 17.14 shows more distinctly his DAR habit. The end of the second line shows only a moderate bend in the French word "*l'anatomie,*" but then halfway down the page the severity of Vincent's habit shows itself more clearly in a group of line-ending words with the word "*complement*" taking an extreme dive to the south. Then there is even another DAR word further down the page.

In a twelve-page letter, Vincent's habit was in full swing on every page. Figure 17.15 shows the many DAR words on page six, with the French word near the bottom, "*changement*," being the most pronounced example. On page nine of the same letter, in figure 17.16, there are some mild examples near the top, and then an extreme example near the bottom with the word "*silencuusement*"—the word bending down to form a half-circle.

In another letter in figure 17.17, Vincent's DAR habit shows itself prominently on three words and slightly on others. Clearly, this was a unique writing habit of Vincent's, but what does it matter unless the same writing habit can be found in Ripper letters?

In the Dear Boss Ripper letter, Vincent had successfully controlled his writing habits and had hidden them well until he slipped up and added the additional paragraph with the uncrossed "f's." He also signaled just as he finished the body of the letter he was holding back his habits and they wanted out. He was tiring from controlling his writing, and when he wrote the last line, as seen in figure 17.11, his DAR habit started to leak out. The word "trade" started to slant downward, and then "name" slanted a little more. It's not severe, but just as Vincent had given his trade name of Jack the Ripper, he also gave his trademark of ending sentences at a downward slant. It's even more so Vincent's trademark because he slanted the words down even though he was nowhere near the edge of the paper.

In the Brixton Road Ripper letter which was found in a pillar box so near to the Loyers' house, Vincent's DAR habit shows more severely, as seen in figure 17.18. The words "whore," "Brixton," and "business" reveal clearly who was behind this Ripper letter. Then again, in the Kentish Town Ripper letter in figure 17.9, Vincent let his habit slip out when he should have tried to control it. He may have thought slanting the entire letter at an angle to the right would hide his habit, but even then he couldn't help running into the edge of the paper and was forced to show himself by turning down the words "catch" and "writing."

After plying Roulin with drinks over the days following his return to Arles on October 9 and beginning to hand him Ripper letters to sneak on the train into the U.K. bin, one of those arrived in London on the 12th. The postmark on the envelope shows it arrived on this date at the E.C. post office, but it wasn't the normal postmark. This one has "OFFICIAL PAID" printed within the circle, which suggests it was flagged for some reason. The envelope has no postage and was addressed to Scotland Yard. On the back were written the words "trade" and "mark" with a hastily drawn image of a knife between the words. A postal worker would have noticed the missing postage. They may have also noticed the knife image. That, together with the letter's destination during a time when all of London was in a stir over the Jack the Ripper murders and letters was enough to cause the worker to hand it over for further inspection.

It was also likely a further mystery because it was brought in to be sorted with letters received from France. If the letter were sent from within London for a London address, the postal worker would have pulled and sorted it with the non-postage letters, which would have then been stamped with a "2d" ink stamp, indicating the city was paying the two pennies for the postage. It would have then been delivered. But finding a letter with no postage and no origination postmark in with the foreign mail must have alerted the worker to have it looked at further.

The official who received it decided to send the letter on its way even though it had no postage and was in with the foreign mail. He chose to stamp it with his "OFFICIAL PAID" stamp instead of the "2d" stamp to show it had been looked at further. The letter arrived at the S.W. District Post Office where it was stamped with their receiving postmark and delivered to Scotland Yard.

Notable within the letter, Vincent's DAR habit shined forth dramatically on the single word "bloodhounds," as seen in figure 17.19.

Vincent wrote Jack the Ripper letters on his visits to London for murder, but he also manipulated a drinking buddy who worked for the French postal system into making it possible for him to send his secret letters from Arles with no way of tracing them back to him. Vincent van Gogh was indeed Jack the Ripper. As the powers of his alter ego expanded, he would crave more Ripper letters and more murder. He would have more of both.

To be continued ....

The case against Vincent van Gogh continues with additional compelling evidence in Volume 2 and Volume 3.

Please visit the book website and subscribe to the email list to stay informed:

https://VincentTheRipper.com

ABOUT THE AUTHOR

Dale Larner graduated with a B.A. in Business from UNC Charlotte and stumbled into the field of computers. But he couldn't let go of his dreams of becoming a writer and artist. Eventually, becoming a writer took over his life, and Larner set out to learn all he could about the craft of creative writing—fully expecting to become a novelist quietly creating adventurous stories filled with fascinating characters.

However, along the way, Larner made a strange discovery about his favorite artist, Vincent van Gogh, and he was compelled to write a non-fiction book about Van Gogh's hidden, murderous side. He didn't expect it to consume his life for so many years, but in the end, he completed *Vincent The Ripper: Vincent Van Gogh Was Jack The Ripper, Case Closed*.

Larner has also written a few short stories and painted a few paintings, which can be viewed at https://DaleLarner.com. He continues to write and paint in his sunny Florida hideaway with his two faithful beagles, Max & Buster, lounging under his feet.

ACKNOWLEDGMENTS

For all who have known about this book and have had to exhibit a patience which would stretch even the most loyal beyond their breaking point. Thank you!

Special gratitude to my family for their enduring patience through my neurotic quest. My Dad didn't get to see this day arrive, but he never wavered in his support for me in this. My Mom, my brothers and their wives—Dan & Debbie and Daryl & Angie, for their support and sticking with me through so much. My brother Dan especially so for using his editing skills to help polish this book. And the two who call me Uncle Dale, Sophie & Zack—they give me inspiration that things will turn out good for the future.

For all those who were on the Jack the Ripper hunt before me, notably Donald Rumbelow for preserving history; Paul Begg and Philip Sugden for building on the story; Patricia Cornwell for expanding the market; and Stewart P. Evans for providing the most thorough facts on the case.

For all those who made the study of Van Gogh their life's work and provided such a commitment to excellence, especially Marc Edo Tralbaut, Jan Hulsker, Ronald Pickvance and Leo Jansen.

The National Archives of the U.K. in Kew, England, with special thanks to Paul Johnson for all his help with acquiring the digital images of the Jack the Ripper letters. I had to have them all!

Gale Inc. and the British Library for digitizing The 19th Century British Newspapers and making them available online. Invaluable resource!

The Van Gogh Museum for their tireless work at preserving everything Van Gogh and making the Van Gogh letters available online.

And for my dogs Max and Buster for reminding me to take a break and go on a walk now and then.

IMAGES USED IN THIS BOOK

All images are available on the book website at:
https://vincenttheripper.com/book-images-volume1-p1

1888 Map of London
New Large-Scale Ordnance Atlas of London & Suburbs, Edited and Published by
George W. Bacon, F.R.G.S., 127 Strand, London, 1888

Chapter 1
Figure 1.1
Theo van Gogh Photo
Van Gogh Museum, Amsterdam

Figure 1.2
Bradshaw Ad, London to Paris
Bradshaw's Continental Railway Guide, W. J. Adams & Sons, 59 Fleet Street,
London, March 1888

Figure 1.3
Van Gogh Self-Portrait, Aug. 1889
National Gallery of Art, Washington, DC

Chapter 2
Figure 2.1
Van Gogh, *The Yellow House*, Sept. 1888
Van Gogh Museum, Amsterdam

Figure 2.2
Van Gogh Letter to John Russell , p 4, June 17, 1888
Solomon R. Guggenheim Museum, New York, Thannhauser Collection, Gift, Justin K.
Thannhauser, 1978

Figure 2.3
Van Gogh Letter to John Russell , p 4, Cut showing "Haha," June 17, 1888
Solomon R. Guggenheim Museum, New York, Thannhauser Collection, Gift, Justin K.
Thannhauser, 1978

Figure 2.4
Van Gogh Letter to John Russell , p 4, Cuts showing "Rip," June 17, 1888
Solomon R. Guggenheim Museum, New York, Thannhauser Collection, Gift, Justin K. Thannhauser, 1978

Chapter 3
Figure 3.1
Uncle Cent Photo
Van Gogh Museum, Amsterdam

Figure 3.2
Martha Tabram Mortuary Photo
The National Archives of the UK (TNA), MEPO 3/140

Figure 3.3
Füdo Print
Van Gogh Museum, Ichiyüsai Kuniyoshi ga, *Füdo*, N421 V/1962

Chapter 4
Figure 4.1
Mary Ann Nichols Mortuary Photo
The National Archives of the UK (TNA), MEPO 3/3155

Figure 4.2
Map of Tabram & Nichols Murder Sites
New Large-Scale Ordnance Atlas of London & Suburbs, Edited and Published by George W. Bacon, F.R.G.S., 127 Strand, London, 1888

Chapter 5
Figure 5.1
Vincent van Gogh Photo at 19
Van Gogh Museum, Amsterdam

Figure 5.2
Relevant London Locations for 1873/74
New Large-Scale Ordnance Atlas of London & Suburbs, Edited and Published by George W. Bacon, F.R.G.S., 127 Strand, London, 1888

Figure 5.3
Vincent's Mother Photo

Van Gogh Museum, Amsterdam

Chapter 6
None.

Chapter 7
Figure 7.1
Annie Chapman Mortuary Photo
The National Archives of the UK (TNA), MEPO 3/3155

Figure 7.2
Map of Murder Sites, Tabram, Nichols & Chapman
New Large-Scale Ordnance Atlas of London & Suburbs, Edited and Published by George W. Bacon, F.R.G.S., 127 Strand, London, 1888

Figure 7.3
Map of Escape Route After Chapman Murder
New Large-Scale Ordnance Atlas of London & Suburbs, Edited and Published by George W. Bacon, F.R.G.S., 127 Strand, London, 1888

Chapter 8
Figure 8.1
Eugenie Loyer Photo
Collection of Mrs. Kathleen Maynard & Ken Wilkie

Chapter 9
Figure 9.1
Van Gogh, *Postman Joseph Roulin*, 1888
Museum of Fine Arts, Boston

Figure 9.2
First Ripper letter Envelope Front/Back
The National Archives of the UK (TNA), MEPO3/142, f. 5

Figure 9.3
First Ripper Letter
The National Archives of the UK (TNA), MEPO3/142, f. 4

Figure 9.4
First Ripper letter, Cut Coffin, Characters Showing

The National Archives of the UK (TNA), MEPO3/142, f. 4

Chapter 10
None.

Chapter 11
Figure 11.1
Kee Vos-Stricker with Son Photo
Van Gogh Museum, Amsterdam

Figure 11.2
Van Gogh Drawing, *Woman With A Child On Her Lap*, March 1883
Van Gogh Museum, Amsterdam

Chapter 12
Figure 12.1
Vincent's Father Photo
Van Gogh Museum, Amsterdam

Figure 12.2
Margo Begemann Photo
Van Gogh Museum, Amsterdam

Chapter 13
Figure 13.1
Map of Murder Sites, Elizabeth Stride & Catherine Eddowes
New Large-Scale Ordnance Atlas of London & Suburbs, Edited and Published by
George W. Bacon, F.R.G.S., 127 Strand, London, 1888

Figure 13.2
Catherine Eddowes Cuts to Face Sketch
The National Archives of the UK (TNA), MEPO 3/141, sketch prepared by Frederick
W. Foster, City Surveyor

Figure 13.3
Elizabeth Stride Mortuary Photo
The National Archives of the UK (TNA), MEPO 3/3155

Figure 13.4
Catherine Eddowes Murder Site Police Sketch

The National Archives of the UK (TNA), MEPO 3/141

Figure 13.5
Catherine Eddowes Mortuary Photo
The National Archives of the UK (TNA), MEPO 3/140, f 3B-6

Figure 13.6
Map of Murder Sites, Tabram, Nichols, Chapman, Stride & Eddowes
New Large-Scale Ordnance Atlas of London & Suburbs, Edited and Published by
George W. Bacon, F.R.G.S., 127 Strand, London, 1888

Chapter 14
Figure 14.1
Map of Vincent Street & Brixton Road Ripper Letter Locations
New Large-Scale Ordnance Atlas of London & Suburbs, Edited and Published by
George W. Bacon, F.R.G.S., 127 Strand, London, 1888

Figure 14.2
Whitehall Torso Illustration
The Illustrated Police News, October 13, 1888

Chapter 15
Figure 15.2
Lille Ripper Letter
The National Archives of the UK (TNA), MEPO3/142, f. 154

Figure 15.3
Vincent's Graph Paper Types
Vincent van Gogh, *Letters of Vincent van Gogh, 1886-1890, A Facsimile Edition*, The
Scolar Press LTD, London, 1977, (623, p 8), (540, p 3), (551, p 3)

Figure 15.4
Vincent Letter, Small Squares Graph Paper
Vincent van Gogh, *Letters of Vincent van Gogh, 1886-1890, A Facsimile Edition*, The
Scolar Press LTD, London, 1977, 551, p 3

Chapter 16
Figure 16.1
Emile Bernard Photo with Vincent (back), Asnières, 1886
Van Gogh Museum, Amsterdam

Handwriting Comparison, Angel of Death & Brixton Road Ripper Letters & Vincent to Russell Letter
Angel of Death: The National Archives of the UK (TNA), MEPO3/142, f. 161
Brixton Road: The National Archives of the UK (TNA), MEPO3/142, f. 300
Russell Letter: Solomon R. Guggenheim Museum, New York, Thannhauser Collection, Gift, Justin K. Thannhauser, 1978
Van Gogh: Vincent van Gogh, *Letters of Vincent van Gogh, 1886-1890, A Facsimile Edition*, The Scolar Press LTD, London, 1977, 502, p

Figure 17.9
Kentish Town Ripper Letter
The National Archives of the UK (TNA), MEPO3/142, f. 173

Figure 17.10
Handwriting Comparison, Kentish Town Ripper Letter to Van Gogh letter to John Russell, pp 1-3, June 17, 1888
Kentish Town Ripper Letter: The National Archives of the UK (TNA), MEPO3/142, f. 173
Russell Letter: Solomon R. Guggenheim Museum, New York, Thannhauser Collection, Gift, Justin K. Thannhauser, 1978

Figure 17.11
Dear Boss Ripper Letter, Cut of Added Paragraph
The National Archives of the UK (TNA), MEPO3/142, f. 3

Figure 17.12
Dear Boss Ripper Letter & Van Gogh to John Russell Letter p 3 Character Comparison to Word "Off"
Dear Boss Ripper Letter: The National Archives of the UK (TNA), MEPO3/142, f. 3
Russell Letter: Solomon R. Guggenheim Museum, New York, Thannhauser Collection, Gift, Justin K. Thannhauser, 1978

Figure 17.13
Van Gogh Letter to John Russell, p 2, June 17, 1888
Solomon R. Guggenheim Museum, New York, Thannhauser Collection, Gift, Justin K. Thannhauser, 1978

Figure 17.14
Van Gogh Letter, DAR Examples

Vincent van Gogh, *Letters of Vincent van Gogh, 1886-1890, A Facsimile Edition*, The Scolar Press LTD, London, 1977, 569, p 3

Figure 17.15
Van Gogh Letter, DAR on Word "Changement"
Vincent van Gogh, *Letters of Vincent van Gogh, 1886-1890, A Facsimile Edition*, The Scolar Press LTD, London, 1977, 571, p 6

Figure 17.16
Van Gogh Letter, DAR on Word "silencuusement"
Vincent van Gogh, *Letters of Vincent van Gogh, 1886-1890, A Facsimile Edition*, The Scolar Press LTD, London, 1977, 571, p 9

Figure 17.17
Van Gogh Letter, DAR on Three Words
Vincent van Gogh, *Letters of Vincent van Gogh, 1886-1890, A Facsimile Edition*, The Scolar Press LTD, London, 1977, 609, p 3

Figure 17.18
Brixton Road Ripper Letter, DAR on Word "whore"
The National Archives of the UK (TNA), MEPO3/142, f. 300

Figure 17.19
You Dogs Ripper Letter, DAR on Word "bloodhounds"
The National Archives of the UK (TNA), MEPO3/142, f. 245

BIBLIOGRAPHY

Van Gogh Letters
VG WebExhibits 2025
Douma, Michael, curator, translated and edited by Robert Harrison. *Van Gogh's Letters: Unabridged & Annotated*. WebExhibits, Public service of the Institute for Dynamic Educational Advancement (IDEA). https://www.webexhibits.org/vangogh/

Jansen 1999
Jansen, Leo, and Jan Robert, eds. *Brief Happiness: The Correspondence of Theo van Gogh and Jo Bonger*. Amsterdam: Van Gogh Museum, 1999.

VG Letters 1958
Van Gogh, Vincent. *The Complete Letters of Vincent van Gogh*. 1958. 3rd ed. 3 vols. Reprint, Boston: Bulfinch Press, 2001.

VG Stone 1958
Van Gogh, Vincent. *Dear Theo: The Autobiography of Vincent van Gogh*. Edited by Irving Stone, with Jean Stone. Reprint, New York: Plume, 1995. First published 1958 by Doubleday.

VG Facsimile 1977
Van Gogh, Vincent. *Letters of Vincent van Gogh 1886-1890: A Facsimile Edition*. 2 vols. London: The Scolar Press, 1977.

VG Bernard 2003
Van Gogh, Vincent. *Van Gogh on Art and Artists: Letters to Emile Bernard*. Edited and translated by Douglas Lord. Mineola, NY: Dover Publications, 2003. First published 1938 by the Museum of Modern Art.

VG Bernard 2007
Van Gogh, Vincent. *Vincent van Gogh, Painted with Words: The Letters to Émile Bernard*. Edited by Leo Jansen, Hans Luijten, and Nienke Bakker. New York: Rizzoli, 2007.

VG Letters 2009
Van Gogh, Vincent. Edited by Leo Jansen, Hans Luijten, & Nienke Bakker. *Vincent van Gogh - The Letters*. Online version. 2009. Amsterdam & The Hague: Van Gogh Museum & Huygens ING. https://vangoghletters.org.

Van Gogh Related
Bailey 1992
Bailey, Martin. *Van Gogh: Portrait of an Artist as a Young Man in England*. London: Barbican Art Gallery, 1992.

Bailey 2005
Bailey, Martin. *Drama at Arles: New Light on Van Gogh's Self-Mutilation*. London: Apollo Magazine, September 1, 2005.

Bonafoux 1990
Bonafoux, Pascal. *Van Gogh*. Translated by Alexandra Campbell. New York: Konecky & Konecky, 1990.

De Leeuw 1997
De Leeuw, Ronald. *Van Gogh Museum*. Zwolle: Waanders Publishers, 1997.

Druick 2001
Druick, Douglas W., and Peter Kort Zegers. *Van Gogh and Gauguin: The Studio of the South*. In collaboration with Britt Salvesen. With contributions to the text by Kristin Hoermann Lister, and assistance of Mary C. Weaver. New York: Thames & Hudson, 2001.

Drutt 2001
Drutt, Matthew, ed. *Thannhauser: The Thannhauser Collection of the Guggenheim Museum*. New York: Guggenheim Museum Publications, 2001.

Du Quesne van Gogh 1913
Du Quesne-van Gogh, Elizabeth. *Personal Recollections of Vincent van Gogh*. Translated by Katherine S. Dreier. Boston: Houghton Mifflin, 1913.

Fell 2004
Fell, Derek. *Van Gogh's Women: His Love Affairs and Journey into Madness*. New York: Carroll & Graf Publishers, 2004.

Field 2006
Field, D.M. *Van Gogh*. NJ: Chartwell Books, Inc., 2006.

Gauguin 1921
Gauguin, Paul. *Gauguin's Intimate Journals*. Translated by Van Wyck Brooks. Mineola, NY: Dover Publications, 1997. First published 1921 by Boni and Liveright.

Gauguin 1949
Gauguin, Paul. *Letters to His Wife and Friends*. Edited by Maurice Malingue. Translated by Henry J. Stenning. Boston: MFA Publications, 2003. First published 1949 by The World Publishing Company.

Homburg 2008
Homburg, Cornelia. *The Treasures of Vincent van Gogh*. New York: Metro Books, 2008.

Hulsker 1980

Hulsker, Jan. *The Complete Van Gogh: Paintings, Drawings, Sketches*. New York: Harrison House/Harry N. Abrams, Inc., 1980.

Hulsker 1990
Hulsker, Jan. *Vincent and Theo Van Gogh: A Dual Biography*. Edited by James M. Miller. Ann Arbor, MI: Fuller Publications, 1990.

Ives 2005
Ives, Colta, and Susan Alyson Stein, Sjraar van Heugten, and Marije Vellekoop. *Vincent van Gogh: The Drawings*. New York: The Metropolitan Museum of Art, 2005.

Lubin 1972
Lubin, Albert J. *Stranger on the Earth: A Psychological Biography of Vincent van Gogh*. New York: Da Capo Press, 1996. First published 1972 by Henry Holt.

Nagera 1967
Nagera, Humberto, M.D. *Vincent van Gogh: A Psychological Study*, Forward by Anna Freud. New York: International Universities Press, Inc, 1967.

Pickvance 1984
Pickvance, Ronald. *Van Gogh in Arles*. New York: The Metropolitan Museum of Art, 1984.

Pickvance 1986
Pickvance, Ronald. *Van Gogh in Saint-Rémy and Auvers*. New York: The Metropolitan Museum of Art, 1986.

Rappard-Boon 1991
Van Rappard-Boon, Charlotte, Willem van Gulik, and Keiko van Bremen-Ito, eds. *Catalogue of the Van Gogh Museum's Collection of Japanese Prints*. Amsterdam: Van Gogh Museum, 1991.

Stein 1986
Stein, Susan Alyson, ed. *Van Gogh: A Retrospective*. Beaux Arts Editions, 1986.

Sweetman 1990
Sweetman, David. *Van Gogh: His Life and His Art*. New York: Crown Publishers, 1990.

Tralbaut 1969
Tralbaut, Marc Edo. *Vincent van Gogh*. Lausanne: Edita, 1969.

Van der Wolk 1987
Van Der Wolk, Johannes. *The Seven Sketchbooks of Vincent van Gogh: A Facsimile Edition*. Translated by Claudia Swan. New York, Harry N. Abrams, 1987.

Walther 2000

Walther, Ingo F., and Rainer Metzger, *Vincent van Gogh: The Complete Paintings*. Köln: Taschen, 2000.

Welsh-Ovcharov 1999
Welsh-Ovcharov, Bogomila. *Van Gogh in Provence and Auvers*. MA: World Publications Group, Inc., 1999.

Wilkie 1978
Wilkie, Ken. *The Van Gogh File: The Myth and the Man*. 3rd ed., rev. London: Souvenir Press, 2004. First published 1978 by Paddington Press as *The Van Gogh Assignment*.

Jack the Ripper Related

Begg 2005
Begg, Paul. *Jack the Ripper: The Facts*. New York: Barnes & Noble Books, 2005.

Dew 1938
Connell, Nicholas, ed. *The Annotated I Caught Crippen: Memoirs of ex-Chief Inspector Walter Dew, C.I.D., of Scotland Yard*. "The Hunt for Jack the Ripper." London: Mango Books, 2018. The main text is a transcription of *I Caught Crippen* by Walter Dew, London: Blackie & Son, 1938.

Cornwell 2003
Cornwell, Patricia. *Portrait of a Killer: Jack the Ripper Case Closed*. New York: Berkley Books, 2003. First published 2002 by G.P. Putman's Sons.

Evans 2000
Evans, Stewart P., and Keith Skinner. *The Ultimate Jack the Ripper Companion: An Illustrated Encyclopedia*. New York: Carroll & Graf Publishers, 2003. First published 2000.

Evans 2001
Evans, Stewart P., and Keith Skinner. *Jack the Ripper: Letters From Hell*. Stroud, England: Sutton Publishing, 2001.

Evans 2006
Evans, Stewart P., and Donald Rumbelow. *Jack the Ripper: Scotland Yard Investigates*. Stroud, England: Sutton Publishing, 2006.

Gordon 2002
Gordon, R. Michael. *The Thames Torso Murders of Victorian London*. North Carolina: McFarland & Company, 2002.

Rumbelow 1975
Rumbelow, Donald. *The Complete Jack the Ripper*. Rev. ed., London: Penguin Books, 1988. First published 1975 by W.H. Allen.

Storey 2004

Storey, Neil R. *A Grim Almanac of Jack the Ripper's London 1870-1900*. Stroud, England: Sutton Publishing, 2004.

Sugden 1994
Sugden, Phillip. *The Complete History of Jack the Ripper*. Revised and reprinted, New York: Carroll & Graf Publishers, 2003. First published 1994 by Robinson Publishing.

Travel and Post
Alcock 1960
Alcock, R.C., and F.C. Holland. *British Postmarks: A Short History and Guide*. Cheltenham, England: R.C. Alcock, 1960.

Bacon 1888
Bacon, George W. Introductory Notes by Ralph Hyde. *The A to Z of Victorian London*. London Topographical Society, 1987. Map first published 1888 by George W. Bacon.

Booth 1889
Booth, Charles. *Charles Booth's Descriptive Map of London Poverty 1889*. Reprint, London Topographical Society, 2006. First reprint 1984.

Bradshaw 1888
Bradshaw's Continental Railway Guide and General Handbook, Illustrated with Local and Other Maps, Special Edition 3/6. London: W. J. Adams & Sons, March 1888.

Dickens 1887
Dickens, Charles. *Dickens's Dictionary of the Thames 1887, From its Source to the Nore: An Unconventional Handbook*. Facsimile of first edition, Moretonhampstead, England: Old House Books Sutton Mead, 1994. Originally compiled by Charles Dickens's son, London: Macmillan & Co., 1887.

Dickens 1888
Dickens, Charles. *Dickens's Dictionary of London 1888: An Unconventional Handbook*. Facsimile of first edition, Moretonhampstead, England: Old House Books, 2006. First facsimile by Old House Books, 1993. Originally compiled by Charles Dickens's son, 1888.

Paris Map 1887
1887 Nouveau Plan De Paris, Lanée Editeur Géographe, 8 Rue De La, Paix, Paris

Westley 1950
Westley, H.C. *The Postal Cancellations of London 1840-1890*. London: H.F. Johnson, 1950.

Psychopath and Serial Killer Profiling
Blair 2005
Blair, James, Derek Mitchell, and Karina Blair. *The Psychopath: Emotion and the Brain*. 2005. 2nd ed. Malden, MA: Blackwell Publishing, 2006.

Campbell 2004
Campbell, John H., and Don DeNevi, eds. *Profilers: Leading Investigators Take You Inside the Criminal Mind*. Amherst, NY: Prometheus Books, 2004.

Hare 1995
Hare, Robert D., Phd. *Without Conscience: The Disturbing World of the Psychopaths Among Us*. New York: The Guilford Press, 1999. First published 1995 by Pocket Books.

Ressler 1995
Ressler, Robert K., Ann W. Burgess, and John E. Douglas. *Sexual Homicide: Patterns and Motives*. NY: The Free Press, 1995.

Vronsky 2004
Vronsky, Peter. *Serial Killers: The Method and Madness of Monsters*. New York: Berkley Books, 2004.

Other Resources
Cain 1964
Cain, Albert C., Ph.D, and Barbara S. Cain, M.S.W. "On Replacing a Child." In *Journal of the American Academy of Child Psychiatry*, 443-456. Vol. 3. Edited by Irene M. Josselyn, M.D. New York: International Universities Press, 1964.

Conrad 1988
Barnaby, Conrad III. *Absinthe: History in a Bottle*. San Francisco: Chronicle Books, 1988.

Hayden 2004
Hayden, Deborah. *Pox: Genius, Madness, and the Mysteries of Syphilis*. 2003. Paperback edition, New York: Basic Books, 2004.

Michelet 1859
Michelet, M.J. *Love*. Translated by J.W. Palmer, M.D. NY: Rudd & Carleton, 1859.

Rose 2001
Rose, Carol. *Giants, Monsters, and Dragons: An Encyclopedia of Folklore, Legend, and Myth*. New York: W.W. Norton & Company, 2001.

Websites
C.B. 2025
Casebook.org, https://www.casebook.org

The Lancet
The Lancet, https://www.thelancet.com/

N.A. 2025

The National Archives of the UK (TNA), website, *The Whitechapel murders: `Jack the Ripper'*, MEPO 3/141, https://discovery.nationalarchives.gov.uk/details/r/C1256550

New York Times
The New York Times, Article Archive 1851-1980:
https://www.nytimes.com/search/?srchst=p

The Paris Catacombs
Les Catacombes De Paris, https://www.catacombes.paris.fr/en

The Times
The Times, London, Article Archive 1785-1985:
https://www.thetimes.com/help/articles/how-do-i-search-the-times-archive

19th Century British Newspapers
The British Newspaper Archive: https://www.britishnewspaperarchive.co.uk

19th Century French Newspapers
Bibliothèque Nationale de France, Gallica Digital Library:
https://gallica.bnf.fr/selections/fr/html/les-principaux-quotidiens

NOTES

For Van Gogh's letters, the numbers and dating established in the first complete English edition from 1958 are used, except when the original dating is missing or has been updated since. In that case, unless otherwise noted, dating established by Pickvance (1984 for Arles period, and 1986 for St. Rémy and Auvers period) is used.

When reference is made to Van Gogh letters in the 2009 edition, the 1958 letter number will follow the 2009 letter number.

All citations of letters include the correspondents' name, date, and reference number, when available. Full citations for abbreviated sources appear in the Bibliography.

Abbreviations provided for names when referencing the "to" and "from" for letters:
V=Vincent, T=Theo, W=Wilhelmina, B=Émile Bernard, R=Anthon G.A. Ridder van Rappard, AB=Andries Bonger, & Jo=Johanna Bonger.

Chapter 1
[1] Druick 2001, p. 57.
[2] Stein 1986, Andries Bonger, "Letters and Art," *Nieuwe Rotterdamsche Courant*, Sept. 5, 1893, p. 105.
[3] V to T, 463.
[4] V to T, 464.
[5] V to T, 482.
[6] V to T, 488.
[7] *Eastern Post*, Apr. 7, 1888.
[8] *Illustrated Police News*, April 7, 1888.
[9] *Lloyd's Weekly London Newspaper,* Apr. 1, 1888.
[10] V to R, R30.
[11] Hulsker 1990, Artist Willem van de Wakker, Dr. Benno J. Stokvis, "Nieuwe nasporingen omtrent Vincent van Gogh in Brabant," *Opgang*, Jan. 1927, p. 188.
[12] VG Letters 1958, Vol. 1, p. XX.
[13] VG WebExhibits 2024, 435b, "Reminiscences of D. Gestel," *Eindhovensch Dagblad*, Oct. 10, 1930.
[14] Ibid., 143a, Louis Piérard, "La vie tragique de Vincent van Gogh," Édition revue, Paris, Éditions *Correa & Cie*, 1939.
[15] Hulsker 1990, p. 192.
[16] V to T, 471.
[17] V to T, 472.

Chapter 2
[1] V to W, W3.
[2] V to T, 480.
[3] V to T, 489.
[4] V to T, 492.
[5] V to T, 480.

[6] V to T, 492.
[7] VG Letters 1958, Vol. 1, p. XXII.
[8] V to G, 494a.
[9] VG Letters 1958, Anton Kerssemakers, "De Groene," *Amsterdam Weekly*, Apr. 14 & 21, 1912, 435c.
[10] V to T, 496.
[11] V to T, 498.
[12] *The Lancet*, "On the Comparative Action of Alcohol and Absinthe," Sept. 19, 1874, p. 410-12, TheLancet.com.
[13] V to John Russell, 501a.
[14] Gauguin Journal 1921, p. 85.
[15] *The Times*, July 11, 1887.
[16] Ibid., Sept. 1, 1887.
[17] *Daily News*, Nov. 6, 1888.
[18] V to W, W4.
[19] V to T, 502.
[20] V to T, 504.
[21] V to B, B9[12].
[22] V to T, 513.
[23] V to T, 514.
[24] V to B, B8[11].
[25] V to T, 506.
[26] V to T, 507.
[27] V to T, 506.
[28] John Russell to V, 501b.
[29] V to T, 513.
[30] V to B, B8[11].
[31] V to T, 506.
[32] V to T, 509.
[33] V to T, 508.
[34] V to T, 509.

Chapter 3
[1] V to W, W5.
[2] V to T, 517.
[3] V to T, 518.
[4] Ibid.
[5] *Daily News*, Aug. 10, 1888.
[6] *The Times*, Aug. 24, 1888.
[7] V to Van Stockum-Haanebeek family, 7 Aug. 1873, 10a.
[8] Rappard-Boon 1991, p. 245.
[9] *Illustrated Police News*, Aug. 18, 1888.
[10] V to T, 519.

Chapter 4
[1] V to T, 350a (author's translation).
[2] V to T, 520.
[3] V to T, 522.
[4] V to T, 358.
[5] V to T, 521.
[6] V to T, 522.
[7] V to T, 523.
[8] V to T, 528.
[9] Stein 1986, Dodge Macknight, "On Van Gogh in Arles," *Lau's Dodge Macknight*, Mar. 20, 1913, p. 108.
[10] Ibid., Pierre Weiller, "We've Tracked Down Van Gogh's Zouave," *Les Lettres Françaises*, Mar. 24-31, 1955, p. 108-11.

11 V to T, 529.
12 *Daily News*, Sept. 3, 1888.
13 *Lloyd's*, Sept. 2, 1888.
14 *The Times*, Sept. 18, 1888.
15 *Reynolds's Newspaper*, Sept. 2, 1888.
16 Evans 2000, p. 25, Ref. MEPO 3/140, ff., p. 239-41.
17 *The Times*, Sept. 4, 1888.
18 *Reynolds's Weekly Newspaper*, Sept. 2, 1888.
19 *Daily News*, Sept. 4, 1888.
20 *Reynolds's*, Sept. 2, 1888.
21 *Bible*, King James Version, 2 Cor. 6:10.
22 V to T, 320.
23 V to T, 530.

Chapter 5
1 VG Letters 1958, Vol. 1, p. XXII.
2 V to T, 13 Dec. 1872, 2.
3 V to T, 18 Jan. 1873, 3.
4 VG Letters 1958, Vol. 1, p. XXIII.
5 V to T, 17 Mar. 1873, 5.
6 VG WebExhibits 2025, Vincent's Father to T, 31 May 1873, p. 17.
7 V to T, 12 June 1873.
8 Sweetman 1990, p. 46.
9 VG WebExhibits 2025, Vincent's Mother to T, 31 May 1873.
10 V to Van Stockum-Haanebeek family, 2 July 1873, 9a.
11 Ibid., 7 Aug. 1873, 10a.
12 Hulsker 1990, Vincent's Father to T, 25 Aug. 1873.
13 *The Times*, Sept. 9, 1873.
14 V to T, 13 Sept. 1973, 11.
15 VG WebExhibits 2025, Vincent's Mother to T, 31 May 1873.
16 *Daily News*, Sept. 10, 1873.
17 V to T, 13 Sept. 1873, 11.

Chapter 6
1 V to T, 531.
2 *Myra's Journal*, Sept. 1, 1888.
3 V to T, 532.

Chapter 7
1 *The Times*, Sept. 14, 1888.
2 *Reynolds's*, Sept. 23, 1888.
3 Evans 2000, p. 74, Ref. HO 144/221/A49301C, ff. 137-45.
4 *The Times*, Sept. 14, 1888.
5 *Reynolds's*, Sept. 23, 1888.
6 *Lloyd's*, Sept. 16, 1888.
7 *Reynolds's*, Sept. 23, 1888.
8 *The Times*, Sept. 27, 1888.
9 *Lloyd's*, Sept. 23, 1888.
10 Ibid.
11 Ibid., Sept. 16, 1888.
12 Ibid.
13 *Reynolds's*, Sept. 16, 1888.
14 *The Times*, Sept. 20, 1888.
15 *Illustrated Police News*, Sept. 29, 1888.
16 *Daily News*, Sept. 10, 1888.
17 *Lloyd's*, Sept. 16, 1888.
18 *The Times*, Sept. 27, 1888.

[19] *Daily News*, Sept. 10, 1888.
[20] Stein 1986, A.S. Hartrick, "A Painter's Pilgrimage Through Fifty Years," 1939, pp. 81-87.
[21] *Daily News*, Sept. 11, 1888.
[22] *The Times*, Sept. 12, 1888.
[23] *Lloyd's*, Sept. 9, 1888.
[24] Ibid.
[25] VG Letters 1958, Vol. 1, April 12, 1912, 126a.
[26] Du Quesne van Gogh 1913, p. 36.
[27] Stein 1986, Emile Bernard, "Vincent van Gogh," *La Plume*, Sept. 1, 1891, p. 282.
[28] *The Times*, Oct. 9, 1888.
[29] *Daily News*, Oct. 3, 1888.
[30] Ibid.
[31] *Reynolds's*, Sept. 16, 1888.
[32] *The Times*, Sept. 12, 1888.
[33] V to T, 533, 8 Sept. 1888.
[34] VG Letters 2009, Siegfried Bing, n5, and Lévy, n16, 637/505.
[35] V to T, 534.

Chapter 8
[1] Michelet 1859, p. 118.
[2] Ibid., p. 151.
[3] V to T, 19 Nov. 1873, 12.
[4] VG Letters 1958, Vol. 1, p. XXIV.
[5] VG WebExhibits 2025, Anna van Gogh to T, 06 Jan. 1974.
[6] V to T, 13 Jan. 1874, 13.
[7] VG WebExhibits 2025, Anna van Gogh to T, 24 Feb. 1974.
[8] V to Van Stockum-Haanebeek family, 3 Mar. 1874, 14a.
[9] V to T, 30 Mar. 1874, 15.
[10] V to T, 13 Apr. 1874, 16.
[11] *Lloyd's*, June 14, 1874.
[12] Ibid.
[13] V to T, 13 Apr. 1874, 16.
[14] V to T, 16 June 1874, 17.
[15] Tralbaut 1969, p. 43.
[16] V to T, 16 June 1874, n2, 17.
[17] VG Letters 1958, Vol. 1, p. XXV.
[18] V to T, 10 Aug. 1874, 21.
[19] VG Letters 1958, Vol. 1, p. XXV.

Chapter 9
[1] V to W, W4.
[2] *Daily News*, Sept. 10, 1888.
[3] *Reynolds's*, Sept. 2, 1888.
[4] *Daily News*, Sept. 10, 1888.
[5] *Pall Mall Gazette*, Sept. 8, 1888.
[6] *Lloyd's*, Sept. 16, 1888.
[7] *The Times*, Sept. 11, 1888.
[8] Ibid., Sept. 12, 1888.
[9] V to T, 534.
[10] V to T, 516.
[11] V to B, B14[19].
[12] V to T, 518.
[13] V to T, 520.
[14] Hulsker 1990, p. 289.
[15] Pickvance 1984, p. 151; Tralbaut 1969, p. 229.
[16] Sweetman 1990, p. 271.
[17] V to T, 541.

[18] V to T, 537.
[19] V to T, 538.
[20] V to T, 540.
[21] V to T, 543.
[22] Ibid.
[23] V to T, 539.
[24] V to T, 535.
[25] V to T, 543.
[26] V to B, B17[14].
[27] V to T, 544.
[28] V to G, 544a.

Chapter 10
[1] Dickens 1888, p. 201.
[2] Alcock 1960, 174.

Chapter 11
[1] Tralbaut 1969, p. 44.
[2] V to T, 18 Apr. 1875, 25.
[3] Tralbaut 1969, p. 44.
[4] V to T, 8 May 1875, 26.
[5] VG Webexhibits 2025, Vincent's Father to T, 09 July 1875.
[6] V to T, 24 July 1875, 32.
[7] Tralbaut 1969, p. 45; V to T, 10 Jan. 1876, 50; VG WebExhibits 2025, Vincent's Father to T, 12 Jan. 1876.
[8] V to T, 23 Nov. 1876, 82a.
[9] Bailey 1992, p. 12.
[10] VG WebExhibits 2025, Elizabeth van Gogh to T, 27 Feb. 1876.
[11] VG Letters 1958, Vol. 1, p. XXVI.
[12] V to T, 17 June 1876, 69.
[13] Ibid.
[14] VG Webexhibits 2025, Vincent's Father to T, 08 Sept. 1876.
[15] VG Webexhibits 2025, Elizabeth van Gogh to T, 18 Aug. 1876.
[16] V to T, 79
[17] V to T, 7 Oct. 1876, 76.
[18] V to T, 17 Nov. 1876, 81.
[19] V to T, 25 Nov. 1876, 82.
[20] V to T, 31 Dec. 1876, 83.
[21] V to T, 30 Oct. 1877, 112.
[22] Hulsker 1990, p. 69.
[23] V to T, 3 Apr. 1878, 121.
[24] VG WebExhibits 2025, Vincent's Father to Theo, 12 May 1878.
[25] Hulsker 1990, p. 70.
[26] VG WebExhibits 2025, Vincent's Mother to T, 07 June 1878.
[27] VG WebExhibits 2025, Vincent's Father and Mother to T, 24 Nov. 1878.
[28] Ibid., Vincent's father to T, 19 July 1879.
[29] VG Letters 1958, Vol. 1, p. 172.
[30] Ibid., Reverend Mr. Pietersen to Vincent's parents, XXIX.
[31] Hulsker 1990, p. 95.
[32] V to T, July 1880, 133.
[33] Hulsker 1990, p. 95.
[34] V to T, 154.
[35] V to T, 155.
[36] V to T, 157.
[37] Bailey 1992, p. 11.
[38] V to T, 154.
[39] V to T, Dec. 1881, 164.

[40] V to T, 18 Nov. 1881, 158.
[41] V to T, 23 Nov. 1881, 161.
[42] Ibid.
[43] V to T, 193.
[44] V to T, Dec. 1881, 164.
[45] V to T, 193.
[46] V to T, 166.
[47] T to V, 5 Jan. 1882, 169.
[48] Ibid.
[49] V to T, 173.
[50] V to T, 181.
[51] V to T, 189.
[52] V to T, 192.
[53] V to T, 193.
[54] V to T, 193a.
[55] Hulsker 1990, p. 122.
[56] V to T, 204.
[57] Hulsker 1990, p. 131-32.
[58] V to T, 201.
[59] V to T, 204.
[60] V to T, 198.
[61] Hulsker 1990, p. 134.
[62] V to T, 206.
[63] Hulsker 1990, p. 140.
[64] V to T, 218.
[65] V to T, 259n.
[66] V to T, 260.
[67] V to T, 332 & 260.
[68] V to T, 326.

Chapter 12
[1] V to T, 345.
[2] VG Letters 1958, Vol. 1, Vincent's father to T, p. XXXV.
[3] V to T, 348.
[4] V to T, 352.
[5] VG Letters 1958, Vol. 1, p. XXXVI.
[6] V to T, 358.
[7] V to T, 360.
[8] V to T, 377.
[9] V to T, 375.
[10] V to T, 377.
[11] VG Letters 1958, Vol. 1, p. XXVII.
[12] V to T, 380.
[13] V to T, 388.
[14] V to T, 390.
[15] V to T, 392.
[16] VG Letters 1958, Vol. 1, Vincent's Father to T, p. XXXVIII.
[17] VG Letters 1958, Vol. 1, p. XXXVIII.
[18] Du Quesne van Gogh 1913, p. 41.
[19] Hulsker 1990, p. 192.
[20] Du Quesne van Gogh 1913, p. 44.
[21] Tralbaut 1969, p. 154.
[22] V to T, 398.
[23] Ibid.
[24] V to T, 204.
[25] V to T, 327.
[26] V to T, 346.

27 V to T, 408.
28 V to T, 423.
29 Tralbaut 1969, p. 159.
30 V to T, 432.
31 V to T, 433.
32 V to T, 434.
33 Ibid.
34 Bailey 1992, p. 13.
35 V to T, 169.

Chapter 13
1 *Lloyd's*, Oct. 7, 1888.
2 *The Times*, Oct. 1, 1888.
3 *Lloyd's*, Oct. 7, 1888.
4 *The Times*, Oct. 1, 1888.
5 *Lloyd's*, Oct. 7, 1888.
6 Ibid.
7 *Reynolds's*, Oct. 7, 1888.
8 *Daily News*, Sept. 30, 1888.
9 *Lloyd's*, Sept. 30, 1888.
10 *Lloyd's*, Oct. 7, 1888.
11 *The Times*, Oct. 3, 1888.
12 *The Times*, Oct. 1, 1888.
13 *Daily News*, Oct. 1, 1888.
14 Evans 2006, p. 110.
15 *Daily News*, Oct. 1, 1888.
16 *The Times*, Oct. 3, 1888.
17 Ibid.
18 *Daily News*, Oct. 1, 1888.
19 *Lloyd's*, Oct. 7, 1888.
20 *The Times*, Oct. 4, 1888.
21 *Daily News*, Oct. 5, 1888.
22 *The Times*, Oct. 1, 1888.
23 *Daily News*, Oct. 5, 1888.
24 *The Times*, Oct. 1, 1888.
25 *Daily News*, Oct. 5, 1888.
26 Ibid.
27 Ibid.
28 *Lloyd's*, Oct. 7, 1888.
29 Ibid.
30 *The Times*, Oct. 3, 1888.
31 *Lloyd's*, Oct. 14, 1888.
32 *The Times*, Oct. 12, 1888.
33 *Lloyd's*, Oct. 14, 1888.
34 *The Times*, Oct. 12, 1888.
35 Ibid.
36 Ibid.
37 Ibid., Oct. 2, 1888.
38 Ibid., Oct. 12, 1888.
39 *Daily News*, Oct. 1, 1888.
40 Ibid.
41 Booth 1889, Map shows synagogue labeled.
42 V to T, c. 16 June 1888, 504.

Chapter 14
1 *Daily News*, Oct. 1, 1888.
2 *The Times*, Oct. 1, 1888.

3 N.A. 2025, MEPO/142, ff. 2-3, 1 Oct. 1888 (author's naming: Postcard Ripper letter).
4 V to T, 317.
5 N.A. 2025, MEPO/142, ff. 4-5, 24 Sept. 1888, (author's naming: First Ripper letter).
6 *The Times*, Oct. 6, 1888.
7 VG Letters 1958, Vol. 1, P.C. Görlitz, May 26, 1914, 94a; VG Letters 1958, Vol. 3, P.C. Görlitz to Frederik van Eeden, A7.
8 N.A. 2025, MEPO3/142, f. 344, 2 Oct. 1888, (author's naming: Mouth Waters Ripper letter).
9 V to B, B9[12].
10 V to T, 544.
11 *The Times*, Oct. 3, 1888; *Daily News*, Oct. 3, 1888.
12 *The Times*, Oct. 9, 1888.
13 Ibid.
14 *The Times*, Oct. 4, 1888.
15 Ibid., Oct. 23, 1888.
16 *Lloyd's*, Oct. 28, 1888.
17 *The Times*, Oct. 4, 1888.
18 *Lloyd's*, Oct. 7, 1888.
19 *Reynolds's*, Oct. 14, 1888.
20 *The Times*, Oct. 9, 1888.

Chapter 15
1 N.A. 2025, MEPO3/142, f. 195, 4 Oct. 1888, (author's naming: Vincent Square Ripper letter).
2 Ibid., MEPO3/142, f. 300, 4 Oct. 1888, (author's naming: Brixton Road Ripper letter).
3 V to T, 85.
4 V to T, 191.
5 N.A. 2025, MEPO3/142, f. 180, 5 Oct. 1888, (author's naming: Churchyard Ripper letter).
6 Ibid., MEPO3/142, f. 491, 5 Oct. 1888, (author's naming: Moab and Midian Ripper letter).
7 Ibid., MEPO3/142, f. 463, 5 Oct. 1888, (author's naming: Thrown in River Ripper letter).
8 *Daily News*, Oct. 18, 1888.
9 N.A. 2025, MEPO3/142, ff. 243-244, 6 Oct. 1888, (author's naming: Clapham Junction Ripper letter).
10 Bradshaw 1888, p. 686.
11 Ibid., p. 12.
12 VG Letters 2009, V to Albert Aurier, 10 Feb. 1890, 853/656a, n5.
13 Ibid.
14 V to T, c. 22 Oct. 1888, 551.
15 V to T, 29 June 1888, 507.
16 V to T, 583 & 589.
17 V to T, 2 July 1889, 598; V to W, 2 July 1889, W13.
18 V to T, c. 10 July 1890, 649.
19 Bradshaw 1888, p. 14.
20 Ibid., pp. 48-49.

Chapter 16
1 Stein 1986, Emile Bernard, "Les Hommes D'Aujourd'hui," 1891, pp. 282-85.
2 Ibid., François Gauzi, "Lautrec et Son Temps," 1954, pp. 71-72.
3 Ibid., A.S. Hartrick, "A Painter's Pilgrimage Through Fifty Years," 1939, pp. 81-87.
4 AB to his parents, 1886, 462a.
5 Ibid., 23 June 1886.
6 V to T, 460n2.
7 Jansen 1999, p. 17.
8 Ibid.
9 V to T, 460.
10 Ibid.
11 Ibid.
12 Ibid., (author's translation).
13 Ibid., (author's translation).

[14] Ibid., (translation from Hulsker 1990, p. 244).
[15] AB to T, 460.
[16] *Le Figaro*, Aug. 5, 1886.
[17] *Le Gaulois*, Aug. 5, 1886.
[18] *Le Figaro*, Aug. 5, 1886.
[19] Ibid., Aug. 7, 1886.
[20] *Le Petit*, Aug. 6, 1886.
[21] *Le Figaro*, Aug. 5, 1886.
[22] Ibid.; *Le Gaulois,* Aug 5, 1886.
[23] *Le Petit*, Aug. 6, 1886.
[24] *Le Figaro*, Aug. 7, 1886.
[25] *Le Gaulois*, Aug. 5, 1886.
[26] *Le Figaro*, Aug. 5, 1886; *Le Petit*, Aug. 6, 1886.
[27] *Le Petit*, Aug. 6, 1886.
[28] *Le Figaro*, Aug. 5, 1886.
[29] *Le Petit*, Aug. 7, 1886.
[30] Ibid., Aug. 6, 1886.
[31] *Le Gaulois*, Aug. 5, 1886.
[32] *Bristol Mercury*, Aug. 9, 1886.
[33] *Le Figaro*, Aug. 6, 1886.
[34] Ibid., Aug. 7, 1886.
[35] Ibid., Aug. 5, 1886.
[36] *Le Petit*, Aug. 6, 1886.
[37] *Le Figaro*, Aug. 15, 1886.
[38] *Le Figaro*, Aug. 5, 1886.
[39] Ibid.; Aug. 6, 1886.
[40] The Paris Catacombs.
[41] *The New York Times*, Aug. 26, 1875.
[42] V to T, 326.
[43] W to Line Kruysse, 27 Aug. 1886; AB to his parents, 26 Aug. 1886.
[44] Jansen 1999, T to Jo, 26 July 1887, 1.

Chapter 17
[1] Bradshaw 1888, p. 49.
[2] V to T, 548.
[3] V to T, 545.
[4] V to T, 546.
[5] V to T, 547.
[6] V to T, 548.
[7] V to W, W8.
[8] V to T, 550.
[9] V to T, 547.
[10] V to T, 549.
[11] V to T, 556.
[12] V to G, 549.
[13] Evans 2001, pp. 74-77.
[14] Ibid., 78 & 105

"Faith without works is dead."